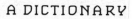
A DICTIONARY

Modern
Critical
Terms

A DICTIONARY OF

Modern Critical Terms

Edited by
Roger Fowler

London and New York

First published in 1973
Revised edition published in 1987
by Routledge & Kegan Paul

Reprinted 1990, 1991, 1993, 1995, 1997, 1999
by Routledge
11 New Fetter Lane, London EC4P 4EE
29 West 35th Street, New York, NY 10001

© Routledge & Kegan Paul 1973, 1987

Set in Imprint, 11 on 12pt with Helvetica
by Inforum Ltd, Portsmouth
Printed by The Guernsey Press Co. Ltd,
Guernsey, Channel Islands

British Library Cataloguing in Publication Data
A catalogue record for this book is available from the British Library

Library of Congress Cataloguing in Publication Data
A catalogue record for this book is available from the Library of Congress

ISBN 0-415-05884-8

Contributors

MJA   Michael Alexander, Senior Lecturer in English, University of Stirling

FWB   F.W. Bateson, late Emeritus Fellow, Corpus Christi College, Oxford

CWEB   C.W.E. Bigsby, Professor of American Studies, University of East Anglia

EJB   Elizabeth Boa, Senior Lecturer in German, University of Nottingham

MSB   Malcolm Bradbury, Professor of American Studies, University of East Anglia

AAAC   Anne Cluysenaar, Senior Lecturer in English, Sheffield City Polytechnic

JC   Jonathan Cook, Lecturer in English, University of East Anglia

EC   Ellman Crasnow, Lecturer in English and American Literature, University of East Anglia

TE   Terry Eagleton, Fellow of Wadham College and Lecturer in English, Oxford University

JWJF   John Fletcher, Professor of Comparative Literature, University of East Anglia

RGF   Roger Fowler, Professor of English and Linguistics, University of East Anglia

AMG   Arnold Goldman, formerly Professor of American Literature, Keele University

GG   Gareth Griffiths, Senior Lecturer in English, Macquarie University

MAH   Michael Hollington, Professor of English, University of New South Wales

GMH   G.M. Hyde, Lecturer in English and Comparative Literature, University of East Anglia

BCL   Brian Lee, Senior Lecturer in American Studies, University of Nottingham

GNL   Geoffrey N. Leech, Professor of Linguistics, University of Lancaster

TM   Timothy Marshall, Lecturer in English, University of East Anglia

PM   Peter Mercer, Lecturer in English, University of East Anglia

MO'T	Michael O'Toole, Professor of Communication Studies, Murdoch University
DJP	D.J. Palmer, Professor of English Literature, University of Manchester
MHP	M.H. Parkinson, Lecturer in French, University of East Anglia
SGP	S.G. Pulman, Lecturer in Computing, University of Cambridge
DGP	David Punter, Professor of English, Chinese University of Hong Kong
AER	Allan Rodway, formerly Reader in English, University of Nottingham
AMR	Angus Ross, Reader in English, University of Sussex
LS	Lorna Sage, Senior Lecturer in English, University of East Anglia
VS	Victor Sage, Senior Lecturer in English, University of East Anglia
CS	Clive Scott, Lecturer in French, University of East Anglia
RWS	Richard Sheppard, Professor of European Literature, University of East Anglia
LSm	Lorna Smith, Part-time Tutor, University of East Anglia
TGW	Todd G. Willy, Professor of Rhetoric, University of California, Berkeley
NZ	Natan Zach, Professor of Comparative Literature, University of Haifa
NCPZ	Nicholas Zurbrugg, Lecturer in Comparative Literature, Griffith University

Note on the style of references

Cross-references give the article to which the reader is referred in SMALL CAPITALS.

Further reading is suggested wherever appropriate, sometimes within the text and sometimes at the end of articles, whichever is stylistically more suitable. Dates of first editions are given when they are significant, but usually the most accessible and convenient modern reprintings and translations are cited.

Preface

This book is directed at an area of the literary catalogue which may seem already rather crowded: there are many 'dictionaries' and 'encyclopaedias' of literature and of critical terminology available, some of them excellent in their own way. But their ways are characteristically different from the approach adopted here. This is not an encyclopaedia, so it does not attempt a comprehensive survey of authors, periods, or genres—though it does explore a number of 'isms' which have been peculiarly vital in the growth of modern literary thought, and it takes a look at some of the major genres which have ordered and shaped European, English and American literature. Nor is this a 'dictionary' in the usual sense, in that its primary concern is not to provide brief working definitions of critical terms. For this reason the student will miss the scores of terms for the labelling of verbal detail, from *acatalectic* to *zeugma*. Although I would not deny that a precise, comprehensible and agreed descriptive vocabulary is essential to the practice of criticism, I have decided to exclude the majority of such terms from this book: there are many other sources where the student can look them up, for example, Babette Deutsch, *Poetry Handbook* (1961), Alex Preminger (ed.), *Encyclopedia of Poetry and Poetics* (1965), Joseph T. Shipley, *Dictionary of World Literary Terms* (3rd ed., 1970). The present work is not designed to replace these terminological handbooks, but to add to and qualify such aids by encouraging a new perspective on literary terminology: to stimulate curiosity about how literary terms work actively for us, rather than to satisfy a utilitarian desire to gain access to their traditional meanings.

Reliable definitions and illustrations of rhetorical terms are not hard to come by. Rhetorical figures and schemes result from certain traditional arrangements of elements of language; the basic elements of language (i.e. language in general) remain constant from age to age, and are unvarying from one individual language to another, thus the range of language devices available to the verbal artist is limited and universal. Though some devices may go out of fashion while others attain a temporary popularity, the verbal bases of the chief and characteristic devices of style and rhetoric are not really vulnerable to the passage of time. It is difficult to imagine a language, or a stage in a language's history, in which metaphor, or paradox, or rhythm, would not be possible, or in which the linguistic causes of these literary devices would need to be completely redefined. For instance, a paradox is a paradox because it embodies one particular type of clash of meanings.

Such a semantic discord is achievable today by using a type of linguistic structure which was available four centuries ago to poets writing according to the rules of rhetoricians such as Puttenham and Wilson or, earlier still, to Cicero writing in Latin. Rhetorical possibilities do not alter substantially, so there is no need for a new glossary of rhetorical terms for each new literary generation. But there are other areas of critical terminology which are more flexible and so more creative. A concept such as 'tension' or 'irony' or 'baroque', for instance, is not tied down by any immutable linguistic rule, and it is such terms which are used creatively by literary communities to explore and define their attitudes to poetic and fictional experience. These terms should receive close scrutiny, and they are the major subject of the present book. New terms suddenly emerge—'apocalypse' and 'fabulation' are modern examples—as critics or writers strive to find a focus for some new perception, some new orientation towards the literary corpus of their culture. Where neologisms or borrowings from non-literary discourse are concerned, it is easy to see that terms are primarily the instruments of investigation and conceptualization, that they are not mere labels for pre-existent components of literature and criticism. It is not so obvious that many established critical terms, perhaps most terms of greater abstractness than the rhetorical ones, are exploratory rather than definitive: that they are used not to fix concepts in utter security, but to derive and to comprehend concepts. Also, of course, as instruments in the process of reading: what particular literary structure a reader perceives depends to a considerable extent on the concepts he has developed in his general, more distant thoughts about literature, his participation in the universe of critical discourse. So the commonest, ostensibly most agreed critical terms may be conceptually 'active' in a reader or critic. What spatial metaphors is he willing to attach to *plot*: simple line, maze, or meander? How concrete is a *theme*: is it a string of images at the surface of a work, or a more abstract, underlying stream of thought?

It seems to me that, if we are going to be at all self-conscious about our critical terminology—and this book implicitly argues for self-consciousness—we must take an openly flexible view about its nature. We should not ask 'what does such-and-such a term mean?', expecting some incontrovertible and memorizable definition, but 'what are the potentialities of this term? What can I do with it?' The contributors to this book were invited to write their entries in this questioning, analytic spirit. Wherever a more or less stable usage is found we have, of course, aimed to reflect it. But we are much more interested in writing about critical concepts in such a way as to open up their potentialities for literary enquiry than we are in providing finished definitions which may give a false impression of the completeness of some line of thought about literature.

We have attempted to be suggestive, informative, but not authoritarian. The book cannot be used as a source of instant definitions, nor as a reference against which one's own use of literary terms can be checked for 'correctness'. The attitudes to literary terminology reflected in a desire to use a book in such ways are, we believe, rather suspect: the student wants an authority to disperse his insecurity; he is unwilling to become conscious of the power of critical terminology to enrich his literary awareness.

Although this book does not aim at complete and definitive coverage of the world of critical terminology, it can nevertheless claim to be 'representative' in a significant way. I have put together essays by a fairly large and varied gathering of critics and teachers: men and women who received their literary education at a range of different universities and in different countries; also—and I regard this as very important—people of different generations. This diversity results in heterogeneity of critical standpoint; but the group is large enough to engender something more valuable than mere disagreement: it is a cross-section of critical attitudes and, I believe, a dramatic representation of the richness of contemporary criticism. This 'dictionary' of the critical lexicon is designed to be read as well as consulted; and it can be read as a picture of literary criticism entering the 1970s as a vital and professional humane discipline.

Preface to the second edition

In the first edition of this book, I took the view that literary studies should be given a pluralistic representation, and I believe that is still appropriate. It would be wrong to say that literary study is a science guided by a single valid theory and set of procedures: I mean, wrong as an empirical description of the state of the art today; many theorists have argued that there could, and should, be a science of 'poetics' or 'theory of literature', and that might indeed be desirable, but no such theory has yet found acceptance.

Since 1970 the field of literary studies has become even more diversified. Traditional assumptions persist, particularly in literary education; but forms of new thinking have been developed which question tradition from several angles. Particularly stimulating have been ideas drawn from other disciplines such as linguistics, anthropology, psychology and politics. Not only have new schools of criticism emerged; whole areas such as narrative analysis have become greatly refined; also, there have been radical revaluations of some basic ideas—concepts as fundamental as 'author', 'reader', and 'language'. As I have indicated, such developments have not displaced earlier conceptions. Generally they have been felt by the traditional critical establishment to be contentious, aesthetically or politically. So debate flourishes today, and the pluralistic model is just as appropriate as it was fifteen years ago.

I am glad to have been given the opportunity to revise and expand this *Dictionary of Modern Critical Terms*, in this situation. New articles have been commissioned to cover as many as possible of the new developments (e.g. AUTHOR, DECONSTRUCTION, MARXIST CRITICISM); and several pieces have been completely rewritten (e.g. METAPHOR, STRUCTURALISM). All the original authors who could be contacted have been given the opportunity to revise and update their contributions; some did not wish to do so, and in such cases I have limited my own editorial intervention to very minor corrections and updatings. So a traditionalist basis is preserved in this book, accurately reflecting the situation in the discipline.

I gratefully acknowledge the cooperation of my fellow-contributors in effecting this revision, and particularly those of my colleagues at the University of East Anglia who have advised and supported me during a period of revision which was unreasonably prolonged by my commitments as Dean. Thanks also to the publishers for waiting patiently for a delayed typescript.

absurd

The theatre of the absurd was a term, derived from Camus and popularized by Martin Esslin's book *The Theatre of the Absurd* (1961), applied to a group of dramatists whose work emerged during the early fifties (though Beckett's *Waiting for Godot* and Ionesco's *The Bald Prima Donna* were actually written in the late forties). In *The Myth of Sisyphus* (1942) Camus defined the absurd as the tension which emerges from man's determination to discover purpose and order in a world which steadfastly refuses to evidence either. To writers like Ionesco and Beckett this paradox leaves man's actions, aspirations and emotions merely ironical. The redeeming message no longer comes from God but is delivered by a deaf mute to a collection of empty chairs (*The Chairs*, 1952); human qualities, such as perseverance and courage, no longer function except as derisory comments on man's impotence (*Happy Days*, 1961); basic instincts and responses, the motor forces of the individual, become the source of his misery (*Act Without Words*, 1957). Camus himself could see a limited transcendence in man's ability to recognize and even exalt in the absurd (*The Outsider,* 1942) or in the minimal consolation of stoicism (*Cross Purpose*, 1944). But he came to feel that absurdity implied a world which appeared to sanction Nazi brutality as easily as it did individual acts of violence. From an examination of the nature of absurdity, therefore, he moved towards liberal humanism: 'The end of the movement of absurdity, of rebellion, etc. . . . is compassion . . . that is to say, in the last analysis, love'. For writers like Beckett and Ionesco such a dialectical shift was simply bad faith. For to the 'absurd' dramatist it is axiomatic that man lives in an entropic world in which communication is impossible and illusion preferred to reality. The individual has no genuine scope for action (Hamm sits lame and blind in *Endgame*, 1958; Winnie is buried to the neck in sand in *Happy Days*; the protagonist of Ionesco's *The New Tenant* (written 1953, produced 1957) is submerged beneath proliferating furniture); he is the victim of his metaphysical situation. Logically, the plays abandon linear plot, plausible character development and rational language. In contrast to Camus' work their style directly reflects their subject.

The term 'absurd drama', applied by Esslin to dramatists as diverse as Beckett, Ionesco, Adamov, Genet, Arrabal and Simpson, is something of a blunt weapon. Esslin had a disturbing if understandable tendency to trace the origins of the absurd in an incredible array of writers some of whom do not properly belong in a theatre which is convinced of the unbridgeable gulf between aspiration and fulfilment, the impossibility of communication, or the futility of human relationships. In other words he is not always completely scrupulous in distinguishing between style and content. In a more recent revision of his book, however, he has shown a commendable desire to underline the deficiencies of a term which, while proving a useful means of approaching dramatists intent on forging new drama, was never intended as a substitute for stringent analysis of the work of individual writers.

CWEB

action, actor
see DRAMA

Aestheticism
A sensibility, a philosophy of life and of art, and an English literary and artistic movement, culminating in the 1890s, with Oscar Wilde as its most extravagant exponent and Walter Pater its acknowledged philosopher. Other names commonly associated are those of the members of the Pre-Raphaelite Brotherhood, Swinburne, Arthur Symons, Ernest Dowson, Lionel Johnson, Andrew Lang, William Sharp, John Addington Symonds and the early Yeats. Aubrey Beardsley and J. McNeill Whistler are representative of the same trend in the fine arts.

For the Aesthete, if his creed is to be derived from Pater's conclusion to *The Renaissance* (1873), reality amounts to sharp, fleeting impressions, images and sensations arrested by the creative individual from an experience in constant flux. The life of art, or the art of life, which the Aesthete wishes to equate, is ideally a form of purified ecstasy that flourishes only when removed from the roughness of the stereotyped world of actuality and the orthodoxy of philosophical systems and fixed points of view. The quest of unadulterated beauty is recommended as the finest occupation man can find for himself during the 'indefinite reprieve' from death which his life is. Pater's phrase, 'the love of art for its own sake', a version of the French *l'art pour l'art*, has served the Aesthetes as a slogan, implying the repudiation of the 'heresy of instruction' (Baudelaire's *l'hérésie de l'enseignement*). Art, Whistler wrote in his 'Ten o'clock' lecture (1885), is 'selfishly occupied with her own perfection only' and has 'no desire to teach'. As a fashionable fad,

English Aestheticism was brought to a halt with the trial of Oscar Wilde in 1896.

Aestheticism, as a stage in the development of Romanticism, is not limited to England. Profoundly a movement of reaction and protest, it reflects the growing apprehension of the nineteenth-century artist at the vulgarization of values and commercialization of art accompanying the rise of the middle class and the spread of democracy ('a new class, who discovered the cheap, and foresaw fortune in the facture of the sham'—Whistler). The hostility of an alienated minority towards bourgeois 'Religion of Progress' ('Industry and Progress,' Baudelaire wrote, 'those despotic enemies of all poetry') prompted an indulgence in the decadent, the archaic and the morbid. The Death of God, as proclaimed by Nietzsche among others, turned the Aesthete towards the occult and the transcendental in an attempt to make a thoroughly spiritualized art substitute for the old faith. The *fin-de-siècle* witnesses the proclamation of an élitist 'new hedonism' determined, in the words of Oscar Wilde, 'never to accept any theory or system that would involve the sacrifice of any mode of passionate experience'.

Philosophy provides the theoretical mainstay of the prevalent moods. Kant's postulate (*Critique of Judgement*, 1790) of the dis-interestedness of the aesthetical judgment, and the irrelevance of concepts to the intuitions of the imagination, is taken up and carried further by Schopenhauer. In the latter's thought, an 'absolute' Art removes the mind from a despicable life and frees it from its bondage to the will. Since music is the most immaterial art, as well as the most removed from quotidian reality, it becomes the ideal. Schopenhauer declares that 'to become like music is the aspiration of all arts', which is echoed by Nietzsche in *The Birth of Tragedy from the Spirit of Music* (1872); by Verlaine in *'de la musique avant toute chose'*, and by Pater in his equally famous 'All art constantly aspires towards the condition of music' (*The Renaissance*, 1873). The ensuing cult of pure or 'essential' form is as characteristic of symbolism and literary Impressionism as it is of the entire English 1890s. This, in turn, leads to the devaluation of the subject-matter in favour of personal, innovatory techniques and the subtleties of exquisite execution.

See Madeleine L. Cazamian, *Le Roman et les idées en Angleterre,* vol. 2: *L'Anti-intellectualisme et l'esthéticisme* (1880–1900) (1935); L. Eckhoff, *The Aesthetic Movement in English Literature* (1959); J. Farmer, *Le Mouvement esthétique et 'décadent' en Angleterre* (1931); W. Gaunt, *The Aesthetic Movement* (1945); Graham Hough, *The Last Romantics* (1949); H. Jackson, *The Eighteen-Nineties* (1913); R. V. Johnson, *Aestheticism* (1969); Louis Rosenblatt, *L'Idée de l'art pour l'art dans la littérature anglaise pendant la période victorienne* (1931); Ruth Zabriskie Temple, *The Critic's Alchemy: A Study of the Introduction of French Symbolism into England* (1953).

NZ

aesthetics

(The study of the beautiful) has developed, especially in Germany, into a formidable subject. Lack of space forbids any attempt to deal with its philosophical and psychological problems here; but some discriminations may be made to clarify and amplify its use as a critical term.

First, *aesthetic pleasure* may be distinguished from other pleasures—according to the Kantian definition now widely accepted—as that which is disinterested, the result of perceiving something not as a means but as an end in itself, not as useful but as ornamental, not as instrument but as achievement. To perceive it so is to perceive its 'beauty' (if it turns out to have any). Such beauty, being the counterpart to use or purpose, which largely depend on content, must spring from formal qualities, as must the special pleasures its perception gives rise to. Non-moral, non-utilitarian, and non-acquisitive, this is the purest of the pleasures, the one least exposed to bias from areas outside the work of art (and therefore the one most appropriate for defining what 'art' is; see ART). Second, aesthetic pleasure may be distinguished from *aesthetic appreciation*. The former emphasizes one's experience of the work, which may be mistaken, untutored or injudicious; the latter emphasizes the characteristics of the work, and implies a critical assessment of their 'beauty'. Third, both presuppose *aesthetic attention*. Unless a work is regarded in the way indicated above—for what it is, not for what it is up to—its aesthetic qualities, if any, are likely to go unperceived. For this reason works where the subject, or manner, deeply involve the reader are less likely to give aesthetic pleasure or to prompt aesthetic appreciation than those that encourage aesthetic attention by formal devices that lend *aesthetic distance*.

Finally, *aesthetic merit* should be distinguished from aesthetic qualities and reactions, for a work might possess genuine aesthetic qualities, properly provide for their appreciation, yet in fact be a poor specimen of its kind. Merit and pleasure, too, are not necessarily related. An untrained or naturally crude sensibility could clearly be aesthetically pleased by a crude work—and so, in certain circumstances, could a trained and refined sensibility (though it would *appreciate* the work for what it was).

Aesthesis (aesthetic perception) is normally a blend of aesthetic pleasure and appreciation, and may be of three kinds: *aesthesis of composition*, resulting from purely formal harmonies of part and part, or parts and whole, and more characteristic of the fine arts than of literature; *aesthesis of complementarity*, resulting from the matching of form and content; and *aesthesis of condensation*, resulting from the perception of aesthetic qualities in part of a work only (a minimal instance, strictly speaking, of either of the other two modes).

The *Aesthetic Movement*, or *Art for art's sake*, which started in France during the latter part of the nineteenth century and flourished in England in the 1880s and 1890s, was less concerned with such niceties than with a general reaction against the Art for morality's sake so characteristic of the earlier part of the century. When Wilde averred that 'all art is quite useless' he spoke truly—if art is defined in aesthetic terms. But the pleasures of literature are usually multiple and its proper appreciation therefore rarely limited to the aesthetic. See also PLEASURE.

See Monroe C. Beardsley, *Aesthetics* (1958); E. F. Carritt, *An Introduction to Aesthetics* (1949); W. Gaunt, *The Aesthetic Adventure* (1945); P. Guyer, *Kant and the Claims of Taste* (1979); John Hospers (ed.), *Introductory Readings in Aesthetics* (1969); H. Osborne, *Aesthetics and Art Theory* (1968); Eliseo Vivas and Murray Krieger (eds), *The Problems of Aesthetics* (1954); *British Journal of Aesthetics (passim)*.

AER

affective fallacy
see EFFECT

aktualisace
see FOREGROUNDING

alienation effect
see CONTRADICTION, EPIC THEATRE

allegory
is a major symbolic mode which has fallen into some critical disrepute this century ('dissociated', 'naive', 'mechanical', 'abstract') though it flourishes in satire, underground literature and science fiction. It is often defined as an 'extended metaphor' in which characters, actions and scenery are systematically symbolic, referring to spiritual, political, psychological confrontations (Bunyan's *Pilgrim's Progress*, Orwell's *1984*). Historically the rise of allegory accompanies the inward-looking psychologizing tendencies of late antiquity and medieval Christianity (see C. S. Lewis, *The Allegory of Love*, 1938). The 'hero' is typically a cypher (Spenser's Guyon, Christian in Bunyan, Winston Smith in *1984*), a proxy for the reader, because the action is assumed to take place in the mind and imagination of the audience; 'characters' other than the hero are, rather like Jonsonian HUMOURS, daemonically possessed by fear, desire or need. (It is often misleadingly suggested that they 'represent' vices and virtues, but when successful they *are*

jealousy, greed, modesty, etc. with intervals of neutrality where they get the plot moving or are spectators to the obsessions of other characters.) Allegory's distinctive feature is that it is a structural, rather than a textural symbolism; it is a large-scale exposition in which problems are conceptualized and analysed into their constituent parts in order to be stated, if not solved. The typical plot is one in which the 'innocent'—Gulliver, Alice, the Lady in Milton's 'Comus', K. in Kafka's *The Castle*—is 'put through' a series of experiences (tests, traps, fantasy gratifications) which add up to an imaginative analysis of contemporary 'reality'.

Many of the attitudes which characterize MODERNISM and NEW CRITICISM are explicitly hostile to the intentionalist and individualist assumptions allegory makes—that the emotive power of literature can be channelled and directed, that the work itself is the means to an end (saving souls, 'to fashion a gentleman', etc.). Pound's strictures against the abstract ('dim lands *of peace*'); Richards's insistence that poetry is 'data' not rationalist scaffolding; Yeats's stress on the mysteriousness of the genuine literary symbol—all seem to label allegory as the product of a now untenable idealism. But the clear-cut distinction between 'the music of ideas' (Richards on Eliot) and the 'dark conceit' of allegory is harder to make in practice than in theory: Yeats's *A Vision* systematizes and expounds the mystery of his symbols much as Spenser did in *The Faerie Queene*. Cleanth Brooks in *The Well Wrought Urn* (1947) allegorizes all the poems he explicates, so that they become 'parables about the nature of poetry', and Northrop Frye in *The Anatomy of Criticism* (1957) summed up this tendency by pointing out that all analysis was covert allegorizing. But though the common distinction between allegory and symbolism falsifies the facts of literary experience when it claims an impossible instantaneity and universality for the symbol (symbolism can be grossly schematic—cf. Hemingway or Steinbeck), and accuses allegory of arid rationalism, there is a genuine distinction to be made.

Two main strands in the modernist aesthetic, the doctrine of the autonomy of the artefact, and the association of literature with collective and recurrent 'myth', combine to leave little room and few terms for allegory. We are equipped to talk about the textural enactment of content, and about the largest (mythic) patterns into which literature falls, but we are not at ease in the area between the two where form and content are often increasingly at odds, and which involves argument, discursiveness, paraphrasable opinion. Allegorists, like satirists (and the two are often the same) employ myths rhetorically, rather than respectfully embodying them (John Barth, *Giles Goat Boy*, 1966). Scholarly analysts—e.g. those dealing with Spenser's political or sexual allegory—are defensive, aware that critical theory somehow contrives to discount their conclusions, because it is embarrassed by meanings in literature that are neither formal nor universal. See also MYTH, SYMBOL.

See Angus Fletcher, *Allegory, the Theory of a Symbolic Mode* (1964); Northrop Frye, 'Levels of meaning in literature', *Kenyon Review,* 1950, 246–62; A. D. Nuttall, *Two Concepts of Allegory* (1967); Edmund Spenser, 'A Letter of the Author's . . . to Sir Walter Raleigh' (1596); Rosemond Tuve, *Allegorical Imagery* (1967); Edgar Wind, *Pagan Mysteries in the Renaissance* (1958).

LS

alliteration
see TEXTURE

ambiguity
Opposed to 'clarity', ambiguity would be considered a fault. Modern criticism has turned it into a virtue, equivalent roughly to 'richness' or 'wit'. This reversal of normal connotations has been made possible by two factors: I. A. Richards's argument that what is required of scientific language (e.g. lucidity) is not necessarily demanded in poetry (see LANGUAGE); and William Empson's promotion of the concept in *Seven Types of Ambiguity*, first published in 1930. Since Empson, ambiguity has come to be regarded as a defining linguistic characteristic of poetry.

Ambiguity is not a specific figurative device which may be chosen at will for decoration; it is not, says Empson, 'a thing to be attempted'. Rather, it is a natural characteristic of language which becomes heightened and significant in verse. The link between content and form is indirect and arbitrary; hence syntactic 'accidents' may occur, syntax realizing two or more meanings in the same signal. Linguists say that one 'surface structure' may conceal two or more 'deep structures' (the reverse situation is PARAPHRASE). Ambiguity is common in ordinary language, but we do not notice it because context usually selects just one of the alternative meanings ('disambiguates'). It is of several kinds: *homophony*, the convergence of unrelated meanings in one form (*bank, plane*); *polysemy*, a scatter of more or less connected meanings around one word (*bachelor, record*); purely syntactic ambiguity, as in *Visiting relatives can be boring* or *old men and women*.

Verse tends to be more ambiguous than prose or conversation, for several reasons: it is less redundant; context is inaccessible or irrelevant; verse displays extra levels of structure and can be 'parsed' more ways. Empson sums this up: 'ambiguity is a phenomenon of compression'. Deletion of words for metrical/stylistic reasons leads to ambivalence, as in Empson's example from Browning:

> I want to know a butcher paints,
> A baker rhymes for his pursuit . . .

So does a line-break at a crucial syntactic point:

> If it were done, when 'tis done, then 'twere well
> It were done quickly.

Since we are disposed to assume multiple meaning in verse, we consent to read in extra meanings. The leaves in Shakespeare's Sonnet 73 ('yellow . . . or none, or few') are simultaneously the leaves of the autumn metaphor and the poet's writings—leaves of a book. The problem is justification, selection; Empson's reading of 'trammel up the consequence' is clearly fantastic. What control is there over the desire to spawn meanings?

The doctrine of ambiguity is not a licence for self-indulgence, free association producing a mushy poem, an arbitrary heap of meanings. Multiple meanings must be justified by their interrelationships. We must neither impose meanings without control, nor reject all meanings but one; instead, we must reject all meanings but those which interact wittily. In the same sonnet we find 'those boughs which shake against the cold'. *Shake* is either passive—the boughs being ravaged by the cold wind—or active and defiant, the shaking of a fist, a gesture against approaching death. This is a common syntactic ambiguity, and the right one for the poem: the diametrically opposed meanings capture the conflict between decay and energy which the poem embodies. Here we have not merely *mentioned* the double meaning, but *used* it in relation to the poem's theme. Ambiguity in this usage resembles (and is the real father of) the New Critics' TENSION, IRONY, PARADOX; it comes nearer than any of them to providing a linguistic explanation for poetic complexity and wit, for it springs from the familiar resources of ordinary language.

RGF

analysis

The purpose of analysis, according to William Empson, 'is to show the modes of action of a poetical effect'. And since the work of Empson (*Seven Types of Ambiguity*, 1930) and Richards (*Practical Criticism*, 1929) it has been a conviction of criticism that these effects are accessible to reason, and not mysteries reserved for silent appreciation. 'The reasons that make a line of verse likely to give pleasure . . . are like the reasons for anything else; one can reason about them' (*Seven Types*). Empson's major achievement was his demonstration that these modes of action were capable of description in terms of effects of language. The conviction that the forms and meanings of literature are linguistically generated gives to the business of analysis its modern centrality. For the classical idea of language as the dress of thought had for long limited literary analysis to the categorization of stylistic features, the description of decorative externals. So long as the reality of the work lay 'beyond' language it had no objective existence, it could not be analysed. Traditional stylistics concerned itself with classification and comparison of types of prosody, diction, imagery, etc. without attempting to show how these features co-operated in creating the 'meaning' of a work. The tradition of *explication de texte* in French education, in which the 'texte' often seems almost incidental to the categorized information that is hung about it, demonstrates the consequences of this dualistic form-content model of language. What is offered is what Ian Watt calls 'explanation . . . a mere making plain by spreading out'; modern critical analysis demands, on the other hand, 'explication . . . a progressive unfolding of a series of literary implications' ('The first paragraph of *The Ambassadors*', *Essays in Criticism*, 10, 1960). But explication, or as W. K. Wimsatt refines it 'the e*xplicit*ation of the implicit or the interpretation of the structural and formal, the truth of the poem under its aspect of coherence' (*The Verbal Icon*, 1954), had to wait upon a language theory that would abandon this dualism and re-define 'meaning' as a totality of linguistic relationships (see LANGUAGE). If language in poetry could be conceived of not as the dress but as the body of meaning, then analysis had access to the fact of the poem, not simply to its incidentals. It could account for its 'modes of action'.

In fact the essential conceptual metaphors had been available to criticism since Coleridge; Romantic theories of poetry as holistic and organic, with their controlling analogies of plants and trees, had supplanted the classical form-content dichotomies. But so long as these vitally interdependent 'parts and whole' were unlocated except as metaphysical abstractions, their relationships remained unanalysable. However, the revolutions in philosophy of Frege and Wittgenstein, and in linguistics of Saussure, substituted for the 'referential' or 'representational' model of language an idea of meaning as a result of complex interaction. Criticism took the point that if the meaning of a word is everything it does in a particular CONTEXT, then analysis of the words of a poem, of their total interinanimation, would be nothing less than an account of the poem itself. The metaphysical abstractions which Romantic theory identified as the form of poetry could now be located as linguistic realities, and since language has a public existence, independent of the psychologies of poet or reader, they were open to analysis.

The analytic tradition that descended from Richards and Empson, known in England (and particularly at the University of Cambridge) as *Practical Criticism* and in America as the NEW CRITICISM, was primarily concerned with semantic explorations. Its key terms—AMBIGUITY, PARADOX, TENSION, gesture—emerged from a new awareness of multiplicity and complexity of meaning in literature. This tradition (and its modern offshoot which relies explicitly on the techniques and conceptual framework of linguistics: see LANGUAGE) has been attacked for its tendency to stick close to the lower levels of verbal structure; for its apparent neglect of value-judgments; for its alleged inability to account for the larger-scale structures of long works; for a necessary preference for short, complex, highly-textured lyric poems. Some of these objections are well-founded; some are based on misconceptions. For instance, Winifred Nowottny's *The Language Poets Use* (1962), although devoted to investigation of arguably 'external' features such as sound-values, rhyme, syntax, diction and lineation, nevertheless succeeds in providing generous and valuable criticism. Moreover, the ideal and the utility of close analysis do not stand or fall by the case for *verbal* analysis. Language provides a stable reference-point (arguably lacking in the work of the CHICAGO CRITICS) and a point of departure for broader structural observations. For one classic and one contemporary example of structural analysis freed from the trammels of purely verbal structure, see Vladimir Propp, *The Morphology of the Folk-Tale* (1st Russian ed., 1928; English trans., 1958; French trans., of the 2nd Russian ed., 1970); Roland Barthes, *S/Z* (1970).

PM

anticlimax
see DENOUEMENT

anti-hero
see HERO

apocalyptic literature
There exists a body of biblical literature, canonical and apocryphal, conventionally called apocalyptic (from the Greek, meaning unveiling, uncovering). The Old Testament Book of Daniel and the New Testament Book of Revelation are the best known of these. They are characterized by an interest in the revelation of future events, as in prophecy. As a kind of systematized prophetic writing, the literature of apocalypse takes a wide view of human history, which it schematizes and periodizes, and an especial interest in eschatology, in the 'latter days', the end of historical time, the last judgment. These revelations are part of a hitherto secret knowledge. They tend to affect an esoteric, visionary, symbolic and fantastic scenario, a cast of animals, angels, stars and numbers, which are to be understood symbolically. The struggle between good and evil powers in the latter days of a terminal period culminates in a final judgment, the resurrection of the dead and the installation of a messianic kingdom. All these elements are not

necessarily present in any one work, and it can be convenient to use the term even where a deliberate frustration of a conventional apocalyptic expectation may be at issue.

Apocalyptic types characterize historical periods of upheaval and crisis, and interest in apocalyptic literature of the past has also occurred in such periods. Similarly, in recent years critics of secular literature have become sensitized to the apocalyptic elements in works not formally of the type, but whose language, particularly imagery, touches on the themes of revelation, renovation and ending. Frank Kermode's *The Sense of an Ending* (1967) is the most notable of these, using the 'ways in which . . . we have imagined the ends of the world' as a taking-off point for a study of fictional endings and fictional structures generally. For him, the literature of apocalypse is a 'radical instance' of fiction, depending 'on a concord of imaginatively recorded past and imaginatively predicted future'. Recent awareness of apocalyptic types in fiction, he claims, has concentrated on 'crisis, decadence and empire, and . . . disconfirmation, the inevitable fate of detailed eschatological predictions'.

In using apocalypse as a type of fiction recent criticism may merely be using a congenial language to define the literature of its own time—including that of the past felt to be 'relevant'—in terms acceptable to its own sense of crisis. It seems also true that there has been a social history of apocalyptic fictions in Anglo-American literature, for while apocalypse seems almost allied with 'progressive' forces in Elizabethan times, as in Spenser's *The Faerie Queene*, it is entertained later with mixed fascination and horror by writers who project the Final End as an image of the abortion rather than the consummation of current trends of history. In his essay, 'The end of the world', reprinted in *Errand Into The Wilderness* (1964), Perry Miller has provided not only a summary of English and American apocalyptic literature, but an insight into the gradual transition in expectations and reasons for the desirability of this typology. He focuses particularly on the period between the Elizabethan and the Modern and on the figures of Jonathan Edwards, 'the greatest artist of the apocalypse' in America, and Edgar Allan Poe, whose eschatological stories pinpoint a transition in the handling of apocalyptic materials, foreshadowing more modern attitudes to a world-consuming holocaust.

AMG

aporia
see DECONSTRUCTION

appreciation
see AESTHETICS, EVALUATION

archaism

is the use of forms whose obsoleteness or obsolescence is manifest and thus immediately subject to the reader's scrutiny. It can be mere whimsical display: Thackeray sometimes lapses into language quaint in his own time and irrelevant to the cast of mind of his characters, his gratuitous mischief evoking a simple, ultimately repetitious response and impeding any probing of the more complex implications of characters and plot. In general, archaism's tendency is to be a simplifying device: one's experience of the language of one's own time and place is of something richly and variously suggestive, closely related to one's experience and knowledge, capable of complexity of organization and delicate flexibility, spontaneously understandable and usable, whereas archaism refers back to a linguistic or cultural system which it cannot totally reconstruct, and archaic forms may thus seem impoverished, rigid and ponderous. The consistent archaism of the Authorized Version (1611) interposes a unified tone of solemnity between the varied subject-matter and the audience, making its response more uniform because more uncomplex. More sophisticated, and richly fruitful, uses of archaic language are commonly found in great authors, invoking and incorporating the values of older literary traditions: Spenser, Shakespeare, Milton, Wordsworth, T. S. Eliot provide many examples.

Since we imagine earlier cultural states to have been, like our childhood, simpler, more manageable, perhaps more desirable than the present, archaism can arouse an often vague delight in the familiar but long forgotten, yet as it refers back to the unknown can also be made frightening: Thomas Mann, in *Doctor Faustus* (1947), exploits this paradox to reveal affinities between cautious, conservative habits of mind and dangerous primitivism.

Except in regionalist writers, cultural archaism is not commonly combined with consistent linguistic archaism, but it too can be a simplifying device: many historical novels exploit our unfamiliarity with the culture described to give an uncomplex, idealized, and sometimes (as in C. F. Meyer) monumental and intriguingly remote impression of human emotions such as heroism, nostalgic yearning and guilt.

See *Cahiers de l'Association internationale des études françaises,* 19 (1967).

MHP

archetype
see MYTH

Aristotelian criticism
see CHICAGO CRITICS

art

Nobody has yet defined art to anyone else's satisfaction. There is general agreement on what art is not; none on what it is. Art, as all know who are in the know, is not Life. Similarly, informed opinion is unanimous in contrasting Art and Craft, Art and Propaganda, Art and Entertainment. But here the difficulties start, since it is evident that if these things are not congruent with art they may well overlap it.

'Art', it seems, like 'good', must be simply a commendatory word covering a multitude of incompatible meanings. The commendatory component is surely what fires controversy in the quest for some common essence to be distilled from the multiplicity of admirable works—a quest inevitably vain. What commends itself to one taste is to another distasteful, for such commendation is subjective: *de gustibus . . .*' Nor can there be agreement about objectively commendatory characteristics, for qualities perfectly appropriate to a good comic drama cannot be so to a love lyric or a tragic novel. In any case commendatory definitions are persuasive, and therefore however descriptive they purport to be are always prescriptive, and thus provocative, in effect.

The pull of common usage is probably too strong to allow this distracting commendatory element to be eliminated, but if the unanswerable question 'What is Art?' were to be dropped in favour of the practical question 'How can "Art" be most *usefully* defined?' it might be easier to diminish and control it. Anyway, it is clearly more useful to go along with common usage as far as it is consonant with the requirements already implied than to flout it completely. Perhaps the following stipulative definition will meet the case: *any work characterized by an obvious aesthetic element is to be deemed a work of art*. This definition is minimally commendatory, for it does not imply that the aesthetic element defining a literary work as 'art' need be its most valuable characteristic, or that all works, even of creative literature, *ought* to be works of 'art' as defined. It is not essentialist in so far as *any* form, whether in drama, narrative or lyric, and *any* content in combination with it, may give rise to aesthetic effects, so allowing dissimilar works all to be classed as works of art yet without the disrespect to their differences that comes from concentrating attention on some alleged metaphysical common property. It is descriptive rather than prescriptive in so far as aesthetic appreciation depends on describable formal qualities (see AESTHETICS). Finally, such a definition is consonant with the commonest use of this word in literary history, 'Art for art's sake'. Nor is it entirely inconsistent with the common contrasts mentioned. Craft, Propaganda, and Entertainment, being intended for use, not ornament, are less likely to be characterized by an obvious aesthetic element than those less instrumental works that can afford to treat the reader more *formally*, keep him at a little distance.

The usefulness of this definition is both negative and positive. Negatively, by drastically reducing the value-connotations of 'art', it avoids that metaphysical discussion which distracts attention from more concrete critical issues. Positively, by leaving open the possibility of good, bad or indifferent art (accordingly to the quality of the aesthetic element) and also by not pre-empting the possibility of factors other than 'art' being more pleasurable or important, it encourages full and varied critical appreciation.

See E. H. Gombrich, *Art and Illusion* (1960); R. Wollheim, *Art and its Objects* (1968); *British Journal of Aesthetics*.

AER

assonance
see TEXTURE

atmosphere
The word 'atmosphere' often occurs in non-literary contexts in vague senses difficult to distinguish satisfactorily from literary uses. Indeed, perhaps its very vagueness makes it a necessary critical term. Unlike almost all others, it reminds us not of the human propensity to arrange phenomena in patterns and think in structures, but of our ability to suspend analytical awareness: 'atmospheric' writing perhaps exploits our delight in an apparent temporary escape from structure.

Atmosphere is created where the overtones of the words and ideas employed reinforce one another; the avoidance of challenging disharmonies reduces the amount of intellectual effort required from the reader and prevents disruption of his sense of the uniformity and continuity of the work. The paradox of 'atmospheric' literature is that although (like almost all writing) it is linear, one word following another, it gives an appearance of stasis. Such German Romantics as Brentano and Eichendorff often use rhyme-words closely related in emotional colouring, so that the second rhyme-word, in recalling the first, includes it; thus a progressively all-engulfing sense of expansion is achieved. This, combined with effects of ebb and flow as one rhyme is replaced by another, eliminates a risk of 'atmospheric' writing, namely that it will seem aimless and meagrely repetitious, and sustains the paradox (exploited more complexly by some authors, e.g. Hardy) of a movement which is no movement.

Atmosphere is often created by the viewing of ordinary events from an unusual angle, giving them an air of mystery: in Alain-Fournier's *Le Grand Meaulnes* (1913) even everyday happenings at school (which themselves evoke nostalgia in the reader) are mysterious because the child's understanding is insufficiently developed to work out to his own satisfaction how they are affecting him.

MHP

author

According to common sense, authors are people who write books. But this is an activity subject to considerable historical variation, and one recent development in criticism has been to attend to this variation: to analyse the shifting identity of the author in relation to different institutions—the church, the court, the publishing house, the university. This analysis includes among its concerns the effects of print technology upon authorship, and the emergence in the nineteenth century of authors as a distinct professional group with legally protected rights of property in what they wrote. Another aspect of this history is the changing cultural image of authorship. Again the variation here is considerable, ranging from the scribe, to the artisan skilled in rhetoric, to the figure who imitates either nature or established models of excellence, to the seer who produces forms of writing deemed equivalent to new forms of consciousness, endowed with powers of prophecy or moral wisdom. This history demonstrates the problematic relationship between writing and authorship: are all writers authors or only some? What, in any given period, makes the difference? Nor is it a history characterized by the simple succession of one image of authorship by another: for example, the fascination with literary works as the product of divinely inspired genius which emerged in late eighteenth-century Europe revives themes found in Longinus and Plato.

The history of the practice and concept of authorship is valuable to students of literature because ideas and fantasies about the author have determined how we read and value literary works. If we regard literature as the product of genius, we approach it with reverence and an expectation of revelation. Or the logic of critical argument could be organized around the idea that the author is the sole or privileged arbiter of meaning. To discover the meaning of a work might be regarded as equivalent to understanding what the author did intend or might have intended in writing it. The problem of how to decode the author's INTENTIONS is itself the subject of extensive critical debate. What is the relevance of biographical information? Can we discern the author's intentions by analysing the literary work as a series of speech acts, each with an intended force? Can we know an author's intention without access to the historical context in which he or she wrote? What are the effects of PSYCHOANALYTIC criticism which introduces the idea of unconscious motivation into an account of authorship?

These questions continue to preoccupy literary critics, testifying to the power of the author in critical argument and in the wider culture.

Our contemporary fascination with authors is long-standing, going back at least to the eighteenth century when Samuel Johnson produced a classic of biographical criticism, *The Lives of the English Poets* (1779–81). ROMANTIC theory introduced the analogy between divine and literary creativity, and this theological aura around authorship was renewed by MODERNIST accounts of the impersonality of the great writer. Authors have become heroic figures in modern culture: whether as rebels or reactionaries, because they write books authors are expected to have wise things to say about a whole range of political and personal dilemmas.

But modern criticism has not simply underwritten the authority of authors. In a famous essay, 'The Intentional Fallacy' (1954), the American critics Wimsatt and Beardsley issued a dictat forbidding critics to refer to authorial intentions in the analysis of literature: a literary work contained all the information necessary for its understanding in the words on the page, so appeals to authorial intention were at best irrelevant, at worst misleading. The argument is valuable in so far as it warns against replacing the interpretation of texts with an interpretation of the author's life. It founders, however, for various reasons: the words on the page do not simply begin and end there, and understanding them requires reference to historical and social contexts, which are not so constant as Wimsatt and Beardsley believe. Nor can meaning be so readily divorced from intention. According to speech act theory, to understand the meaning of an utterance requires that we understand the intention of someone in uttering it. The problem with literary texts is identifying who that someone is, given the multiple displacements of the author into narrator, persona, characters, statements of traditional wisdom and other forms of quotation. Where do we find Dostoevsky amid the multiple voices which make up *Crime and Punishment*? Where do we find Chaucer in the *Canterbury Tales*?

The impossibility of answering these questions is the starting point for Roland Barthes's polemical essay 'The Death of the Author'. According to Barthes the author is an ideological construct whose purpose is to legitimate a practice of writing and reading which always pursues 'the voice of a single person, the author "confiding" in us'. Barthes proposes an alternative account: the text is irreducibly plural, a weave of voices or codes which cannot be tied to a single point of expressive origin in the author. Reading is not about the discovery of a single hidden voice or meaning, but a production working with the multiple codes that compose a text. Traditional assumptions about the origin and the unity of·a text are reversed:

> The reader is the space on which all the quotations that make up a
> writing are inscribed without any of them being lost; a text's unity

lies not in its origin but in its destination. Yet this destination cannot any longer be personal: the reader is without history, biography, psychology; he is simply that someone who holds together in a single field all the traces by which the text is constituted.

Barthes's stress upon the anonymity of the reader recalls T. S. Eliot's earlier account of the impersonality of the author in 'Tradition and the Individual Talent' (1919). Barthes shifts the terms of a MODERNIST poetics on to the side of the READER; the meaning of a text is volatile, varying according to the different occasions of reading and without reference to an authority which will fix meaning. Barthes's paradoxical transformation of authors into readers liberates us from the oppressive reverence for authorial creativity and wisdom, but it excludes important questions from the critical agenda: what is it that brings a particular person at a particular time to write? What do we make of the phenomenon of originality or of the fact that literary works have stylistic signatures which enable us to distinguish the work of one author from another? Turning authors into cults is not going to answer these questions, but neither is banishing them altogether from the discourse of literary criticism. See also CREATION, DECONSTRUCTION, DIALOGIC STRUCTURE, DISCOURSE, READER.

See J. Bayley, *The Characters of Love* (1960); R. Barthes, 'The Death of the Author' in *Image-Music-Text* (trans. 1977) and *S/Z* (1970, trans. 1975); M. Foucault, 'What is an author?' (1969) in *Language, Counter-Memory and Practice* (1977); P. Parrinder, *Authors and Authority* (1977). JC

autobiography
see BIOGRAPHY

B

ballad

The term has three meanings of different scope. The widest, of no literary significance, is that of any set of words for a tune. The narrowest refers to the English and Scottish *traditional ballad*, a specific form of narrative poem which became a part of the larger world of folk-song. The ballad is not peculiar to England and Scotland, but is found throughout Europe and in post-settlement America. In Britain, the traditional ballad first appears in the later Middle Ages, probably in the fifteenth century, when the minstrels, declining in social status and circulation, began to carry to a wider audience their narrative art in folk-songs based on strong symmetrically constructed stories in a simplified four-line stanza. Then ballads were increasingly sung at every level of society by non-professionals. By the end of the seventeenth century, emphasis had shifted to the music as the prime formative constituent and more ballads used refrains, meaningless vocables like 'fal-lal', common-places and formulae, 'filler lines' to give the singer time to arrange the next stanza, and the peculiarly effective structure known as 'incremental repetition':

> He was a braw gallant,
>   And he rade at the ring;
> And the bonny Earl of Murray
>   Oh he might have been a king!
>
> He was a braw gallant
>   And he played at the ba;
> And the bonny Earl of Murray
>   Was the flower among them a'.

The traditional ballads as a whole have certain well-marked and justly admired characteristics. They deal with episodes of well-known stories, condensed and impersonally presented, often by means of juxtaposed pictures or direct speech of the persons involved:

> The king sits in Dunfermline town
>   Drinking the blude-red wine;

> 'O whare will I get a skeely skipper
> To sail this new ship o' mine?' . . .
>
> Our king has written a braid letter,
> And seal'd it with his hand,
> And sent it to Sir Patrick Spens,
> Was walking on the strand . . .

There is little psychological comment, and the 'meaning' is realized through directly rendered action, and cryptic references to the larger context of related events. There is a 'ballad form' and a 'ballad world', both of supreme imaginative interest. The traditional ballads became admired literary objects in the eighteenth century, and numerous collections were made and published from then on. The most famous is Francis J. Child's five volumes of *The English and Scottish Popular Ballads* (1882–98). Such study tended to treat the ballads as timeless, though later discussion, based on the invaluable work of scores of collectors such as Bishop Percy (*Reliques of Ancient English Poetry*, 1765), Sir Walter Scott (*Minstrelsy of the Scottish Borders*, 1802–3) and Child himself, has begun to establish one of the most complex and interesting socio-aesthetic facts in English art, the evolution of style in the ballads. The Romantics were interested in the ballads as folk-art and monuments of the heroic past. The *literary ballad*, with no music, had a vogue at the end of the eighteenth century and for another century, the best-known of such works being Coleridge's *Ancient Mariner* and Keats's 'La Belle Dame sans Merci'. The older study of ballads had the disadvantage of treating 'collected' ballads both as written texts—though any written form poorly represents the 'performed' ballad in its musical and dramatic strength—and as fossil objects of a dead art. A revival of popular interest in traditional song, dating in Britain from the 1950s, has however brought to general attention the fact that traditional ballads are still being sung by expert performers, and are still being composed and renewed.

Before the end of the eighteenth century the third meaning of the word was the most common: any doggerel verses set to one of several well-known tunes such as 'Packington's Pound'. These were the sheet ballads, broadside ballads sold in roughly printed sheets, or stall-ballads hawked around the countryside at fairs or from door to door. The ballad-singer sang to collect customers for his wares, which dealt with murders, political events, prodigies. Such ballads were 'low-falutin', mostly realistic, irreverent, ironic, sometimes seditious. From this kind of production come the miners' ballads, work songs, protest songs, party political attacks which have had popular revival on the contemporary 'folk scene'.

The European settlement of America has also produced large bodies of distinctive ballads in the New World, particularly in the United States. The ballads in English consist either of transplanted traditional ballads which successive waves of immigrants, to Virginia in the seventeenth and eighteenth centuries, for example, have taken with them, or of indigenous ballads which have been and still are produced among West Virginian miners, the cowboys of the South West or the blacks. Many versions of traditional ballads have been collected in the remoter parts and more isolated communities of the United States, such as portions of the Atlantic coast and the Central West, or the mountain people of the Appalachians, and these have been an important source for British as well as American ballad scholars. The changes which took place in the texts by transmission in America, modifications, for example, of the importance of rank in the narrative and modulations of names, provide valuable material for the study of ballad tradition. American sources often preserve archaic forms of European tunes, and musical works are rich and distinguished. The words, it has been said, are often preserved in relatively impoverished forms. An interesting reverse transplanting of traditional material is to be noticed in the way modern American recordings frequently introduce Scottish and English listeners and singers to forgotten or half-forgotten ballads. Indigenous American ballads include broadsides of the Revolutionary Period and the Civil War.

See B. H. Bronson, *The Traditional Tunes of the Child Ballads* (1959–62); W. J. Entwistle, *European Balladry* (revised ed., 1951); D. C. Fowler, *A Literary History of the Popular Ballad* (1968); Hamish Henderson, 'Scots ballad and folk song recordings', *Scottish Literary News*, 1 (2), January 1971; M. J. C. Hodgart, *The Ballads* (1950); V. de Sola Pinto and A. E. Rodway, *The Common Muse* (1950).

AMR

baroque

A term denoting a distinctive style deeply characteristic of the seventeenth century, long since firmly established for critics of art and music, whose usefulness for literary critics must still be regarded as problematic and controversial. However, its increasing popularity amongst critics of many persuasions seems likely to make it a word, like 'Romanticism', that must at least be lived with; it offers possibilities for exciting analysis of a broadly cultural nature, and all the attendant dangers. Like ROMANTICISM again, it submits to an enormous number of seemingly disconnected and even contradictory usages, as phrases like 'Baroque grandeur', 'Baroque eccentricity', 'Baroque mysticism', 'Baroque exuberance' attest; it is even more polymorphously perverse in its frequent appearances outside the seventeenth century in labels like 'The Contemporary Baroque'.

Art historians generally now agree to regard the Baroque as the third Renaissance style, setting in around 1600, with its centre in Rome and its quintessential representative in Bernini, and with important Catholic and post-tridentine tendencies. Musicologists associate the Baroque with the advent of Monteverdi, the birth of operatic recitative and *concertante* style, and with figured bass. The essential features of the works of art produced can perhaps best be suggested in a short space by means of semantic clusters, obviously shading into each other, with appropriate illustrations: *solidity*, massiveness, size, intimidation (St Peter's, Rome); *ornament*, playfulness, wit, fancifulness (Bavarian and Austrian Baroque); *mysticism*, ecstasy, inwardness, transcendence (Bernini's St Teresa); *drama*, human warmth, fleshiness (the paintings of Caravaggio); *illusion, trompe l'oeil* (the Heaven Room in Burghley House). It is important to add, as a further defining feature, that Baroque works of art unify, or attempt to unify, such elements in simple, massive organization: solidity *carries* ornament, for instance, rather than being swamped by it (consider Baroque columns, or the function of the figured bass in Bach).

Most critical importers of the term fall down on one of two counts. On the one hand, the temptation to be over-cautious and literal: the study of reference to works of art (establishing for instance that Pandemonium is a Baroque building) or of relations between literary and pictorial iconography is a very useful but limited activity. On the other hand, the opposite danger of over-ambition, betraying itself very often in loose metaphoric talk of the 'architecture' of a poem, its 'illusory perspectives', its use of space or light. The most fruitful approach to the relations between literature and other arts is likely to be one that attempts to 'translate' the stylistic elements of one art form into those of another. To give examples: it seems legitimate and useful to regard the frequent literary use of oxymoron and paradox in the seventeenth century as a counterpart to the dramatic use of chiaroscuro in Baroque painting, or to see a correspondence between the 'play within a play' form in seventeenth-century drama and the construction of Bernini's St Teresa chapel. But a great deal of systematic work along these lines needs to be done.

In the case of Baroque, however, having got this far in his importations, the critic may need to go further—to explore in particular the term MANNERISM. A good deal of vagueness or confusion is often disseminated by the literary critic's ignorance of this concept; the features of Donne's poetry, for instance, that are sometimes referred to as 'Baroque' might more fruitfully be considered in relation to the art of Parmigianino or Giulio Romano.

Besides setting a challenge of an interdisciplinary nature, the use of the word *baroque* outside the seventeenth-century context involves other problems that reach out as far as the theory of history. Some critics (e.g. Hauser, *Mannerism*, 1965) see 'Baroque' as a recurrent phenomenon, a constant tendency of the human spirit. This requires very cautious handling indeed; if one can posit a 'Baroque spirit' it seems most fruitful to regard it as historically activated, as a last energetic assertion of the Renaissance faith in the fundamental inter-connectedness of phenomena—one that is conveyed above all in a fleshly solidity of realization, accessible (and unavoidable!) to a wider audience than were the *arcanae* of Florentine neo-Platonists.

There is none the less a contemporary vogue of Baroque imitation and pastiche, with exemplars like John Barth, Iris Murdoch, Günther Grass; our current self-conscious preoccupation with illusion and sham makes this unsurprising. In many ways, however, it is failed Baroque—the inflated or sentimental rhetoric that generated, for instance, the stylistic conventions of religious kitsch—that fascinates and stimulates the camp use of the self-evidently bad or hollow. The best Baroque art—the work of Bernini, Rembrandt, Milton, Monteverdi, Bach—is of a different order of intensity and coherent grandeur altogether, and one should not readily assume its recurrence.

See L. L. Martz, *The Wit of Love* (1969); W. Sypher, *Four Stages of Renaissance Style* (1955); René Wellek, 'The concept of Baroque in literary scholarship', *Journal of Aesthetics and Art Criticism,* 5 (1946), 77–109, reprinted with a Postscript in *Concepts of Criticism* (1963).

MAH

belief

Reading is a conscious or unconscious confrontation or symbiosis of one's own beliefs, assumptions and angle of vision with another's. A writer may seek to disguise this (e.g. by concealing his attitudes, adopting uncontroversial ones, or appealing to apparently non-moral desires), but even his omissions may imply much.

Since I. A. Richards's *Principles of Literary Criticism* (1924), critics have usually been wary of detailed explorations into reader psychology: 'willing suspension of disbelief' (Coleridge) is now more often alluded to than investigated. It implies a contract between author and reader: the reader is encouraged to imagine that what is portrayed is real or possible rather than remain querulously aware of its fictionality and impossibility, and hopes thereby to attain satisfactions and discoveries for which involvement, not distance, is required. Total delusion is rarely achieved (we do not rush on stage to whisper in the tragic hero's ear) and would probably be psychologically damaging: literature may help us to recognize and explore our fantasies without giving way to them. But as J. R. R. Tolkien's current popularity and some early reactions to the philosophizing of Wordsworth and Lamartine show, the desire to believe is often strong, even (as sceptics would see it) manipulable into extreme gullibility or regressive escapism. Perhaps an opportunity to believe in something, even hypothetically and with only part of oneself, is sufficient palliation for human insecurity to be a desired goal. The wish to participate in a beautiful, perfectly ordered universe, where one's expectations are harmoniously satisfied even though what will come next is not fully predictable and thus preserves the charm of surprise, a wish some requite by listening to Mozart, can also be satisfied by literature. Some would attach a religious significance to this.

The means by which belief is encouraged are diverse. Perhaps the best known is *verisimilitude*, an attempt to satisfy even the rational, sceptical reader that the events and characters portrayed are very possible (e.g. typical of a certain milieu or recurrent human tendencies). Other means are less rational, e.g. 'metaphysical pathos' (A. O. Lovejoy, *The Great Chain of Being*, 1936 reprinted 1961, 10–14), the non-intellectual appeal of intellectual ideas, sometimes reinforced by incidental sensuous and motor attractiveness (e.g. the power, lilt and sound-quality of Hugo's verse is sometimes seen as giving convincingness—ultimately spurious—to his ideas). Another, frequent in tragedy and linked to wish-fulfilment, is an appeal to the desire to believe in human dignity and value. Belief may be sustained by the continuous presentation of a coherent universe (Tolkien's Middle Earth has a highly complex and detailed coherence); sometimes (as in Kafka) the coherence is strongly marked but (as in some dreams) difficult to identify, thus creating an impression of threat.

The human willingness to believe provides various possibilities for manipulating responses. Some writers (e.g. Arnim and Hoffmann in their use of 'Romantic irony', and many comic novelists in their alternations of sympathy and mocking distance) use techniques which destroy belief, or which continually play off our wish to believe against our wish to be sceptical, calling both in question and requiring a complex, questioning response. Some (e.g. Céline) display an innocuousness which at first creates uncritical belief but of whose implications the reader becomes increasingly suspicious. Others, by undermining confidence in the world presented, induce us to transfer our belief to the narrator or author as the only reliable authority. In short, it is difficult to imagine a form of literature to which the concept of belief would be irrelevant.

MHP

biography

In post-classical Europe the literary recording of people's lives begins with the search for example in the Lives of the Saints and the stories of the rise and fall of princes. Medieval historians like Geoffrey of Monmouth, Matthew Paris and others, bring a concern with human failings and strengths to their histories which often overrides their objectivity. But it is not until the sixteenth century that the first recognizable biographies appear. Cardinal Morton's *Life of Richard III* (1513?), wrongly attributed to Thomas More; Roper's *Life of More* (1535?); and Cavendish's *Life of Wolsey* (1554–7) are varously claimed as the first true biography, though no one could claim that the genre is established in the eyes of a readership. The seventeenth century saw Bacon's *Life of Henry VIII* (1621), Walton's *Lives* (1640–78) and, best known of all perhaps, Aubrey's *Minutes of Lives* which he began collecting in the 1660s and in which he persisted till his death. It is in Aubrey that we first hear the real human voice commenting with a sly smugness, a gossipy humour and a delight in the oddity of human nature on the affairs and misalliances of those he minuted. But it is in the eighteenth century and with Dr Johnson's *Lives of the Poets* (1779–81) that the form is established beyond a doubt with his claim for its recognition as a literary form in its own right and his insistence on its peculiar virtue being that it alone of literary forms seeks to tell the literal, unvarnished truth. It was fitting that the founder of the form should be repaid by becoming the subject of what is perhaps the best known of all biographies, Boswell's *Life of Johnson* (1791).

In the nineteenth century, biography continued to flourish (e.g. Lockhart's *Life of Scott* (1837, 1838), Gilchrist's *Life of Blake* (1863)) but now it was also showing its potential influence on the structures of fiction. Wordsworth's *Prelude*, the novels of Dickens and those of the Brontës all show in various ways the intimacy which grew up between experience and invention during and after the Romantic period. This process continued until the end of the century, culminating perhaps in that most literary of biographies, Gosse's *Father and Son* (1907) and that most biographical of novels, Butler's *The Way of All Flesh* (1903). But if the hybrids flourished so did the thing itself, and Lytton Strachey's *Eminent Victorians* (1918) established the standards both in reasoned objectivity and in witty skill for all those who were to follow him. The modern biography was established.

The main claim of the modern biographer is his objectivity towards his subject. He asserts by choosing the form that he deals in *fact*, not fiction. This claim may seem dubious if we compare his methods and presuppositions with his close relation, the autobiographer, who also claims to tell the whole truth and nothing but the truth. (Vladimir Nabokov has great fun with this claim in his autobiography *Speak Memory*, 1966). A much more naïve judgment emerges from H. G. Wells's *Experiment in Autobiography* (1934) when he wishes the novel could more closely resemble the biography since the latter is more 'truthful': 'Who would read a novel if we were permitted to write biography all out?' This completely begs the question of the selection and presentation of the material; it presupposes that the only limitations to the biographer's truth-telling are the range of his knowledge and licence of his society to publish it. It ignores the central issue of what kind of reality language can sustain.

Recently a wide interest has been shown in the interchangeability of fictional and documentary techniques. Novelists have experimented with 'factual subjects' (e.g. Truman Capote's *In Cold Blood*, 1966), while social scientists have gone to the novel for structures which enable them to relate patterns of behaviour not amenable to the sequential logic of analytic prose discourse (e.g. Oscar Lewis, *The Children of Sanchez*, 1962). The traditional distinctions between biography, personal history (diary/confession) and novel (especially first-person narrative and/or tape-recorded novels) are coming to be questioned. For many new writers—for example in the emerging African countries (Achebe, Ngugi, Soyinka) and in Negro American circles (Baldwin, John Williams, Jean Tooner)—autobiographical art is not a device for summing up the accumulated wisdom of a lifetime but a means of defining identity. The distinction between novel and autobiography becomes almost meaningless in this context. A novel like Ralph Ellison's *Invisible Man* (1965) and an autobiography like J. P. Clark's *America, Their America* (1964) are united beyond their different forms in a single gesture of passionate self-exposure.

Recent work in England has begun to show this influence too: Alexander Trocchi's *Cain's Book* (1960) and Jeff Nuttall's *Bomb Culture* (1968) continue a tradition whose roots run back through Kerouac to Henry Miller. It seems likely that this trend will continue and that the future will see an extension of the 'hybrid' book whose format disdains to answer the query, fact or fiction? See also FICTION, NOVEL.

See Leon Edel, *Literary Biography* (1957); Paul Murray Kendall, *The Art of Biography* (1965); H. G. Nicholson, *The Development of English Biography* (1959); Lytton Strachey, *Biographical Essays* (modern collection, 1969).

GG

burlesque

see PARODY

C

cacophony
see TEXTURE

caricature
see PARODY

carnival
see DIALOGIC STRUCTURE

catastrophe
see DENOUEMENT, DRAMA

catharsis
The most disputed part of Aristotle's definition of tragedy is his statement that it is an action 'through pity and fear effecting a catharsis of these emotions'. Traditionally *catharsis* is rendered as 'purgation' and refers to the psychological effect of tragedy on the audience. Against Plato's condemnation of art for unhealthily stimulating emotions which should be suppressed, Aristotle argues that audiences are not inflamed or depressed by the spectacle of suffering in tragedy, but in some way released. Our subjective, potentially morbid, emotions are extended outward, through pity for the tragic hero, in an enlargement, a leading out, of the soul (*psychogogia*). So tragedy moves us towards psychic harmony. A related, but less psychological, interpretation puts catharsis into the context of Aristotle's argument that the pleasure peculiar to tragedy arises from the fact that our emotion is authorized and released by an intellectually conditioned structure of action. In fiction, unlike reality, we feel the emotion *and* see its place in a sequence of probability and necessity.

   Alternatively catharsis may be seen, as by G. Else (*Aristotle's 'Poetics'*, 1957), not as the end result, but as a process operating through the 'structure of events' which purifies, not the audience, but the events themselves. The tragic hero's pollution (typically from the murder of a blood-relation) which makes him abhorrent is shown, through the structure of discovery and recognition, and his subsequent remorse, to be in some measure undeserved. So catharsis is the purification of the hero which enables us to go beyond *fear*, our horror at the events, to *pity* born of understanding; the poet's structure leads our reason to judge our emotion. See also PLOT, TRAGEDY.

See Humphry House, *Aristotle's 'Poetics'* (1956).

PM

cento(nism)

see PASTICHE

character,

the fictional representation of a person, is likely to change, both as a presence in literature and as an object of critical attention, much as it changes in society. Ideas of the place of man in the social order, of his individuality, his capacity to determine his own fortunes, the extent to which he is assumed to dominate his own life and motives or be dominated by forces outside himself—the entire basis of identity in short—clearly shift historically; and this is often mimed in literature by the relation of characters to actions or webs of story. The idea of character often attaches, therefore, to the personalizing or humanizing dimension of literature; thus naturalism, which tends to create plots in which men are not self-determining agents but in ironic relationships to larger sequences of force, seems a remarkably impersonal writing. Yet individual identity is often partly an attribute of social interaction, of the play of the social drama; this too is mimed in the dramatic character of much literature. In plays the paradox is compounded by the fact that characters are not simply represented verbally but impersonated by actors—a situation often used (as in much Shakespearean drama) to explore the paradoxes of being or identity themselves.

If the idea of character undergoes variation in different phases of literature, so it does in criticism. Neo-classical criticism tends to interpret characters as representatives of general human types and roles; romantic, to isolate and humanize them (see A. C. Bradley, *Shakespearean Tragedy*, 1904) and even separate them from the surrounding fictional determinants or dramatic design as 'living' people; modern, to regard them as humanized outcroppings from some larger verbal design. 'Characters' are by definition in determined contexts (i.e. they are parts of a literary sequence, involved in a plot), and can hence arouse liberal issues about the individualism of selves: as has happened latterly (in, e.g. John Bayley, *The Characters of Love*, 1960 and W. J. Harvey, *Character and the Novel,* 1965) where an intrinsic association between humanist realism and literature has been suggested, and the loss in contemporary fiction of what Iris Murdoch has called 'the difficulty and complexity of the moral life and the opacity of persons' explored. Indeed 'liberal' character has been a central aspect of artistic attention: hence, perhaps, Henry James's attempt (in parallel to that of his character Ralph Touchett) to set Isobel Archer 'free' in *The Portrait of a Lady*. Many fictional actions are in this sense portraits, aspects of the tendency of literature to personalize experience, in which the following out of the growth of a character is a primary cause of the work, the basis of its form.

But (as James indicates) there are characters and characters in fiction; we recognize some as of the centre and others as of the circumference. Some are characters in the Aristotelian sense (i.e. detailed figures with their own motives and capacity for distinctive speech and independent action); some are enabling aspects of story, minor figures, stereotypes; there are some to whose perceptions we give credence (from poetic speakers to characters like Anne Elliot in *Persuasion*) and some we regard as a contextual society; some who partake in and are changed in the action (heroes, protagonists) and confidantes or devices. Literature is dramatic as well as personal; and the dramatic play of characters in a sequence frequently involves various levels of aesthetic impersonality. Hence there are always variables of closeness to and distance from them (a fact which has enabled much Shakespearean criticism). The complex of impersonation, role and mask; the complex of the personality and impersonality of identity or of the dimensions of the unconscious; the complex of that spectrum running from character as separate existence to character as qualities, moral attributes: all of these have been essential areas of exploration for drama, poetry, fiction.

'Character' is perhaps the most mimetic term in the critical vocabulary, and hence one of the most difficult to contain within the fictional environment; yet it is an essential condition of fictional existence that a character is so contained. In this sense the representation of persons in literature is a simultaneous process of their humanization and their dehumanization. See also DIALOGIC STRUCTURE, HERO, NARRATIVE.

See Northrop Frye, *Anatomy of Criticism* (1957); Erving Goffman, *The Presentation of Self in Everyday Life* (1959); Leo Lowenthal, *Literature and the Image of Man* (1957); Ortega y Gasset, *The Dehumanisation of Art* (1948).

More recently the concept of 'character' has come under attack for methodological and ideological reasons in STRUCTURALIST and POST-STRUCTURALIST theory. In the work of Roland Barthes, for example, we find 'character' dispersed into the constitutive 'indices' or 'semes' of narrative discourse. See Barthes, 'Introduction to the structural analysis of narratives' (1966), trans. in *Image-Music-Text* (1977) and *S/Z* (1970, trans. 1975). Representative of a more radical critique of this humanistic notion is H. Cixous, 'The character of "character" ', *New Literary History*, 5 (1978).

MSB

Chicago critics

A group of critics, literary scholars and philosophers who came together first at the University of Chicago in the middle 1930s; included R. S. Crane, W. R. Keast, Richard McKeon, Norman Maclean, Elder Olson and Bernard Weinberg; are best-known through the collective volume *Critics and Criticism* (1952); and have had a strong and continuing influence on modern criticism. Their contribution to literary study lies in the philosophical clarity with which they attempted two main tasks. One was a close analysis, historical and synchronic, of criticism itself, to find out the kind of thing it was and the kind of thing it was studying; the second was an attempt to derive from that analysis a usable, coherent poetics. Participating in the general tendency of modern American criticism toward theory (as compared with the English tendency toward critical pragmatism), these critics dissented from several NEW CRITICAL emphases—stress on symbolism, paradox and the iconic nature of literature and the pre-eminent concern with lyric rather than narrative or dramatic forms. What distinguishes 'Chicago' theory is that it is holistic (concerned with the complete, dynamic structure of works) and typificatory (concerned to identify general kinds or species of works). It is thus that it is *neo*-Aristotelian: following Aristotle's ideal of a poetics always being derived from existing works, it is empirically plural, regarding criticism as secondary analysis, and so continually opened by the ever-growing variety of literature. Neo-Aristotelian poetics goes beyond the Aristotelian base to the extent that it draws on a vastly larger and more various literary corpus than Aristotle knew.

The neo-Aristotelian attitude in criticism is this: critical discourse, ostensibly a dialogue, actually conceals a multitude of differing presumptions about the genesis, nature and effect of a poem (i.e. any fiction) and sees it according to a wide variety of metaphors and analogies, often derived from extra-literary schemes of knowledge, and often dependent on self-invigorating dialectical pairs (form-content, tenor-vehicle, structure-texture) which are at best local expedients of composition rather than central features of artistic ordering. For critical dialogue, we have to know what kind of thing a poem is, to have a poetics based on the nature of the object. Hence the need for a pluralizable and pragmatic poetics which is still a poetics capable of emerging with general principles, a responsive theory of parts which are capable of creating concrete wholes in the given case, but will not predetermine the basis of coherence according to prescriptive assumption. The neo-Aristotelian poetics turns primarily on the notion of plot as a complex of matter *and* means: the basis of unifying coherence which has reference both to composition, to significant authorial choice, *and* the range of matters imitated. The result is a remarkably sophisticated notion of the relation of parts to wholes—one of the most promising modern bases for deriving a *literary* (as opposed to a linguistically or scientifically based) ontology. The risk is that the approach can become a ponderous applied method rather than a critical sympathy; it has led to some rather heavy works (Sheldon Sacks, *Fiction and the Shape of Belief,* 1964) as well as some very elegant critical endeavours (Wayne C. Booth, *The Rhetoric of Fiction,* 1961). Crane, especially in *The Languages of Criticism and the Structure of Poetry* (1953) and some essays in *The Idea of the Humanities* (1966), remains the best exemplar; also see Elder Olson, *The Poetry of Dylan Thomas* (1962) and *Tragedy and the Theory of Drama* (1961) and Bernard Weinberg, *History of Literary Criticism in the Italian Renaissance* (1961). For an unsympathetic view see W. K. Wimsatt, Jr, *The Verbal Icon* (1954), 41–65.

MSB

chorus

A band of dancers and singers at the festivals of the gods; also, their song. According to Aristotle, Greek tragedy evolved from the choric song of the Dithyramb. Incorporated in fifth-century drama, the chorus, male or female, represents the voice of a collective personality commenting on events and interpreting the moral and religious wisdom of the play. In Aeschylus, it still has some direct influence on the action. With Euripides, who curtailed its function, it loses some of its mythic solemnity but takes on a new lyrical beauty. In post-Euripidean tragedy, it apparently became mere ornamental interlude.

In later drama, the chorus was never to regain its original significance. In Elizabethan tragedy, it is sometimes reduced to a single actor, but larger choruses also exist (e.g. Norton and Sackville's *Gorboduc*). Milton (*Samson Agonistes*), Racine (*Esther, Athalie*) and in the nineteenth century, Swinburne (*Atalanta in Calydon, Erectheus*) use it in an attempt to revive or imitate the spirit and procedures of the Greek theatre. Rare in twentieth-century drama, it appears in Eliot's *Murder in the Cathedral*, and in *The Family Reunion*, where the cast itself assumes the role of chorus. But it survives in the opera.

Interpretations of the nature and function of the chorus vary. A. W. Schlegel considered it the 'idealized spectator'. Nietzsche, who attacked the democratic conception of the chorus as representing the populace over and against the noble realm of the play, maintained that it posits a reality set apart from quotidian reality, affirming the timeless, indestructible force of Nature. English critics, such as Lowes Dickin-

son and Gilbert Murray, point out that through the chorus the poet
could speak in his own person and impose upon the whole tragedy any
tone he desired.

NZ

classic

Matthew Arnold, in *The Study of Poetry*, says that 'the true and right
meaning of the word *classic, classical*, is that the work in question
belongs to the class of the very best'; and as T. S. Eliot observed (*What
is a Classic?*) classic status can be known 'only by hindsight and in
historical perspective'. A critic for whom the term *classic* is important is
likely to be a conserver of the canons of art: and the scholars of
Alexandria who invented the classic status of earlier Greek literature
held it fast in an elaborate mesh of formal rules which they then tried to
use as the basis of their own work, thus ensuring its own classic status.
The Romans, inheriting this classificatory system of rhetorical terms,
based their own upon them and reinforced the 'classic' status of Greek
literature, which they imitated with a recurrent sense of inferiority. For
us 'the classics' means first the literature of both Greece and Rome: but
'a classic' is nowadays likely to signify a work about the status of which
there is general agreement, often unenthusiastic (Arnold perhaps used
the term thus when he called Dryden and Pope 'classics of our prose').
A turning-point in the conception of classic status may have occurred in
the neo-classical eighteenth century when deference to the rules of
rhetoric, enshrined in the much-imitated *Ars Poetica* of Horace and in
Aristotle's *Poetics* and sustaining an aristocratic culture, gave way to
that sense of cultural diffusion that enabled Dr Johnson to invoke the
general admiration for Gray's 'Elegy' as real evidence of its excellence.
Since Arnold's time the term *classic* has lost effectiveness in proportion
as moral criticism has waned. Where there is no critical consensus or (in
Johnson's phrase) 'common pursuit of true judgement' the term is of
doubtful use. Eliot, in *What is a Classic?* cites 'a very interesting book
called *A Guide to the Classics* which tells you how to pick the Derby
winner': and his own argument for the classic status of Virgil is clearly
shaped by extra-literary concerns. In general the term is too readily
used as a substitute for criticism, and to endorse received judgments.

Nevertheless an impulse towards *classicism* as fostering the virtues of
formal discipline, impersonality, objectivity, and the eschewal of the
eccentric and self-indulgent has since the time of Goethe (who defined
the classical as the healthy, the romantic as the sick) served to check the
individualistic aesthetics of romantic conceptions of 'genius'. Pushkin's
work displays a classicism of this kind, often manifesting itself through
satire, as in the case of much eighteenth-century neo-classical writing.
The revolt of many twentieth-century writers against their late romantic

predecessors either enlisted the literature of classical antiquity as an aid to objectivity or universality (Joyce's use of Homer in *Ulysses*, or Pound's of Sextus Propertius) or contained lyric sensibility within the disciplined forms of a deliberate doctrine of classical impersonality. Eliot's theory of the OBJECTIVE CORRELATIVE is neo-classical in this sense, as is his insistence on the separation in great literature of the man who suffers from the mind which creates. A neo-classicism of this kind also underlies IMAGIST theory and practice. It was Eliot's elaboration of this new classicism into a Virgilian absolutism and orthodoxy extending beyond the frontiers of literature that prompted D. H. Lawrence's expostulation that 'This classiosity is bunkum, and still more *cowardice*' (*Collected Letters*, p. 753); and it is true that such modern neo-classical phenomena as neo-Aristotelianism in criticism, of J. V. Cunningham's homage to Horace in 'The quest of the opal' run deliberately counter to the eclecticism of the culture they spring from, rather than constituting an authoritative definition of literary norms (as did the neo-classicism of Dryden, Pope and Boileau). Such phenomena amount in essence to a renewed emphasis on the importance of careful craftsmanship and technique.

See Matthew Arnold, *Essays in Criticism, Second Series* (1888); J. V. Cunningham, 'The quest of the opal', in *The Journal of John Cardan* (1964); T. S. Eliot, *Selected Essays* (3rd ed., 1951); T. S. Eliot, *What is a Classic?* (1945); H. M. Peyre, *Qu'est-ce que le classicisme?* (1933); S. Vines, *The Course of English Classicism* (1930).

GMH

closure
see DECONSTRUCTION

code
see CREATION, SEMIOTICS

cohesion
see DISCOURSE

comedy
Arouses and vicariously satisfies the human instinct for mischief. The playing of tricks on unsuspecting victims, whether by other characters (e.g. Palaestrio in Plautus' *Miles Gloriosus*) or quirks of chance (e.g. Goldoni's *I due Gemelli veneziani*) or both, recurs continually in comedy. The tendency to derive delight from watching characters who come to find situations difficult and problematical (although to the audience they are clear and simple) can go beyond mischief and draw on more dubious emotions, such as delight in sadistic and voyeuristic observation of another's discomfiture. A situation which to a comic

character seems dangerous (likely to erode or destroy his self-esteem, comfort, amatory adventures or worldly success), but which implies no great threat to the audience or humanity in general, is a typical comic situation. Indeed, one characteristic of comedy (especially of comic drama, since it is frequently enacted at speed) is its ability to blur the distinction between harmless mischievous enjoyment and sado-voyeuristic satisfaction. When (as frequently in Molière) a master beats his servant, or when a fop is humiliated in a Restoration comedy, our amusement is spontaneous and unreflecting. This casts doubt on the supposedly intellectual and unemotional appeal of comedy which, according to some, derives from the absence of any deep sympathy and the distance which comedy sets up between characters and audience. The tempo leaves us no time to puzzle over our reactions and motives.

Rapidity can also be exploited more positively. If we are made to associate things which at first seemed dissimilar, the enjoyment of comedy can become more than an exercise in self-indulgence. A comic dramatist may choose simply to indulge our preconceptions of the comic: those who watch a third Whitehall farce know from the previous two exactly what forms of enjoyment to expect. But he may also aim to extend our awareness of comedy, so that we see analogies between what we regard as ridiculous and what previously we regarded as having value. The effect of this may sometimes be to blur distinctions (e.g. Aristophanes, in *The Clouds*, falsely equates Socrates's style of philosophy with that of the sophists); at other times self-seeking and self-adulation can be revealed behind an impressive exterior (Molière's treatment of a hypocrite in *Tartuffe*, and Kleist's of a village magistrate in *Der zerbrochene Krug*, illustrate ways in which respected social roles can be manipulated and misused). Comedy in itself is thus neither morally useful nor immoral: it can perpetuate and extend misconceptions as well as ridicule them. Sometimes, however, dramatists use the irresponsible instinctual speed of comedy to lead the audience to a more complex intellectual awareness. Besides manipulating audience responses, many comic writers have developed various devices for making us conscious that manipulations of various sorts are taking place and roles being adopted: the use of disguise and masks is an obvious example (*Love's Labour's Lost*).

Such awareness of complexities, when it occurs, is normally available only to the audience; rarely does it leave an imprint of uneasiness on the language of the plays. The language of comedy is fluent and articulate: characters do not feel a need to develop exploratory, stretching uses of language to account for themselves and the world around them, but are satisfied that the relationships between them and the world are simple and comprehensible. Unlike the tragic hero, the comic character does not face up to the task of reconciling inconsistencies in his own nature

(Harpagon, in Molière's *L'Avare*, feels no discrepancy between his selfish avarice and his desire to marry an emotionally lively young woman). The comic character is, however, usually more than willing to face up to the task of defending himself, particularly in the cut-and-thrust of dramatic dialogue. Even comic butts share this articulateness: they may be fools, but they are normally capable of speaking the same language as their more perspicacious opponents (e.g. the language of abuse in Molière or the language of pun and conceit in Shakespeare). Comic dialogue is frequently a battle which needs evenly balanced opponents to sustain its momentum. With dialogue and characterization, as with other aspects of comedy, it is perhaps by examining an author's capacity to generate pace, and the repetitiveness or increasing subtlety of the ways in which he exploits it, that one can best arrive at an assessment of him as a comic dramatist. See also FARCE.

See Henri Bergson, *Le Rire* (1899); Maurice Charney, *Comedy High and Low* (1978); Robert W. Corrigan (ed.), *Comedy: Meaning and Form* (1965); Paul Lauter (ed.), *Theories of Comedy* (1964); Elder Olson, *The Theory of Comedy* (1968).

MHP

comedy of manners
see MANNERS

comparative literature
Techniques of comparison form a natural part of the literary critic's analytic and evaluative process: in discussing one work, critics frequently have in mind, and almost as frequently appeal to, works in the same or another language. Comparative literature systematically extends this latter tendency, aiming to enhance awareness of the qualities of one work by using the products of another linguistic culture as an illuminating context; or studying some broad topic or theme as it is realized ('transformed') in the literatures of different languages. It is worth insisting on comparative literature's kinship with criticism in general, for there is evidently a danger that its exponents may seek to argue an unnatural distinctiveness in their activities (this urge to establish a distinct identity is the source of many unfruitfully abstract justifications of comparative literature); and on the other hand a danger that its opponents may regard the discipline as nothing more than demonstration of 'affinities' and 'influences' among different literatures—an activity which is not critical at all, belonging rather to the categorizing spirit of literary history.

Comparative literature is often discussed as if it were analogous with comparative philology or comparative religion: but it lacks, fortunately or unfortunately, the academic establishment of these disciplines. The idea that a work of literature yields a richer significance when placed alongside another, each serving as a way of talking about the other, has more to do with the NEW CRITICISM, and with Eliot's assertion that 'comparison and analysis are the chief tools of the critic', than with traditional literary scholarship, since intrinsic criteria of value help to shape such comparisons. This is not to deny, of course, that an imposing family tree is available to show how a shared European culture in medieval times (and later) took for granted what must now be painfully recreated: a culture in which to consider Chaucer, for instance, only in an English context would have seemed as senseless as to explain him away by reference to his French or Italian sources. On the world-historical showing the nationalist nineteenth century and the critical aftermath, stressing the need for a high degree of linguistic and cultural inwardness on the part of the reader—who cannot, the argument goes, be expected to attain this in a foreign culture except in unusual circumstances—can be seen as a Romantic aberration, wrongly at odds with the internationalist aspirations of European man which received their supreme formulation in the Enlightenment. But although an ideology of internationalism underlies comparative literary studies, and many of its more impressive exponents have been European Marxists, such studies clearly need to assimilate, not reject, the admirable critical work done, for example, in England by critics whose high degree of sensitivity to literature in their own language has not been accompanied by a developed critical interest in another literature. There seems little hope of a rapprochement between cultural history and practical criticism: yet this is the area where the need for discussion is most urgent. Practical criticism becomes niggling and circumscribed if it lacks authoritative generalization; cross-cultural literary history becomes pompous and empty if its practitioners are not critics. Tolstoy matters to an English reader at least as much as George Eliot does, and the objection that he is not truly accessible to the reader without Russian seems trifling. But how does one resolve the methodological problems involved in comparing the work of the English novelist with the translated work of the Russian with whom she has so much in common? Must we try to forget that Tolstoy did not write in English?

The presumptuousness of this may be avoided if emphasis is shifted from the smaller units of the literary work ('texture') to the larger ('structure'). Style can be described in terms of chapters as well as sentences: and the failure of many critics who approach novels as 'dramatic poems' can be explained as a consequence of over-insistent application to the minutiae of metaphoric language. The analogy with linguistics is fruitful: one needs as exact as possible an apparatus for describing the structure of a literary work, its 'grammar'. The term 'morphology' was appropriated by the Russian anthropologist Vladimir

Propp (*The Morphology of the Folk-Tale*, first published 1928, translated 1958) to describe the large metamorphoses undergone by certain themes or topoi in folk narratives, when it became clear to him that it was unproductive to compare (or indeed to describe) 'images' or 'characters'—local and partial phenomena. He discovered that one tale about a rabbit, for instance, might be radically different from another such: but that one could compare tales in terms of *patterns* of activities, what one might call 'fields', generated by the topos as it underwent changes of role and relationship: its morphology, in fact. It is evident that where narrative fiction is concerned a close study of the style of any given episode of a large structure will be of questionable validity unless the analysis can refer to the relationship of this episode to the whole work conceived as a coherent utterance: and that this pattern, often unperceived, is likely to yield more significance than local texture minutely analysed. In other words, a satisfactory account of a novel could consist, more than is usually the case, in an account of its 'plot' (the morphology of its fable, the pattern of formal changes), and there is no reason why this should not be perceived and described in a translated text as well as in a text in the original. Characteristic devices can be perceived in works which are products of similar phases of civilization (the devices used by Tolstoy and George Eliot to assert the religious significance of life against the small agnostic ego are comparable). To such a degree may this comparability exist that comparative analysis may need to invoke a concept of an underlying MYTH which has structured the works in a given way: Lévi-Strauss may become a potent force in literary studies. In the case of poetry, too, verbal texture needs to be considered as one manifestation of the total structure of the poem if comparative criticism is to be possible: but since many forms and stanza-patterns are common to the whole European tradition, where they engender comparable formal problems, comparative analysis will be rewarding to the critic who reads the language in question. In many cases the study of translations becomes a comparative critical exercise of great value, even for readers who lack the original: intelligent students of literature can benefit from a systematic comparison of three significant translations of Homer (e.g. Dryden, Pope and Cowper) even if they do not know Greek. The Chomskyan concept of deep structure may offer a new impetus to comparative criticism, since it would seem to facilitate the comparison of works whose surface structures may be dissimilar (an example that springs to mind is Melville's *Bartleby* and Gogol's *The Overcoat*: dissimilar in detail, these two masterpieces have a profound kinship which seems inadequately described in terms of 'theme' but may be more convincingly described in terms of generative grammar).

Certainly, we lack comparative studies of the stature of (say) the work of Empson or Leavis on English literature: and one must guard against throwing into relief the dearth of comparative studies in English by pointing to their abundance in French and German, since so many of these are unrewarding. Comparative literary studies are hampered by self-conscious theoreticians, especially in the English-speaking world, where they feel the need to assert themselves in the face of an impressive native criticism that is analytic rather than synthetic. Against this, the apparent decline of the English tradition of severe ANALYSIS may be interpreted as symptomatic of the end of English isolation in cultural as well as in political matters.

See Henry Gifford, *Comparative Literature* (1969); Marius Guyard, *La Littérature comparée* (1961); Leo Spitzer, *Linguistics and Literary History* (1948); N. P. Stallknecht and H. Frenz, *Comparative Literature: Method and Perspective* (1961); René Wellek and Austin Warren, *Theory of Literature* (1963). Relevant journals include *Comparative Criticism, Comparative Literature, Comparative Literature Studies, Comparison*.

GMH

competence, literary
see POETICS, STRUCTURALISM

complaint
see ELEGY

conceit
A characteristic feature of much Renaissance lyric poetry, the conceit is a way of apprehending and expressing the subject which pleases and illuminates by its ingenious aptness. It belongs therefore to a kind of poetry which is avowedly artificial, which is not 'the spontaneous overflow of powerful feeling' but instead invites the reader's appreciation of virtuosity and inventiveness. Like WIT and 'fancy', terms to which it is closely related, the word 'conceit' itself refers to the mental act of conception or understanding, and it implies an artful varying of the ordinary, not only in verbal expression, but in the way the subject has been conceived.

Although conceits may take the form of paradox ('The truest poetry is the most feigning') or hyperbole ('An hundred years should go to praise/Thine Eyes, and on thy Forehead Gaze'), they commonly involve metaphorical or analogical correspondences, which may be paradoxical or hyperbolical in character, e.g.:

> Full gently now she takes him by the hand,
> A lily prison'd in a gaol of snow,

Or ivory in an alabaster band;
So white a friend engirts so white a foe.
(Shakespeare)

For I am every dead thing,
In whom love wrought new Alchimie.
For his art did expresse
A quintessence even from nothingnesse,
From dull privations, and leane emptinesse:
He ruin'd mee, and I am re-begot
Of absence, darknesse, death; things which are not.
(Donne)

As these examples illustrate, the conceit belongs as much to the courtly style of the Elizabethans as it does to the wit of the Metaphysical poets; yet the former presents a series of emblematic pictures, while the latter realizes its object in the conceptual terms of a philosophical definition.

A single conceit may provide the basis of a whole poem (as in Sidney's sonnet, 'With how sad steps, O moon, thou climb'st the skies', or in Donne's 'The Flea'), or a poem may consist of a string of different conceits on a single subject (Crashaw's 'The Weeper', Herbert's 'Prayer'). The conceit may be sustained and elaborated at length, especially if it derives from a familiar or conventional motif (such as the innumerable variations on the 'blazon' or descriptive praise of the lady in Elizabethan love sonnets), or it may be confined to a single striking figure (such as Marvell's image of the fishermen carrying their coracles over their heads: 'Have shod their heads in their canoes/Like the Antipodes in shoes'). It may even be altogether implicit, like the unspoken pun on 'host' which underlies Herbert's 'Love'.

The conceit went out of fashion when it was generally felt that ingenuity or surprise were effects less suited to poetry than a sense of the natural. Like the pun, which suffered disfavour at the same time, it came to be regarded as a form of bad taste. But in our own age, with its taste for singularity and shock in art, the conceit has returned to poetry, nowhere more so than in the work of T. S. Eliot, himself a great admirer of seventeenth-century wit. The famous image from the beginning of 'The Love Song of J. Alfred Prufrock' describing the evening 'spread out against the sky / Like a patient etherised upon a table', is a good modern example of the conceit's appeal to the reader's mental acuity as much as to his feeling. For as the Renaissance itself insisted, however far-fetched or elaborate the conceit, its success depends upon how appropriate its extravagance and ingenuity are. True artifice in this kind of poetry demands of the poet a precise balance of fancy and judgment. See also WIT.

See M. Praz, *Studies in Seventeenth-Century Imagery* (1964);

K. K. Ruthven, *The Conceit* (1969); R. Tuve, *Elizabethan and Metaphysical Imagery* (1961).

DJP

concrete poetry

conceives of the poem as ideogram; as an instantly assimilable, visually ordered text in which the word stands both as physical spatial object, and as a plurality of simultaneously existing meanings. Preoccupations with both typographical form and semantic content have created confusions in which the text is seen as being somehow 'between poetry and painting', the reader being unsure whether he is confronted with a picture for reading, or a poem for looking at. At its mimetic extreme, the structure of the concrete poem either echoes its semantic content, in the manner of Apollinaire's '*Il pleut*', or else becomes its semantic content; in the words of the painter Stella: 'a picture of its own structure':

backwards

The concrete poem's aesthetic is not that of accumulative, discursive, linear writing, but that of the 'constellation'; Max Bense explains: 'It is not the awareness of words following one after the other that is its primary constructive principle, but the perception of its togetherness. The word is not used as an intentional carrier of meaning'. Bense's 'abstract' texts seem very close to the 'silence of form' that Roland Barthes believes attainable 'only by the complete abandonment of communication'.

Despite such formal preoccupations not all concrete poetry rejects communication; indeed the semantic extremes of concrete poetry, via its spatial 'grammar', come closer than any other mode of writing to the elusive meaningful semantic simultaneity that Barthes lauds as 'colourless writing'; writing in which each word is 'an unexpected object, a Pandora's box from which fly all the potentialities of language'. The elusiveness of 'writing degree zero' may be explained by the fact that traditional syntax, and the logical form of linear writing, simply do not permit a statement of the several simultaneously existing semantic realities making up the 'potentialities' of the word.

The eye may perceive two objects, the mind may conceive two concepts, but such pluralistic observations transcend the possibilities and patterns of linear language which must choose to record first one observation and then the other; a distortion which turns simultaneity into the sequential. Attempting to simultaneously evoke all the potentialities of language, rejecting the internal ordering of sequential linear language, yet still working within its confines, the Surrealists abandoned logical order for the 'super-real' semantic impressionism of 'automatic writing', while Joyce, Helms, Eliot and Burroughs re-mixed fragments of words and phrases in order to exchange old semantic potentialities for those of their new hybrid creations. Mallarmé achieved a relatively non-sequential and non-linear simultaneity of pluralistic semantic potentialities in his poem '*Un Coup de Dés . . .*' whose pages, though precisely sequentially ordered, proffered scattered spatially punctuated words permitting permutation in a number of non-sequential readings.

Concrete Poetry finally attained a truly poly-semantic 'Pandora's box' of potentialities of meaning, synthesizing the typographical discoveries of the DADA and Futurist poetries, and adopting the single page as 'working area', transcending the sequential, and creating simultaneity, by rejecting linear order and spatially punctuating the liberated word, henceforth an object to be read freely in all directions, and as such a semantic object capable of presenting both vertical and horizontal linguistic potentialities. Whilst the scale of Concrete Poetry (one page) marks this genre with the limitations of minimal rather than of epic literature, it is significantly symptomatic of a new mode of writing permitting the presentation of unprecedented semantic simultaneity. If Concrete Poetry has yet to produce a universally accepted masterpiece, it has offered important pointers to a visual writing transcending the limitations of sequential language.

See Stephen Bann (ed.), *Concrete Poetry: An International Anthology* (1967); Mary Ellen Solt; *Concrete Poetry: A World View* (1968); Emmett Williams (ed.), *An Anthology of Concrete Poetry* (1967).

NCPZ

consonance
see TEXTURE

context
is a central notion in modern philosophical linguistics and by extension, in modern literary criticism too. Contextual theories of meaning assert that concept precedes percept; that association can only take place between universals, not discrete impressions; and that all discourse is over-determined, having a multiplicity of meaning. In literary criticism the effect of these doctrines has been to extend the use of the word 'meaning' to cover all aspects of interpretation and to apply the false dictum 'The meaning of a word is its use in the language'. What should be substituted for this is the sentence 'The interpretation of an utterance is dependent upon a knowledge of the contexts within which

it occurs'. The problem may be seen at its most acute in the use of puns, and is discussed by Paul Ziff in his brilliant study, *Semantic Analysis* (1960). As Ziff points out, knowing the meaning of the words will not help one to understand the remark 'England had at least one laudable bishop'. It is also necessary to catch the pun. The range of contexts within which utterances occur extends from the narrowly linguistic (phonetic or morphological) to the broadly philosophical, and the task of literary criticism can be seen, in part, as the need to relate words, phrases, sentences and other parts of literary works to their linguistic contexts. The other, more open-ended part of criticism involves relating literary works themselves to their relevant psychological, social, and historical contexts. The obvious difficulty of interpretation arises from the need to assess the claims of conflicting contexts.

The development of contextual theories of meaning has produced, in this century, revival of a neo-Romantic criticism which focuses primarily on the various kinds of ambiguity in language, such as metaphor, symbolism, paradox and irony, and on the techniques used for controlling them. Among important contributions to such knowledge are William Empson's *Seven Types of Ambiguity* (2nd ed., 1947), and *The Structure of Complex Words* (1952), the latter book being intended to supplement and extend the function of a dictionary in relation to literary language. One of the more important and readable theoretical discussions of the problems dealt with here is I. A. Richards's *Philosophy of Rhetoric* (1936). See also DISCOURSE.

BCL

contradiction

From Aristotle to Coleridge, Hegel to T. S. Eliot, literary criticism has tended to conceive of the literary work as an achieved unity, often of an ORGANIC or 'spontaneous' kind. Recent developments in MARXIST, SEMIOTIC and DECONSTRUCTIVE criticism have queried this view, regarding it as a misleading, and potentially mystifying, account of the nature of literary texts. Emphasis has shifted instead to the multiple, conflicting and uneven character of such texts, which may well *attempt* to resolve into harmony materials which nevertheless remain stubbornly various and irreducible.

Deconstructive criticism, as practised by Jacques Derrida and his disciples, has characteristically fastened upon those aspects of a literary work which appear to an orthodox eye fragmentary, marginal or contingent, and shown how the implications of such fragments may begin to deconstruct or unravel the 'official', unifying logic on which the work is founded. Expelled by that logic to the text's boundaries, such unconsidered trifles return to plague and subvert the literary work's ruling categories. For Marxist criticism, this process has ideological relevance. Literary texts, like all ideological practices, seek an imaginary reconciliation of real contradictions; the classical REALIST work, in particular, strives for a symmetrical 'closure' or 'totality' within which such contradictions can be contained. But in its striving for such unity, a literary work may paradoxically begin to highlight its limits, throwing into relief those irresolvable problems or incompatible interests which nothing short of an *historical* transformation could adequately tackle. In granting ideology a determinate form, the work unwittingly reveals that ideology's absences and silences, those things of which it must at all cost not speak, and so begins to come apart at the seams. All ideologies are constituted by certain definite exclusions, certain 'not-saids' which they could not articulate without risk to the power-systems they support. In daily life, this is not often obvious; but once an ideology is objectified in literature, its limits—and consequently that which it excludes—also become more visible. A literary text, then, may find itself twisting into incoherence or self-contradiction, struggling unsuccessfully to unify its conflicting elements.

For much Marxist and deconstructive criticism, this is true of any literary writing whatsoever. But there are also literary works which are, as it were, conscious of this fact, which renounce the illusory ideal of unity in order to expose contradictions and leave them unresolved. In much MODERNIST writing, the fundamental contradiction of all realist literature—that it is at once FICTION and pretends not to be—is candidly put on show, so that the text becomes as much about its own process of production as about a stable reality beyond it. In the hands of Marxist artists, such devices have been turned to political use. For Bertolt Brecht, the point of theatre is not to provide the audience with a neatly unified product to be unproblematically consumed, but to reflect in its own conflicting, irregular forms something of the contradictory character of social reality itself. 'Montage'—the abrupt linking of discrete images—and the 'alienation effect', in which the actor at once exposes a reality and reveals that his exposure is fictional, are examples of such techniques. By articulating contradictions, the Brechtian drama hopes to throw the audience into conflict and division, undermining their consoling expectations of harmony and forcing them to ponder the many-sided, dialectical nature of history itself. See also EPIC THEATRE.

See Leon Trotsky, *Literature and Revolution* (1971); Lucien Goldmann, *The Hidden God* (1967); Christopher Caudwell, *Illusion and Reality* (1937).

TE

convention

is a generalizing term which isolates frequently occurring similarities in a large number of works. If the critic is concerned to categorize a work, he will describe it as belonging within a convention which in this sense is a sub-category of TRADITION. If, on the other hand, he is more concerned to describe the individual work, he will point out that this or that element is conventional without implying that the whole work is thus defined as belonging within that convention. *As You Like It* 'belongs within the pastoral convention': or *As You Like It* 'has this or that element of pastoral', but is more usefully categorized in some other way. Clearly it is largely a matter of how all-pervasive the conventional element is.

It is tempting to distinguish between conventions of form and conventional content. A convention in the first sense is any accepted manner, hallowed by long practice, of conveying meaning. The second sense coincides with ordinary usage and means a generally accepted, standard, view or attitude. But it is as difficult to keep these two meanings separate as it is generally to separate medium and meaning. Take an example of what seems a purely technical convention: the invisible fourth wall separating the real world of the theatre audience from the imaginary world of the play. Even in this case it might be argued, as Brecht argues, that the technical convention tends to express, and foster as immutable truth, views which are mere conventions in the second sense.

The pastoral convention shows clearly how manner and meaning are inextricably entwined, and demonstrates too the positive and negative values of both aspects. The conventionality of meaning allows for stylistic brilliance. We are so familiar with the broad meaning that we can appreciate aesthetically the subtle expression of fine nuances—the variations on a theme—as we cannot so easily in new un-assimilated areas of discourse. On the other hand, the conventional style or form may function like a shorthand. It allows an author to introduce huge areas of meaning very concisely by virtue of the accretions of connotation and resonance it has acquired. In a negative way, such manipulation of a literary convention is a powerful weapon of the ironist.

The drawbacks are obvious. The convention may become exhausted, the language and form too mannered: a stylistic rigor mortis revealing dead attitudes and emotions (see MANNERISM). The accretions of meaning may be too heavy or centrifugal, so that works seem abstruse or vague. The language may be so weighed down by conventional associations that it cannot absorb and express new meaning, even through irony. Conventional attitudes from the past may blind to present truths. *Conventional* commonly has such pejorative undertones and in this sense is opposed to *original* (see ORIGINALITY).

See M. C. Bradbrook, *Themes and Conventions of Elizabethan*

Tragedy (1952); Bertolt Brecht, trans. and ed. J. Willett, *Brecht on Theatre* (1964); W. Empson, *Some Versions of Pastoral* (1935).

EJB

couplet

In English verse, a unit consisting of a pair of lines of the same length, linked by rhyme. The couplet may be *closed* if the sense and syntax are complete within the metrical unit, or *open* if the couplet is itself a part of a longer unit. There are two chief kinds of couplets; other experiments have proved unsuccessful. The older in English is the *octosyllabic* or *four-stress* couplet, perhaps based on a common Latin hymn metre, which became a staple form of English medieval narrative verse in works like *The Lay of Havelock the Dane*, remaining a popular form into the eighteenth century. The two great practitioners of the four-stress couplet both show the strengths of the couplet as a form: pithy memorability of wit in closed units, and sinuous flexibility in the open structure. The craggy couplets of Samuel Butler's influential work, *Hudibras* (1663–78) became known as 'Hudibrastics':

> And Pulpit, Drum Ecclesiastick,
> Was beat with Fist, instead of a stick.

Swift forms a link with the older masters of the shorter couplet in his satirical narratives like *Baucis and Philemon*, or in straight satire ('Verses on the death of Dr Swift'):

> My female Friends, whose tender Hearts
> Have better learn'd to act their Parts,
> Receive the News in *doleful* Dumps:
> 'The Dean is dead, (and what is Trumps?)
> The Lord have Mercy on his Soul!'
> (Ladies I'll venture for the *Vole*.*)

* grand slam

The *decasyllabic* or *five-stress* couplet is most commonly thought of as the English couplet form. It seems to have been introduced into English by Chaucer in the 'Prologue to the Legend of Good Women' (c. 1375), as an imitation of a French metre. In the Restoration theatre, it became the staple equivalent of the French dramatic Alexandrines of Racine and others: hence the term, from its association with those heroic tragedies, 'heroic couplet'. Early in the seventeenth century, Waller adjusted and regularized the syllabic structure to match English stress structure, and in the hands of Dryden and Pope the 'heroic couplet' became one of the most disciplined and effective verse forms. As with all formalist art, it allows great sophistication and power to develop from almost imperceptible signals, such as small variations in placing the *caesura* or pause, or from pressing the strict form into unusual uses (Pope, 'Epistle to Bathurst'):

> 'God cannot love (says Blunt, with tearless eyes)
> The wretch he starves'—and piously denies:
> But the good Bishop, with a meeker air,
> Admits, and leaves them, Providence's care.

AMR

creation

The metaphor of creation has traditionally dominated discussions of literary authorship, with strong implications of the mysterious, possibly transcendental nature of such activity. Recent MARXIST CRITICISM has identified the roots of the notion as essentially theological: the hidden model of literary creativity is the Divine Author, conjuring his handiwork—the world—*ex nihilo*. Viewing such an idea as a fundamental mystification of the process of writing, Marxist criticism (in particular the work of Pierre Macherey) has preferred to substitute the concept of literary production, which suggests the essentially ordinary, accessible nature of fiction-making. Production is understood as the general activity of purposive transformation of raw materials, whether this be economic, political, cultural or theoretical; and it is seen as possessing a triple structure. All production entails:

1 certain specific raw materials to be transformed;
2 certain determinate techniques of transformation; and
3 a definitive product.

Because of the intervention of stage 2, this product can in no way be reduced to the 'expression', 'reflection' or mere *re*production of the initial raw materials.

Literary raw materials, for Marxist criticism, are essentially of two kinds. On the one hand there is the specific historical experience available to a given writer, which will always be *ideologically* informed, directly or indirectly relevant to the processes of political, cultural and sexual power. On the other hand there are previous writings, equally ideologically formed, which the writer, in that practice known as *intertextuality*, may also transform. These raw materials are never 'innocent' or easily pliable: they come to the literary productive process with specific degrees of resistance, particular valences and tendencies of their own. The 'techniques of literary production,', always part of a certain LITERARY MODE OF PRODUCTION, can then be grasped as the codes, conventions and devices historically available to a particular literary producer. These techniques, equally, are never ideologically neutral: they encode and secrete particular ways of seeing which have complex relations to social power-systems and power-struggles. Since a particular literary device or convention may belong to an ideology other than that to which its raw material belongs, one can expect that the ideology of the end-product is especially complex.

Such a view of literary production renders writing amenable to analysis by 'decentring' the individual AUTHOR, who can then be seen not as the unique, privileged and perhaps mysterious 'creator' of the text, but as a particular analysable element in its constitution, a 'code' or ideological sub-formation in itself. How important this 'authorial ideology' is in the production of the text will be generically and historically variable: more important, obviously, in ROMANTIC lyricism than in medieval religious verse. Such a decentring of the author finds parallels in STRUCTURALIST, POST-STRUCTURALIST and DECONSTRUCTIVE criticism, where the 'author' is no more than one text among others; the 'author's life' will not provide us with a firm foundation for the meaning of the work, since this itself is only textually available to us. Post-structuralist criticism, in its concern with the potentially infinite productivity of language, and PSYCHOANALYSIS, which sees the dream as itself the product of a 'dream-work' or determinate process of labour, both tend to converge with Marxist criticism in its dethronement—to many still scandalous—of the 'creative author'.

See L. Althusser, *Lenin and Philosophy* (1971); R. Coward and J. Ellis, *Language and Materialism* (1977); T. Eagleton, *Criticism and Ideology* (1976); F. Jameson, *The Political Unconscious* (1981); P. Macherey, *A Theory of Literary Production* (1978); P. Macherey and E. Balibar, 'Literature as ideological form', in R. Young (ed.), *Untying the Text* (1981).

TE

criticism

'To criticize', etymologically, meant 'to analyse' and later, 'to judge'. If today's usage were to be restricted to both these meanings some coherence could be given to a now dangerously over-extended term. Literary *scholarship* and literary *history*, then, should be so named and should be regarded as complementary to literary *criticism*, not as part of it. *Critical theory* too should be distinguished from criticism, since it concerns itself with the analysis and judgment of concepts rather than works. It is a philosophical activity which should underlie criticism but, again, should not be regarded as part of it. Similarly, *metacriticism* is probably the better name for what is often called *extrinsic criticism*: the practice of using literary works for some extra-literary end, such as gaining insight into the author or his readers or society, amplifying studies of ethics, religion, psychology and so on. Modern *structural criticism*, so called, since it regards literature only as a manifestation of

its environment and is therefore intent on using it merely as evidence—
a piece in the jigsaw 'structure' of society—is a type of metacriticism,
though certain critics, especially in France, mistake it for criticism
itself, and indeed for the whole of it. In fact, (*intrinsic*) *criticism* must
precede metacriticism, as no literary work can constitute valid evidence
in any more general field until its own nature has been rightly assessed.
For many works, of course, it is desirable that critical appreciation of
meaning should be complemented by metacritical study of relevant
significance; that a grasp of literary identity should lead to discussion of
extra-literary relationships. But the two activities, despite some overlapping, should not be confounded under one term; nor should the
extra-literary end in view be allowed to bias the critical activity (by
pre-selecting the aspects considered to be central) or to blind the
metacritic to the possibility of other significances, other standards (for
literary works are multifaceted and multivalent).

'Extrinsic criticism' is often used for that criticism which relies
heavily on information drawn from outside the literary work, and is
contrasted with an 'intrinsic criticism' which does not. Sometimes the
same terms are also used to distinguish criticism that deals mainly with
content (attitudes, ideas, subject-matter) from that dealing mainly with
form. These usages evidently do not correspond to the difference
between metacriticism and criticism, since a work grasped without the
aid of external scholarship could then be put to some metacritical end
and, contrariwise, a good deal of scholarly information might be
necessary to appreciate a work in and for itself. The distinction
therefore is between two critical approaches to a work, not between a
critical and an extra-critical use of it. *External criticism* and *internal
criticism* thus seem to be preferable terms. And the second distinction
mentioned is made more clearly by the terms *contentual criticism* and
formal criticism. The term 'extrinsic criticism' is better used, if at all,
only as a synonym for metacriticism, and '(intrinsic) criticism', with or
without the brackets, only as the contrary of metacriticism.

The distinction of *ends*, which marks off various kinds of criticism
from various kinds of metacriticism, may be matched by a broad
distinction of *means: objective* or *subjective*. Metacriticism can
obviously attain objectivity more easily than criticism (but has to be
based on the latter). External criticism seems to encourage objectivity,
internal criticism subjectivity. But within the field of internal criticism,
though, it is clearly easier to be objective about form (as formal
criticism is technical) than about content. Equally clearly, none of these
approaches actually compels the critic to adopt one attitude or the
other. However, *impressionistic criticism* and *affective criticism*—since
they limit themselves by definition to judgment from immediate personal reaction—are necessarily subjective. *Practical criticism* and

judicial criticism—since they aim at consensus-judgments based on analytical or other evidence—are necessarily objective. What is called *Freudian* criticism, or (to take another example) *Marxist* criticism, usually turns out to be metacriticism, but where the critic is in fact moving *inwards* from Freud or Marx to the work itself his (intrinsic) criticism will be objective, though limited.

As with metacriticism and criticism, there is inevitably some overlapping of objective and subjective methods. Objectivity, in the arts, can be defined only as the attempt to be unbiased, uneccentric, about personal reactions, the attempt to get them right, so that they may constitute valid evidence not mere opinion. It cannot imply their exclusion; criticism that excluded them would not be criticism at all, for they *are* much of the literary work. Similarly the most impressionistic of critics must refer, at least implicitly, to some recognizable (and therefore objective) characteristics of the work if his impressions of it are to carry any weight as criticism and not be discounted as mere autobiography. Nevertheless, the existence of objective criticism has led to claims that criticism is, or should be, a science. As literary art, unlike nature, is not uniform, not amenable to the experimental method, and not mathematically quantifiable, it is not, and cannot be. The existence of subjective criticism has led to claims that criticism is, or should be, an art, parallel to literature rather than a commentary parasitic upon it. But both the etymology of the word, its current uses, and all the various traditional practices that have come under it, indicate 'criticism' to be an activity dealing with fictions but not itself fictional; it has never been considered strictly creative, but at most re-creative (and then only to aid appreciation of the original creative work). So creative writing that uses other literature as its raw material in the same way that literature uses life should be seen for what it is, a secondary art that is an extreme form of subjective metacriticism. This is something quite different from the task of analysis or judgment, or both—a task already varied enough to strain the viability of 'criticism' as a useful term. See also ANALYSIS, CRITIQUE, DECONSTRUCTION, EVALUATION, HERMENEUTICS.

See E. D. Hirsch, Jr, *Validity in Interpretation* (1967); Allan Rodway, *The Truths of Fiction* (1970); R. Wellek, *A History of Modern Criticism* (1961); René Wellek and Austin Warren, *Theory of Literature* (3rd ed., 1963); W. K. Wimsatt, Jr, and C. Brooks, *Literary Criticism: A Short History* (1962); D. Daiches, *Critical Approaches to Literature* (2nd ed., 1981); D. Lodge (ed.), *Twentieth Century Literary Criticism* (1972); A. Jefferson and D. Robey (eds), *Modern Literary Theory* (1982). See C. Belsey, *Critical Practice* (1980) or R. Fowler, *Linguistic Criticism* (1986) for alternative conceptions of 'criticism'.

AER

critique

is a word that comes into the English language from French early in the eighteenth century. The *Oxford English Dictionary* cites, among other examples, the following quotation from Addison: 'I should as soon expect to see a Critique on the Posie of a Ring, as on the inscription of a medal'. Here 'critique' refers to a piece of writing, in the manner of an essay or review, concerned with the description and judgment of a work of art or literature. The connection with writing about literature is maintained in the transfer of the word from noun to verb, as in the further example from the *OED*, 'Hogg's tales are critiqued by himself in Blackwoods' (1831). This usage, although it has died out in England, continues in the United States where it is still possible to 'critique' a poem and to write a 'critique' of a novel.

The precise reasons for borrowing 'critique' from French are difficult to discern. The word appears in English during a period when a new form of literary culture is appearing, marked by the emergence of reviews such as the *Spectator* and the *Tatler*, and by new audiences for literary works, who are felt to need guidance in matters of taste and judgment. Literature becomes a two-fold process: the production of novels, plays, poetry and works of philosophy and history, and the production of a commentary on them in the form of essays and reviews. Critique, then, may have been a useful word to describe this relatively new kind of writing, a literature about literature, concerned with matters of taste, judgment, and advertisement, a new form for the promotion and circulation of opinion.

A new meaning for critique emerged in England during the nineteenth century, and again, the reasons for this have to do with intellectual developments outside England. In the late eighteenth century the German philosopher Kant published a series of what, in translation, became known as critiques. A word recently borrowed from French was used to translate the German word *Kritik*. The provenance of critique moved away from literature and toward philosophy, where it designated a mode of inquiry designed to reveal the conditions of existence for certain ideas and perceptions. Kantian critique was concerned to discover the nature and limits of human understanding, and found these in what were claimed as the fundamental structures of the human mind. Marx changed the direction of critique by locating such fundamental structures not in the human mind but in the economic organization of society. This became, however mediately, the explanatory ground for why we think, feel and act the way we do, and in Marx's writing critique became closely concerned with *ideology*: the purpose of critique was to reveal ideology at work in thought by referring it to its base in economically determined antagonisms of class. Marx's writing forms one episode in the transformation of Kantian critique into what has subsequently become known as the sociology of knowledge. Weber and Durkheim are also central figures in the transformation. Although the three writers do not necessarily agree about what the relevant social context is for explaining why we think as we do, they do share a sense that it is in some concept of social structure that an explanation is to be found.

Literary criticism has developed various affiliations with the different modes of critique. An early equivalent for the Kantian critique can be found in ROMANTIC theories of IMAGINATION which attempt to locate the origins of literature in a faculty which is ambiguously placed between a human and a divine mind. More recently, the different modalities of critique—Marxism, feminism, linguistics, structuralism, psychoanalysis—have all, in combination or separately, produced critical theory which is concerned not only with the detailed analysis and evaluation of literary works but also with their conditions of existence, whether these are discovered in the structures of culture or language, in the laws of narrative, or the ideologies produced by class-divided societies. It is possible, therefore, to distinguish between those forms of literary criticism which bear some affiliation to critique and those which do not concern themselves with reflexive thought, preferring instead to carry out routine maintenance of a literary canon whose own creation is not subject to inquiry. But there are other and equally important kinds of distinction to be made, notably between those kinds of critique and criticism which put in question forms of political power, and those which locate the fundamental questions outside the realm of politics, in certain (claimed) invariant properties of culture, language, or the human unconscious. Critique reproduces today a division—and a point of transgression—which characterized its eighteenth-century origins. As Paul Connerton has noted (Introduction to *Critical Sociology*, 1976), in the eighteenth century 'The process of critique claimed to subject to its judgment all spheres of life which were accessible to reason; but it renounced any attempt to touch on the political sphere'. But this self-denying ordinance was not maintained for long. Critique increasingly concerned itself with politics and laid the intellectual foundations for the French Revolution. Then, as now, when critique, and the forms of literary criticism associated with it, question the prevailing distribution of political power, the alarm bells start to ring. By contrast,the apolitical forms of critique are a tolerated part of the intellectual scene. But this distinction between the political and the apolitical is not itself invariable and we cannot necessarily know in advance what form of critique will strike a political nerve. See also DECONSTRUCTION, DISCOURSE, FEMINIST CRITICISM, MARXIST CRITICISM, PSYCHOLOGY AND PSYCHOANALYSIS, and references.

Some examples of work which, in various ways, presupposes critique

as a goal, would include C. Belsey, *Critical Practice* (1980);
T. Eagleton, *Criticism and Ideology* (1976); A. Easthope, *Poetry as
Discourse* (1983); R. Fowler, *Literature as Social Discourse* (1981),
Linguistic Criticism (1986); P. Widdowson (ed.), *Re-Reading English*
(1982).

JC

culture

Metaphorically, a cultivation (*agri-cultura*); the cultivation of values;
by extension, a body of values cultivated. See Raymond Williams,
Culture and Society, 1780–1950 (1959) and *The Long Revolution*
(1961). More recently, sociologists and anthropologists have employed
the term to denote the totality of customs and institutions of a human
group (cf. SOCIETY).

Literary criticism has traditionally concerned itself with culture as a
body of values, especially those values transmitted from the past to the
future through the imaginative works of men. Culture in this sense
implies the accumulation of discriminations. It implies a selective social
structure, since it distinguishes passive recipients of social perspectives
from those who cultivate an awareness of such perspectives. This, in
turn, implies a teaching and learning process, and generates theories of
a distinctive class with a duty to protect and disseminate traditions.
Such an embodiment of the standards reinforces the traditional personal dimension of culture, as implicit in the underlying metaphoric
skein (a 'cultivated' or 'cultured' man). It becomes simultaneously a
code of values and a mode of perception. So, concepts like SENSIBILITY
and taste evolve. Matthew Arnold (*Culture and Anarchy*, 1869 and
Essays in Criticism, 1889) represents the classic statement of this view
of culture.

At first this version of culture seems isolated from the alternative,
'scientific' version, namely, culture as the totality of human habits,
customs and artefacts. See, for example, M. F. Ashley Montague,
Culture and the Evolution of Man (1962) and *Culture: Man's Adaptive
Dimension* (1968). But the critical and scientific definitions overlap,
despite the apparent central difference that one claims to be evaluatory
and the other descriptive. It is arguable that the distinctions depend on
the isolation of certain phenomena as expressions of human value, and
the false rejection of others (institutions, social habits, political movements, etc.). We might ask whether a communal act, e.g. the founding
of the trades unions, clearly part of the sociological dimension of
'culture', is not also an embodiment of cultural *values* as much as a
novel or a painting. It certainly involves a radical change of sensibility
and may be said to be an expression of cultural advancement in the
widest sense. Judgment of such issues is obscured by the tendency to

confuse *sensibility* and *manners*, in the narrow social sense: few objections might be advanced if for the trades unions we substituted the English country house!

Confusion has increased with the growth of mass communication. Films, television, paperbacks—the whole range of devices for the distribution of images and information—call into question traditional standards and accepted forms. In the face of this threat to its standards, criticism failed to create the necessary models to investigate the new phenomena. Critics discovered that it was necessary to turn to other disciplines, such as sociology, to find tools to aid their work. A pioneer in this field was Richard Hoggart, whose *The Uses of Literacy* (1957) led to a widespread interest in what had been dismissed by all but the most acute (e.g. George Orwell) as trivial pulp-art. Cross-fertilization between mass- and minority-art, and between its audiences, necessitated rejection of the old pyramidical structure of high-, middle- and low-brow, as conceived by the first critical response (e.g. Q. D. Leavis's *Fiction and the Reading Public,* 1932). As all art-forms begin to overlap it becomes increasingly apparent that pigeon-holing is not enough. As one critic has said, the mass-minority split is not the cure of our plight but its symptom (Raymond Williams, *Communications,* revised ed., 1966). Modern cultural discussions stress the rejection of the past, the increasing disengagement of modernist and post-modernist thought (Bernard Bergonzi (ed.), *Innovations,* 1968). Our central cultural metaphor of unfolding growth may disappear entirely in an age wedded increasingly to violent change. See also SOCIETY.

For the etymology and semantic development of the term, see R. Williams, 'Culture' in his *Keywords* (1976); his *Culture* (1981) is a book-length treatment with full bibliography. See also C. W. E. Bigsby (ed.), *Approaches to Popular Culture* (1976); Dick Hebdidge, *Subculture: The Meaning of Style* (1979); D. Punter (ed.), *Introduction to Contemporary Cultural Studies* (1986).

GG

D

Dada,

which received its enigmatic name in February 1916, was a reaction against the brutality of war, the expediency of art and literature and the dangerous inadequacy of rational thought; in fact it spat out its contempt for the spiritual and moral decadence of a whole intellectual, cultural and social system. Born in neutral Zurich in the middle of the anarchic destruction of modern warfare, it expressed its disgust with a morally culpable bourgeoisie and a spiritually nerveless art which had no objective beyond a simplistic social photography, a faith in its own function as anodyne and a reprehensible dedication to self-fulfilment. With unabashed relish Dada declared its negative intent: it wished, apparently, to destroy art along with bourgeois society, but in truth it opposed itself to the abuse of art rather than art itself, to society rather than humanity. Its exponents were poets and artists (Marcel Duchamp, Hugo Ball, Tristan Tzara, Richard Huelsenbeck, Man Ray, Max Ernst) who professed to despise art and literature but who, paradoxically, expressed their contempt in terms which identified them as part of the modernist movement. Its chief weapons—manifesto, phonetic poetry, simultaneous poem, noise music and provocative public spectacle—were all borrowed directly from the Futurists and stood as an image of the dissolution which seemed the central fact of modern existence. Their commitment to experimental modes, and the vitality of their performances, however, seemed to indicate a more fundamental faith in the possibility of opposing historical entropy with energy and concern if not with the self-contained structure of art itself. When Dada found itself outflanked by the more coherent and purposeful experiments of the Surrealists it was laid to rest in 1922. But, as an attitude of mind rather than a formal movement, its subversive energy could not be contained by the incantations of a mock funeral service. In the 1960s American artists, writers, actors and musicians laid claim to the excitement and commitment of Futurists, Dadaists and Surrealists alike and approximated their experiments in the technique of Pop Art, happenings and the multi-media performance. See also SURREALISM.

See C. W. E. Bigsby, *Dada and Surrealism* (1972); Hans Richter, *Dada: Art and Anti-art* (1965); William S. Rubin, *Dada, Surrealism and their Heritage* (1968); S. Foster and R. Kuenzl (eds), *Dada Spectrum* (1979) (contains extensive bibliography); M. A. Caws, *The Poetry of Dada and Surrealism* (1970); R. W. Lust, *German Dadaist Literature* (1973); R. Sheppard (ed.), *Dada: Studies of a Movement* (1979), (ed.), *New Studies in Dada* (1981); R. Short, *Dada and Surrealism* (1980); D. Tashjian, *Skyscraper Primitives* (1975).

CWEB

decentring
see AUTHOR, CREATION, DECONSTRUCTION, DISCOURSE

deconstruction
Refers to a philosophical activity initiated by Jacques Derrida in France; the first major publications appeared in the late 1960s. It is a critique of concepts and hierarchies which, according to Derrida, are essential to traditional criteria of certainty, identity and truth; but which, nevertheless, achieve their status only by repressing and forgetting other elements which thus become the un-thought, and sometimes the unthinkable, of Western philosophy. Derrida, following Nietzsche and Heidegger, tries to expose and explain this partiality, which he calls 'logocentrism'. Both aspects of this name—the fact of being centred, and of the logos as centre—are significant. Logos is a Greek term that can specifically mean 'word', but also carries implications of rationality and wisdom in general, and is sometimes reified as a cosmic intellectual principle. Early Christianity, in its drive to contain and supplant classical philosophy, adapted logos for the Word of God, thus annexing the principle of wisdom to the creative divine utterance, as in the Fourth Gospel. God is the only self-sufficient being; his word, as both source and standard of meaning, is the only self-sufficient discourse.

The logos casts a long shadow: a whole series of preferences is seen to derive, nostalgically, from its value judgments. Speech, as unmediated expression, is privileged in relation to writing, which appears as a suspect supplement to the authenticity of utterance—a distinction already evident in Greek thought. A desire for self-sufficiency, for the unqualified and unmediated, shows itself in attitudes to meaning, in the search for absolute knowledge, original truth, or determinate signification; and in attitudes to existence, in the search for unified being or a self-knowing reflexive consciousness. It is as if the urge of every entity— signified or existent— is to be *present to itself* in a way that makes it self-confirming and self-sufficient. 'Presence' is thus a prime value for logocentrism, which itself forms 'the matrix of every idealism'. And the various systems which function as 'centrisms' of whatever kind are attempts to delimit realms of security in which the proliferating play of meaning is closed by the presence of a centre as guarantor of signification.

Now, Derrida's approach to these desires is sceptical; but simply to equate deconstruction and scepticism is to miss the point. The critique of logocentrism or of a metaphysics of presence cannot take place from a privileged position outside the traditions it questions, for there is no such outside; the traces are too deep in language and thought. But (luckily for the critic) just because ideal logocentrism is never actually achieved, the language will also carry traces of its repressed other, of the un-thought. And hence Derrida's philosophical practice involves a close textual criticism in order to trace the contradiction that shadows the text's coherence and 'expresses the force of a desire'. This under-mining from within is the first stage of deconstruction, and usually subverts a privileged term: thus 'nature' is shown as always already contaminated by 'culture', 'speech' by 'writing', and so on. Writing (*écriture*), necessarily caught up in the play of signification, takes the place of pure speech as a norm for language. But Derrida is not concerned with simple binary reversals of value, which would merely offer another centred structure. He therefore releases his 'undecide-ables', radically unstable terms which act to disrupt systematization. The most important of these is 'differance', a coinage which plays on two meanings of the French *différer*: difference—between signs as the basis of signification (see SEMIOTICS), and deferment—deferment of presence by the sign which always refers to another sign, not to the thing itself. Derrida's mis-spelling cannot be heard in French pronun-ciation; it exists only as written, emphasizing writing and textuality at the expense of speech. And so that 'differance' cannot be recuperated as a centre, he insists that it is neither word, concept nor origin: at most, a condition of the possibility of meaning, which resists hypostatization. The artifice and even frivolity of its neologism act to prevent it being taken as a master key to any structure. Indeed, the use of neologisms, puns and etymologies, as well as individually opaque styles, is common among deconstructive writers. It strikes readers as exemplary or as infuriating; sometimes as both.

As we have seen, the power of logocentrism it not total. Certain texts appear 'to mark and to organize a structure of resistance to the philosophical conceptuality that allegedly dominated or comprehended them'. There is a distinction between this latter group and those texts that simply contain an inherent contradiction or *aporia*. The *aporia* is a built-in deconstruction, as it were; but the 'resistant' texts go further and begin their own critique. They include (only in part) the writings of Nietzsche and Heidegger, Freud and Saussure. They also include some 'literary' texts—Derrida distrusts the category, but finds in Artaud, Mallarmé and others 'the demonstration and practical deconstruction of the *representation* of what was done with literature'.

The relevance to literary studies, then, is not through a critical method (which isn't on offer as such) nor in the finality of given interpretations (there are no final interpretations) but in the theoretical and conceptual insights of deconstruction. There are specific points at which Derrida's argument overlaps with more narrow literary concerns: the treatment of nature in Rousseau, for example (*Of Grammatology*, 1967, trans. 1976); or the treatment of mimesis in Mallarmé (*Dissemination*, 1972, trans. 1981). A great deal of modern writing has turned around problems of representation and consciousness, and these are extensively discussed by Derrida through his critical involvement with phenomenology, semiotics and psychoanalysis. Many critical issues are open to a deconstructive approach; thus our concern with authors evinces a desire for origin, to serve as interpretive closure; and realist representation is precisely an illusion of presence. In general, Derrida's way of thinking will radically revise what a reader expects to do with a text.

The specific use of deconstruction in literary argument has grown in the United States, following pioneer work by Paul de Man and J. Hillis Miller at Yale. There is a dubious tendency in de Man to privilege literature in general as a self-deconstructing discourse; but this does not destroy the brilliance of individual readings which, in their aporetic ensemble, make the text 'unreadable' in terms of closure (*Allegories of Reading*, 1979). Similarly, Hillis Miller argues that 'The fault of premature closure is intrinsic to criticism' (*Fiction and Repetition*, 1982). Besides generating new readings, mainly of nineteenth- and twentieth-century material, American deconstruction has enlivened debate about critical principles. The refusal of final meaning has caused a certain institutional anxiety about anarchic individualism—understandably so, perhaps, in view of the polemical mannerism of deconstructionist style (as seen by those who don't enjoy it). But the absence of absolute criteria for interpretation does not mean total freedom; it is precisely the pressure of pre-existent discourse that deconstruction re-marks in its critique of origin. In a recent interview, Derrida says that 'Meaning . . . does not depend on the subjective identity but on the field of different forces, which produce interpretations.' (*The Literary Review* 14, 1980, p.21)

Deconstruction, as a set of popular clichés, soon palls. Simply to demonstrate logocentrism becomes a tautologous exercise. But the major examples of deconstructive practice retain their power. Few theoretical approaches have combined such challenging abstraction with such intense textual work. Not the least of its values lies in the learning and wit of its principal practitioners. 'To write on their plan, it was at least necessary to read and think.' See also DISCOURSE, PSYCHOLOGY AND PSYCHOANALYSIS.

For a concise account see D. C. Wood, 'An Introduction to Derrida',

Radical Philosophy 21, Spring 1979. The most approachable of Derrida's texts is *Positions* (1972, trans. 1981); there are excellent translators' introductions to the English versions of *Dissemination* (Barbara Johnson) and *Of Grammatology* (Gayatri Spivak). The 1980 Derrida colloquium at Cerisy, directed by Ph. Lacoue-Labarthe and J.-L. Nancy, is published as *Les Fins de l'homme* (1981); it includes deconstructive thinking in many different areas. Vincent Descombes, *Modern French Philosophy* (1979, trans. 1980) is a brilliant background study; Christopher Norris, *Deconstruction: Theory and Practice* (1982) is a general account from a literary standpoint. For examples of effects on criticism see Barbara Johnson, *The Critical Difference: Essays in the Contemporary Rhetoric of Reading* (1980) and Gregory L. Ulmer, *Applied Grammatology: Post(e)-Pedagogy from Jacques Derrida to Joseph Beuys* (1985). Relevant journals include *Glyph* and the *Oxford Literary Review*.

EC

decorum

—appropriateness of manner to ideas or situation—defined by the Elizabethan critic Puttenham as 'this good grace of every thing in his kinde', is primarily associated with the tradition of classical rhetoric and courtly values underlying Renaissance literature. Nevertheless, as a principle of propriety and appropriateness its validity is not confined to one period. It has, too, both aesthetic and moral considerations, as a criterion of right relationships whether between style and subject-matter or in the fulfilment of social obligations.

Sensitivity to decorum is likely to be greater when and where the observance of formal conventions is felt to be important; in art and life the concept of what is fitting implies a sense of established or accepted values. Thus by the critical canons of neo-classicism, decorum regulated the distinctions between literary genres, determining what kinds of style and subject were in keeping with each other: an elevated style for epic, for instance, to match the heroic proportions of character and action, but a mean style for comedy, in which ignoble vices and follies were ridiculed. By such canons Shakespeare's drama was held to be essentially indecorous, since it persistently mingled tragedy with comedy, and high style with low; Dr Johnson's objection to the word 'blanket' in *Macbeth* is a celebrated example of what neo-classical taste felt to be a breach of decorum.

The vagaries of Shakespeare's critical reputation illustrate how the principle of decorum can atrophy and become mechanical in its application. Indeed an application of inappropriate critical criteria is in itself a form of indecorum, and in this respect we can understand why writers in any age who depart radically from accepted conventions are likely to be judged indecorous by their contemporaries. Donne, whose love poetry 'perplexes the minds of the fair sex with nice speculations about philosophy', as Dryden put it, deliberately flouted the established decorum of courtly tradition, while the Wordsworth of *Lyrical Ballads* and the Eliot of 'The Waste Land' were felt by most of their first readers not only to be abandoning conventional ideas of decorum but also to be defying any principle whatsoever of fitness and formal coherence. Such cases remind us that the sense of decorum lies not in the rigid prescription of absolute law but in a tactful and flexible judgment. 'For otherwise seems the decorum,' wrote Puttenham, 'to a weake and ignorant judgement then it doth to one of better knowledge and experience; which sheweth that it resteth in the discerning part of the minde.'

DJP

defamiliarization
see FORMALISM

dénouement
French metaphor, literally 'unravelling', derived from the Latin for 'knot'; synonym 'catastrophe'. First used in French with reference to drama in 1636, adopted in English in 1752, to denote the neat end of a plot, the final resolution of all conflicts in a play, the tying up of loose ends, usually in the last act or even scene. Like all conclusions, dénouements have a reputation for difficulty, and even great playwrights (such as Shakespeare and Molière) have been criticized for the unconvincing artificiality of theirs. But as with other elements of dramaturgy once thought essential, the traditional type of dénouement is generally avoided by contemporary writers, e.g. Samuel Beckett in *Waiting for Godot* (1955) and Harold Pinter in *The Caretaker* (1960) both opt for open, ambiguous endings which resolve nothing— anticlimax in place of striking climax. By extension, the term 'dénouement' is also applied sometimes to the unravelling of plots in narrative fiction. See also NARRATIVE STRUCTURE.

See William Archer, *Play-Making* (1912), 253.

JWJF

deviation
see FOREGROUNDING, POETIC LICENCE

dialogic structure
The term 'dialogic' is uniquely associated with the work of the Russian scholar Mikhail Bakhtin, and in particular his theorization of the novel in *Problems of Dostoevsky's Poetics*. The dialogic principle is central to Bakhtin's extensive and polemical theory of language and consciousness. Dialogue, he writes

is not a means for revealing, for bringing to the surface the already ready-made character of a person; no, in dialogue a person not only shows himself outwardly, but he becomes for the first time that which he is, not only for others but for himself as well. To be means to communicate dialogically.

There can be no such ready-made character existing somehow prior to the linguistic, social operations of the dialogue with the other. And likewise, before we can use words for inner self-expression we must have developed language through dialogue with other people. Bakhtin is not merely talking about dialogue in the ordinary sense in which two or more people talk with each other. He is addressing the prior issue as to how such dialogues are in the first place enabled or even possible. They are so because, in his view, language is constitutively intersubjective (therefore social) and logically precedes subjectivity. It is never neutral, unaddressed, exempt from the aspirations of others. In his word, it is dialogic.

The polemical thrust of Bakhtin's theory lies in his pervasive suggestion that our hallowed autonomous individuality is an illusion; that in fact the 'I' that speaks is speaking simultaneously a polyphony of languages derived from diverse social contexts and origins. In reality each of us is a 'we' and not an 'I'. Without ever using religious terminology, Bakhtin nonetheless assigns to this fact of life an exalted value: and he turns to the study of genre in literature, to the novel in particular, to raise the question of the degree to which texts embrace or efface this value. He uses the term *monological* to designate the reduction of potentially multiple 'voices' (or characters) into a single authoritative voice. This voice is sometimes inescapable. The apparent polyphony of drama, for example, remains tied to the fact that the dramatist imposes upon his characters what they must say. But the technical resources of narrative in prose (the varieties of indirect discourse in particular) do have an inherent capacity to represent languages other than the author's. Bakhtin celebrates the novel as the genre most capable of technically dismantling the dictatorial authorial voice that regulates and resolves any interplay of other voices in the text.

The dialogical text remains, nonetheless, the exception rather than the norm; it is perhaps better described as an experimental possibility: the writer thinking, as it were, in points of view, consciousnesses, voices, as for example Richardson did in the epistolary form of *Clarissa*. In Bakhtin's account, however, this possibility has a long and rich historical foundation in the genres of the Socratic dialogue and the ancient Menippean satire, the latter being directly rooted in the world of *carnival* folklore. In the carnival the social hierarchies of everyday life—their solemnities and pieties and etiquettes as well as all ready-made truths—are profaned and literally outspoken by normally suppressed voices and energies demanding equal dialogic status. In this world-turned-upside-down, ideas and truths are endlessly tested and contested, and thus de-privileged. In Dostoevsky Bakhtin found a paradigmatic polyphonic structure where the other voices in the text come into their own, as it were; they acquire the status of fully-fledged verbal and conceptual centres whose relationship, both amongst themselves and with the author's voice, is dialogic and carnivalized, and thus not susceptible to subordination or reification. Raskolnikov, as with all the other characters, is a subject and not an object: therefore never exhaustively known or defined as he would be were the implied author to have the first and last word about him.

The dialogic or polyphonic text thus puts the much argued issue of the author's so-called 'disappearance' into a significantly new light. The character ceases to be the object of the choices and plans open to the implied author. Many critics in the Western tradition have argued (Wayne C. Booth, for example, in *The Rhetoric of Fiction*) that only these choices and plans can guarantee the 'unity' of the text and justify the ways of the author to the reader. Bakhtin challenges these long-held assumptions radically: the monological text is a partial report. There is even an attractive value-judgment implicit in Bakhtin's constant invitation to us to distinguish more keenly between those techniques that favour polyphony and those that easily give the final word to the monologue.

See M. Bakhtin, trans. C. Emerson, *Problems of Dostoevsky's Poetics* (1984); M. Bakhtin, *Rabelais and his World* (1965); V. N. Voloshinov, *Marxism and the Philosophy of Language* (1973); M. Holquist, (ed.), *The Dialogic Imagination: Four Essays by M. Bakhtin* (1981); K. Clark and M. Holquist, *Mikhail Bakhtin* (1984); T. Todorov, *Mikhail Bakhtin: The Dialogical Principle* (1984).

TM

diction

Aristotle's low ranking of diction (*lexis*) among the six elements of tragedy implies an idea of the poet clothing the essential form, the structure of action, character and thought, in appropriate language: the selection of words is secondary to the imaginative design. This dualistic view of language as the dress of thought lies behind traditional critical attitudes to diction in poetry. It is customary to speak of the archaic diction in *The Faerie Queene* or the Latinate diction of *Paradise Lost* as if these were stylistic incidentals. In the eighteenth century, the idea of 'poetic diction' emerged: poets like Thomas Gray asserted that the language of poetry was necessarily specialized and remote from 'ordinary' language. It was this 'poetic diction', with its elaborate devices of archaism, Latinity and circumlocution, that Wordsworth attacked as artificial and unnatural; he denied any 'essential difference between the language of prose and metrical composition'. But the idea that there is a special language for poetry persists; I. A. Richards, in *Principles of Literary Criticism* (1924), attempts to separate poetry from other forms of discourse in his theory of the emotive and scientific uses of language. However, as Elder Olson points out, 'there are no necessary differences between poetic diction, as diction, and the diction of any other kind of composition. There are no devices of language which can be pointed to as distinctively poetic' ('William Empson, contemporary criticism, and poetic diction' in R. S. Crane's *Critics and Criticism*, 1957). But Olson's neo-Aristotelian relegation of language to the least important place among the parts of poetry revives the dualism that generated the concept of 'poetic diction'. His argument that 'the chair is not wood but wooden; poetry is not words but verbal' suggests that the 'matter' of poetry, language, is as incidental to its essential form as wood to the chair; chairs can be made out of many materials and remain chairs. But it is difficult to imagine poetry 'made out of' anything other than language. In fact modern descriptive criticism would prefer the organic analogies of Romantic poetics, and assert that language is no more incidental to poetry than wood is to *trees*.

The new attitudes to language of the later Richards (*Philosophy of Rhetoric*, 1936) and William Empson (*Seven Types of Ambiguity*, 1930) relocate diction at the centre of critical attention. For if 'meaning' is the result of the total activity of all the words in a context, and not something pre-existing expression, then statements about the meaning and form of poems are implicitly statements about organizations of words: diction, the choice of words, is a fundamental element of meaning. Winifred Nowottny (*The Language Poets Use*, 1962) points out that diction determines the personae of poetry, the voices the poet adopts, and argues that poetry differs from other utterances in its ability to create its own context, to speak with any voice. Indeed, far from being restricted to a 'poetic diction', it is uniquely free 'to raid other forms of language at will'; poetry can take its words from any style of language, literary or other. Once in the poem, however, words are characteristically 'used to induce or define attitudes other than those in which everyday language allows us inertly to rest'. See also ANALYSIS, CHICAGO CRITICS, LANGUAGE, NEW CRITICISM.

PM

differance

see DECONSTRUCTION, FEMINIST CRITICISM

dirge
see ELEGY

disbelief
see BELIEF

discourse

Twenty years ago, 'discourse' had its traditional meaning: the ordered exposition in writing or speech of a particular subject, a practice familiarly associated with writers such as Descartes and Machiavelli. Recently the term has been used with increasing frequency and with new kinds of meaning, reflecting in part the effect on critical vocabulary of work done within and across the boundaries of various disciplines: linguistics, philosophy, literary criticism, history, psychoanalysis and sociology. The term has come to represent the meeting-ground for diverse inquiries into the nature and use of language; but it means different things when it is spoken in a French or an Anglo-American accent.

A basic motive in the formulation of discourse in Anglo-American research has been to discover the regularities and constraints at work in units of language larger than the sentence. This has meant a redefinition of the goals of linguistic inquiry as formulated by Chomsky. Whereas Chomsky had given priority to a description of our knowledge of the grammaticality of sentences, work on discourse stressed the importance of a description of communicative competence, our ability to combine sentences, to relate them coherently to the topics of discourse, and to say the right thing at the right time. A string of grammatically well-formed sentences does not necessarily constitute a successful act of communication. To reply to the question 'What is your name?' by saying 'The cows are under the bridge' is not, ordinarily, to respond appropriately, even though both question and answer are grammatically correct. Such an exchange might make sense in the context of a surrealist novel or of schizophrenic language, but normally discourse is cohesive, and one of the aims of discourse analysis is to show how a knowledge of conventions for links between sentences and for links with context is a necessary condition of successful communication (see M. A. K. Halliday and R. Hasan, *Cohesion in English*, 1976).

A concern for understanding language in the context of communicative use has been central to the contemporary conception of discourse. What is understood as the context of communication has varied from one field of inquiry to another. In the philosophy of language, the theory of the speech act, notably developed in the work of Austin and Searle, has been incorporated into this expanded definition of discourse. Speech act theory is, in part, a reaction against the impoverished conception of language inherited from logical positivism whereby the meaningful use of language consists in the utterance of statements about the world which can be either confirmed or disconfirmed. Austin and then Searle proposed that language use was not simply a matter of making true or false statements about the world, but also a kind of action, the expression of an intention in relation to a person or state of affairs. To understand the meaning of an utterance requires more than knowing what it refers to; it is also to understand its 'force', whether it be promising, commanding, questioning, or any one of a number of what Austin and Searle called 'illocutionary acts'. Although working with invented examples of utterance, speech act theory has made a good case for describing the necessary conditions for a successful or 'felicitous' act of communication, a task neglected not only by linguistic philosophy but also by the Chomskyan grammar of sentences. (See J. R. Searle, *Speech Acts*, 1969.)

Three other related areas of inquiry need to be noted: the ethnography of speaking, conversational analysis, and functional linguistics. The first of these, through the development of such concepts as speech community and speech style, has refined our understanding of language as a force in social life, and notably the way that language contributes to the definition of social identity and difference. (See J. J. Gumperz and D. Hymes, *Directions in Sociolinguistics*, 1972.) Conversational analysis poses various questions—what are the constitutive events in a conversation, how do we recognize that it is our turn to speak, who controls the topic of conversation—in an effort to identify the regularities and constraints at work in examples of actual conversation. (M. Coulthard, *Introduction to Discourse Analysis*, 1977; M. Coulthard and M. Montgomery, *Studies in Discourse Analysis*, 1981.) The premiss of functional linguistics has been usefully described by its principal exponent, M. A. K. Halliday: 'The particular form taken by the grammatical system of language is closely related to the social and personal needs that language is required to serve'. Given that our language allows us to make the same proposition in different forms—'John loved Mary', 'Mary was loved by John'—functional linguistics investigates what it is that determines one realization over another. The question of determination here is complex: preference for one grammatical form can be partly understood in terms of the immediate speech context, but implicated in that and surrounding it are other contexts of power and politics. Functional linguistics can alert us to the operations of ideology in language, whether it be in everyday usage or in literature. For example, the use of nominalization and personification—'The stock market had a good day today'—can obscure the issue of who immediately profits; compare as an alternative realization 'Today a number of stock brokers and speculators made a lot of money.' Besides enriching our understanding of the social context of communication, functional linguistics, conversational analysis, and the ethnography of speaking have opened up a critical potential for discourse analysis because of their capacity to illuminate language use as a process in which inequalities of power and position are negotiated and contested. (M. A. K. Halliday, *Language as Social Semiotic*, 1978; R. Fowler, R. Hodge, G. Kress and T. Trew, *Language and Control*, 1979.)

The work described above has had a considerable effect on literary study. At one level the refinement of the analysis of spoken language has contributed a new set of techniques for the close reading of literary language. Work done in the analysis of conversation has allowed a more discriminating description of dialogue in drama (D. Burton, *Dialogue and Discourse*, 1980). Speech act theory has produced a diversified if unstable set of categories which can be used in the analysis of the intentions and verbal actions encoded in the rhetorical strategies of literature (R. Ohmann, 'Speech, action and style,' in S. Chatman (ed.), *Literary Style: A Symposium*, 1971). At another level discourse analysis has provided a global model for literature itself, one which describes literary works not as iconic objects set apart from a world of intention and effect, but as a socially determined communicative practice between reader and writer, and, as such, analogous to other forms of communication (R. Fowler, *Literature as Social Discourse*, 1981).

Working from a different perspective, discourse is a key term in the writings of the French philosopher and historian, Michel Foucault. The place of discourse in Foucault's own work can be crudely described through two intertwined concerns. The first is with discourse as an historical phenomenon, an emphasis that has been marginal to the main body of Anglo-American work. For Foucault there is no general theory of discourse or language, only the historically grounded description of various discourses or 'discursive practices'. These latter consist in a certain regularity of statements which then define an object—whether it be sexuality or madness, criminality or economics—and supply a set of concepts which can be used to analyse the object, to delimit what can and cannot be said about it, and to demarcate who can say it. But the regularity which produces a discursive practice should not be confused with a logical or systematic coherence. It is an historical event, not the realization of some pre-existent system. The analysis of discourse is a matter of research into the historical conditions which permitted, but did not guarantee, its appearance. As discourse defines its object, there are no criteria of truth external to it: the truth of a discourse is, according to Foucault, akin to a rhetorical imposition. We believe a discourse about sexuality to be true because we have no alternative. Truth is the unrecognized fiction of a successful discourse.

The second concern, already indicated in Foucault's attitude toward the concept of truth, is a radical scepticism about many basic assumptions in intellectual history, literary criticism and linguistics. In literary criticism Foucault has unpacked and criticized the assumptions at work in such terms as 'tradition' and 'author'. Foucault sees the idea of tradition as bestowing a specious unity upon works whose difference is then obscured for the sake of a myth of a unified development of literature which transcends the abrupt discontinuities between diverse social formations. Similarly, the idea of the 'author' is historicized: 'Even within our civilization the same type of texts have not always required authors; there was a time when these texts which we now call "literary" (stories, folk-tales, epics, and tragedies) were accepted, circulated, and valorized without any question about the identity of their author' (M. Foucault, 'What is an author?' 1969; see AUTHOR). The fact that literature and authors have become so closely identified needs to be explained as the condition of a discursive practice which may itself be historically transient.

Foucault's critique of our common sense about authors is consonant with another important component of his conception of discourse. For Foucault, discourse is at once a denial and a critique of a canonical assumption in our thinking about literature and language, the assumption that these are expressive activities, either in the sense that they express emotions and ideas 'within' the individual, or in the sense that acts of expression, and notably acts of literary expression, are a means of self-realization. The different 'discursive practices' within a society afford various 'subject positions' which permit us to write or speak in certain ways about certain subjects. But this cannot be equated with acts of expression or self-realization. The opposite is true: 'discourse is not the majestically unfolding manifestation of a thinking, knowing subject, but on the contrary, a totality in which the dispersion of the subject, and his discontinuity with himself may be determined' (Foucault, *The Archaeology of Knowledge*, 1969, trans. 1972). This account of discourse expressly challenges the commonly held assumption that literature is the expressive use of language *par excellence*. For Foucault this would simply be another myth about literature in our cultural epoch, one that could be traced in the genealogy of an ideal of expressive selfhood in the forms of lyric poetry. Conceived as discourse, literature no more expresses us, either as writers or readers, than do the leaves on a tree express themselves when they are blown by the wind.

Although Foucaultian discourse is the enemy of traditional conceptions of the literary, his work can be read as the theoretical equivalent of a contemporary practice of literary writing which itself traces the disappearance of the expressive subject (the works of the American writers John Ashberry and Thomas Pynchon would be a case in point).

More generally, work done around a conception of discourse has permitted a rethinking of notions of literary form. Instead of seeing the literary work as an ideal aesthetic harmony, or the equally ideal resolution of psychological tensions in the author or reader, discourse theory conceives of the literary work as an instance of the historically variable institution of literature, an institution which mediates relations between writer and reader in different ways at different times, and in so doing, echoes, transforms, or challenges the uneven distribution of power within societies. See also C. Belsey, *Critical Practice* (1980); A. Easthope, *Poetry as Discourse* (1983).

JC

dissociation of sensibility

A term coined by T. S. Eliot in 'The Metaphysical Poets', originally an anonymous review in *TLS* (1921) of Grierson's anthology, *Metaphysical Lyrics and Poems of the Seventeenth Century*. Its success dates from its reprinting under Eliot's name in 1924. The essay concludes: 'The poets of the seventeenth century . . . possessed a mechanism of sensibility which could devour any kind of experience. . . . [But with Milton and Dryden] a dissociation set in, from which we have never recovered . . .' This malady of English poetry allegedly stemmed from a separation of the 'thinking' and 'feeling' parts of the poets' consciousness, an inability to accommodate intellection in the poetic synthesis. Thus thought and emotion in poetry appeared embarrassingly raw. A unified sensibility, such as Donne's, was able, on the other hand, to feel a thought, 'as immediately as the odour of a rose'. The poetry of the 'moderns' was to recapture this unified sensibility: 'The Waste Land' is a kind of pattern for the poetic amalgamation of disparate elements. Coleridge's synthesizing IMAGINATION is at the back of this idea, but the terms and concept derive from the French symbolist critic Remy de Gourmont, and Eliot sees in Baudelaire, Laforgue and Corbière a similar unification (which was also present by implication in Pound and Eliot himself). By 1931 Eliot was detecting the dissociation even in Donne, but in his last reference to the problem (in 1947) he reaffirmed the original doctrine, though in more general terms: 'All we can say is, that something like this did happen; that it had something to do with the Civil War . . . that we must seek the causes in Europe, not in England alone . . .' Cleanth Brooks attributes the dissociation to Hobbes and L. C. Knights to Bacon, but Frank Kermode, in a masterly chapter on the doctrine in *Romantic Image* (1957), may well be right in describing the concept as 'quite useless historically'.

FWB

documentary

see BIOGRAPHY

dominant
see POETICS

double irony
see IRONY

drama
has been studied for centuries as a form of literature, 'a poem written for representation' (Johnson). In other words, it has been judged primarily as a poem, and all that peculiarly belongs to the stage— acting, production, scenery, effects—has been subsumed under the vague term 'representation'. The alternative is to invert that position, and stress the representation before the poem. In the theatre, the poet's art is only one among many, and it is not an essential one: indeed, words at all are not essential. In Greek the term meant simply to act or perform, and the definition is still valid; all others are derivative and of limited historical significance. The dictionary offers 'a set of events . . . leading to catastrophe or consummation'; but that relates to Victorian theatre and to a Victorian view of Greek tragedy. The dancing and flute-playing which Aristotle discussed are not events, and do not lead to catastrophe; nor does the Fool in *Lear*, nor the tramps in *Waiting for Godot*. Beckett's play is constructed against an expectation of con-summation, but its positive qualities are vested in the tramps, who are clowns. Their performance derives for us from the circus, or more specifically from Charlie Chaplin, but the association of clown and outcast is ancient, recurrent, and common to most societies.

The clown invites our laughter, and through it our derision. His opposite is the heroic actor, who invites admiration (naïvely, emulation or identification). His identity is established by his presence on the stage, his physical power to dominate the scene and the audience; but he, far more than the clown, depends on words, and can use them. For such an actor (Alleyn), Marlowe created the language of Tamburlaine. Hamlet's language rarely displays such authority, and readers have doubted Ophelia's view of him as a noble mind o'erthrown; Shakespeare sets what he *is* (leading actor) against what he *says*, and makes that the focus of his relation to the player king. A heroic actor relies on projecting his role through his own personality, which means that the 'character' he presents depends on his own. The clown, on the other hand, like the character actor, appears to be quite other than himself. But king and clown are equally roles that men play (as fathers do to their children): the actor's relation to his audience is a double one: he must imitate men and women as they appear to be, and he must represent our urge to play a role—the paradox that we can only 'be ourselves' when we can find a role to play. For the first, his language must resemble speech, for the second it will not; hence the duality observable even in Aeschylus, where the reader may concentrate on elements of human utterance which the actor will find to be only inflections in a poetry whose general condition is close to recitative. Lear can attack the storm with tremendous rhetoric; his Fool can use snatches of folk song and ballad. The relation of king to fool is profoundly disturbing in *Hamlet*, acutely painful in *Lear*.

The range of a great dramatic text, then, derives from the roles that actors play. The peculiar richness of Shakespeare's drama depends on the derivation of his company from the multiplicity of talents masquerading in the Middle Ages under the general term of minstrels (and the status of vagabonds). The impoverishment of drama representing upper-middle-class drawing-rooms did not derive only from its social narrowness, but also from its lack of theatrical range. The problem for Elizabethan dramatists was to unify the diversity at their disposal (dancing and fooling would happen whether it was part of the play or not). Marlowe wrote great poetry only for those moments when it would be needed; for others, only the necessary words for what was largely silent action; for the clowns it seems likely that he provided only a scenario to be fulfilled with improvisation. Shakespeare seems always to have provided a fuller text, but in *Romeo and Juliet*, Peter and the musicians must have been relied on to do more than was set down for them; by the time of *Hamlet* he requires even clowns to perform strictly within the 'necessary questions of the play', which have become too consistently intricate for undisciplined expansion.

Drama, then, is not a poem; not even a dramatic poem. But prose is only in special circumstances adequate to its nature. It cannot be defined in literary terms, or if it must be, they take on a different meaning in the theatre. Action in a novel is the journeys and battles in which men engage; in drama that is only a secondary sense, action must primarily mean the movement of actors on the stage. It is not enlightening to offer a map of Scotland in an edition of *Macbeth*: he does not travel from Glamis to Forres, but enters and exits on the stage. Drama depends on actors with an audience. Performances, even of the same production with the same cast, will vary, sometimes radically, from night to night; and the variation will primarily depend on the different audiences, and the actors' response to them. There is no such consistent object to abide our criticism as a painting, or a printed poem; nor can there be an 'ideal theatre of the mind'. Actual performance is inherent in drama. So *King Lear* may be one night a rather abstract dissertation on Nature, the next an overwhelming experience whose end is silence. Dramatic criticism has to reckon with this variability and actuality; but it must not be defeated by it; the variables are neither infinite nor arbitrary. *King Lear* is never *Endgame*.

See S. W. Dawson, *Drama and the Dramatic* (1970); Clifford Leech, *The Dramatist's Experience* (1970); Stanley Wells, *Literature and Drama* (1970).

NSB

dramatic irony
see IRONY

E

écriture
see DECONSTRUCTION

effect
Concentration of critical attention on the psychological effect of poetry on the reader is attacked by W. K. Wimsatt and Monroe C. Beardsley, in their essay 'The affective fallacy' (*The Verbal Icon*, 1954), as encouraging impressionism and relativism much as the 'Intentional Fallacy' (see INTENTION) encourages biography and relativism. They relate the practice to the nineteenth-century tradition of affective criticism in which the critic was concerned to exhibit and record his emotional responses, to catch the intensity of his experience of a work without bothering to investigate the causes of the experience. This habit of regarding poetry as an exclusively emotional affair arises from the Romantic distinction of psychological events into 'thought' and 'feeling', 'reason' and 'emotion': in such a scheme poetry is always the expression of feeling or emotion. I. A. Richards, in *Principles of Literary Criticism* (1924), continued to associate poetry with an 'emotive' as opposed to a 'scientific' use of language, and attempted to apply behavioural psychology to analysis of the effects of poetry. His failure to find terms in which the psychological processes of the reader could be described meant that descriptive criticism had to seek explanations not in psychology but in language. Thus Wimsatt and Beardsley argue that emotive import depends on the descriptive and contextual aspects of a word; it is not something added on but a function of meaning. So for an emotion we have not merely a cause, but an object, a reason—one is angry *because* one thinks a thing is false, insulting or unjust. The emotion aroused by poetry is felt in response to an organization of meaning. The descriptive critic seeks to describe the *reasons* for emotion, the meaning of the poem as a structure of language.

An absurd misunderstanding of this argument concludes that poems have no effect, no emotional quality, are merely objects to be 'objectively' analysed. But the critic could hardly hope to account for an effect he had not experienced. Wimsatt and Beardsley rightly insist that in explaining the reasons for his response to a work—in any case a more complex mental event than a state of 'feeling'—the critic must seek terms which relate to the public object, the poem as a pattern of knowledge. See also FEELING, PLEASURE, READER, SINCERITY.

PM

eiron
see IRONY

elegy
Some genres, such as EPIC and SONNET, are fairly unequivocal in classical and/or modern European literature: the first of these two examples is identified by its scale, its subject-matter, and its manner of handling that subject-matter; the second must obey stringent metrical rules. 'Elegy' illustrates a different type of genre-term: ultimately classical in origin, transplanted into modern European terminology only as a word, without the classical formal basis, unrestricted as to structure (except for the minimal requirement that it be a VERSE composition), overlapping with a number of similarly inexplicit terms (complaint, dirge, lament, monody, threnody), yet conventionally tied to a limited range of subject-matters and styles (death and plaintive musing), and readily comprehensible to educated readers. In these respects, a most typical genre-term.

Elegia in Greek and Latin was a type of metre, not a type of poem—a couplet consisting of a dactylic hexameter followed by a pentameter. Since this verse-form was used for all kinds of subjects, the classical ancestry is relevant to modern elegy principally in an etymological way.

From the English Renaissance, 'elegy' or 'elegie' referred to a poem mourning the death of a particular individual. Spenser's 'Daphnaida' (1591) and 'Astrophel' ('A Pastorall Elegie upon the death of the most noble and valorous Knight, Sir Philip Sidney', 1595) are influential early examples; Donne uses the word in the same sense (e.g. 'A Funerall Elegie' in *An Anatomy of the World*, and the titles of several poems in the collection *Epicedes and Obsequies upon the Deaths of Sundry Personages*); then there are the 'Elegies upon the Author' by several hands appended to the 1633 edition of Donne's poems. But since Donne also uses the word for his collection of twenty 'Elegies', casual, erotic and satirical poems on various topics, the precise 'funeral elegy' sense was obviously not securely established.

Milton's 'Lycidas' mourning the death of Edward King (1637) revives the pastoral form, with its apparatus of shepherds, nymphs and satyrs, and sets the pattern for the modern English elegiac tradition. The best-known poems in this mode are Shelley's 'Adonais' on Keats (1821) and Matthew Arnold's 'Thyrsis' on Clough (1867). (Milton and Arnold refer to their poems as 'monodies', not 'elegies'.) Tennyson's 'In

Memoriam' on the death of Arthur Hallam (1833–50) is not pastoral, but introspective and personal.

The language of funeral elegies provided opportunity for plaintive, melancholy generalizations on death or on the state of the world: there are signs of this appropriation of the mode for general complaint already in 'Lycidas', where the author 'by occasion foretells the ruin of our corrupted clergy'. Thomas Gray's 'Elegy Written in a Country Churchyard' (1750) is the archetypal general meditation on the passing of life, unconnected with any particular death. Coleridge departicularized the definition still further when he stated that the elegy 'is the form of poetry natural to the reflective mind'—so elegy came to be a mood, or a style, as well as a poem for a specific dead person. This second, looser, definition of elegy is invoked by literary historians to characterize assorted melancholy poems of any period, e.g. the so-called 'Anglo-Saxon elegies' including 'The Wanderer' and 'The Seafarer', both tales of personal deprivation shading into regretful meditations on the mutability of the world and seeking divine consolation.

As long as we are clear that there is a strict and a loose definition of 'elegy', that there is slender classical warrant for the term in either of its two familiar modern senses, and that we perforce apply it to works which were not thought of by their authors as 'elegies' (remember that the paradigm elegy 'Lycidas' is called a 'monody'), we have a useful exploratory genre term.

See T. P. Harrison, Jr, and H. J. Leon (eds), *The Pastoral Elegy: An Anthology* (1939); Mary Lloyd (ed.), *Elegies, Ancient and Modern* (1903); A. F. Potts, *The Elegiac Mode* (1967).

RGF

emblem

'Emblem,' wrote Bacon in 1605, 'reduceth conceits intellectual to images sensible.' In its fullest development the emblem comprised a symbolic picture plus motto and explanation; familiar moral and religious paradoxes were encoded in popular books like Francis Quarles's *Emblemes* (1635), and poetic emulation of such 'silent parables' (cf. ALLEGORY, CONCEIT) helped stimulate 'concreteness' and palpability in metaphor, and witty, reflexive verbal texture. (See J. A. Mazzeo, 'A critique of some modern theories of metaphysical poetry', 1952, reprinted in W. R. Keast (ed.), *17th Century Poetry*, 1962.) 'Emblem' or 'Device' came to signify a complex of meaning enacted through analogy (whether in paint or words or spectacle); a compressed poem-within-a-poem, or a central motto or hieroglyphic epitomizing the poem's intention. It might be traditional (the insignia of saints or nations) or bizarrely original, simultaneously announcing and hiding its meaning, assuming the portentousness of a talismanic sign.

Modern use of the term has been vexed by the ambiguous 'concreteness' it implies (see IMAGE); also by the awareness that, no matter how personal its communicative intention, 'emblem' suggests an arrogantly intentionalist aesthetic at odds with current critical thinking ('a Device' said Puttenham (1589) 'such as a man may put into letters of gold and send to his mistresses for a token'). Post-romantic distrust of the 'frigidity' of calculation, combined with the discredit of analogical thinking, has inhibited our reactions to emblematic techniques. They exist however: in *Coole Park and Ballylee*, 1931, Yeats exclaims 'Another emblem there!' with the assurance that characterizes public and explicit image-making.

See Rosemary Freeman, *English Emblem Books* (1948); Erwin Panofsky, *Studies in Iconology* (1962); George Puttenham, *The Art of English Poesie* (1589), Book 2, ch. 11; Austin Warren, *Richard Crashaw: A Study in Baroque Sensibility* (1939); Edgar Wind, *Pagan Mysteries in the Renaissance* (1958).

LS

epic

European literature was described by Samuel Johnson as a series of footnotes to Homer; and Keats's 'On first looking into Chapman's Homer' expresses a delight that has not often been felt since by those who have to read Homer in less golden translations. The *Iliad* has remained the type of classical epic ever since Aristotle's *Poetics*, and the romantic fascinations of the *Odyssey* have not been exhausted by *Ulysses* and the *Cantos*. Virgil's *Aeneid*, recapitulating the themes of *Odyssey* and *Iliad*, consecrated the epic as the supreme literary form of antiquity, and so it remained for Dante and for the Renaissance humanists. The Christian epic *Paradise Lost* was the consummation of Renaissance efforts to soar 'above the Aonian mount'; it was also the last. Dryden and Pope chose to translate rather than to emulate Virgil and Homer; Arnold lectured on the Grand Style.

Victorian definitions of epic used to speak of 'national themes' (usually war) and invoked Milton's 'great argument' and 'answerable style'. Classically trained critics, expecting art to see life steadily and see it whole, look for an idealized realism and debar folklore and romance elements. W. P. Ker disqualified *Beowulf* because its hero fights monsters and not men; Tolkien defends it on the same grounds. Bowra (*Heroic Poetry*) held that heroic poetry, for all the power of the gods, is centred on the human level, and that magic should not play a determining role. Modern advances in the study of non-classical heroic and oral poetry (Chadwick, Bowra, Parry, Lord) have illuminated the connection of epic with 'heroic ages' where the warrior-lord of a pastoral society is the shepherd of his people in peace, and in war achieves glory by a life of action. 'Breaker of cities' and 'tamer of horses' are equally complimentary epithets; and death *is* better than dishonour. So it was with the men at Thebes and at Troy; so with Beowulf, with Charlemagne, with Myo Cid; so perhaps with Gilgamesh and with King David. So it was in the days of our grandfathers, as Nestor reminds us. A heroic age lasts very few generations, and is firmly integrated about a few central places and figures.

The stories of these particular heroes are known to us through writing; the heroes of the Old English *Widsith* remain names. It is only recently that the techniques of oral composition were definitively analysed by Milman Parry; his work shows in minute detail how the text of Homer has the same formal characteristics as the improvised oral epics of modern Yugoslavia; both verbal phrase and type-scene and overall structural patterning are part of a repertoire of stock formulae, a tradition which evolved in response to the conditions of oral improvisation. Parry's methods are being applied to the products of other cultures. But the consequences of his work for the poetics of an epic written in an 'oral' style have not yet been worked out critically. There is, after all, a qualitative difference between Homer's epic and the Yugoslav *epos*; their compositional mechanics may be the same, but their aesthetic effects differ, at least in degree, and the difference may be due in part to a literate finishing of the *epea pteroenta*, Homer's 'winged words'.

Between Homer and Virgil lies a world of difference, and again between Virgil and Milton; critics speak of primary, secondary and tertiary epic. The verbal art of Virgil refines and transmutes the clear and inevitable directness of Homer into something softer; the laughter of his gods, when heard, is less uncontrollable. For all the sternness of its ethos and beauty of its surface, his world has a fuller moral and psychological dimension, and a more personal reverberation, than Homer's. Milton himself and his concerns as a Renaissance humanist and Protestant are so powerful in *Paradise Lost*, and it contains in baroque form so much of the extravagance of the so-called romantic epics of Ariosto, Tasso and Spenser, that the usefulness of the term 'epic' may be disputed. The epic surely cannot be an individual's personal view of the world?

The point about epic, Frye argues, is its encyclopaedic scope and its cyclic structure; the anger of Achilles, the journeys of Odysseus and Aeneas—these stories in their resolution recapitulate the life of the individual and of the race. The note of epic is its objectivity:

It is hardly possible to overestimate the importance for Western literature of the Iliad's demonstration that the fall of an enemy, no less than of a friend or leader, is tragic and not comic. With the *Iliad*, once for all, an objective and disinterested element enters into the poet's vision of human life. With this element . . . poetry acquires the authority that since the *Iliad* it has never lost, an authority based, like the authority of science, on the vision of nature as an impersonal order.

Frye argues well for this pattern and this authority in Virgil and Milton; he also considers the Bible an epic.

It is this objectivity and authority that Joyce sought and Brecht wanted in his 'epic theatre'. The epic qualities achieved by Tolstoy, aimed at by Steinbeck and travestied by Cecil B. de Mille are based on the idea of epic presenting the whole of the life of a society against a natural background with simplicity, grandeur and authority. The fate of a character is part of the pattern: like the others, when he falls to the ground, his armour clatters upon him; but he comes from a particular family and place, had a brother or an orchard. 'The lives of men are like the generations of leaves' or an incident in battle is 'as when a shepherd in the mountains sees a thundercloud (or a wolf) . . .' The coherence of the pattern of life is maintained by these traditional epic similes; there is the feeling that the whole is more than the part you are reading, and that you know, in general, what the whole is like. Aristotle remarks that Homer leaves the stage to his characters; this impersonality of narrative technique stems from the fact that Frye's 'poet's vision' is the traditional vision of a preliterate society. Hence the *aidos* of epic, its respect for the given facts of nature and human life, which it crystallizes into generic type-scenes and verbal formulae; hence its pattern, beauty and authority.

See Erich Auerbach, trans. W. Trask, *Mimesis* (1953); Maurice Bowra, *Heroic Poetry* (1952); Maurice Bowra, *Virgil to Milton* (1945); H. M. and N. K. Chadwick, *The Growth of Literature* (reprinted 1968); Northrop Frye, *Anatomy of Criticism* (1957); W. P. Ker, *Epic and Romance* (1896); G. S. Kirk, *Homer and the Epic* (1965); C. S. Lewis, *A Preface to Paradise Lost* (1942); A. B. Lord, *The Singer of Tales* (1964); Milman Parry, ed. A. Parry, *The Making of Homeric Verse* (1971).

MJA

epic theatre

The cardinal concept of the work of Bertolt Brecht (*the* classic MOD-ERNIST, and currently, after Shakespeare, the most frequently performed of all dramatists), 'epic theatre' means, simply, a theatre that narrates, rather than represents. Stemming from the period in which

Brecht first began to study Marx, with *The Threepenny Opera* of 1928 as its first major exhibit, the theory is grounded in historical and political propositions—in the view, espoused by mentors like the sociologist Fritz Sternberg and the critic Walter Benjamin as well as by Brecht himself, that the workings of modern industrial civilization, and the essentially 'inorganic' cities spawned by it, are too abstract and complex to be visually apprehended, or immanently represented upon the stage. Upon such premisses Brecht built a 'scientific' theory of a radical drama in which experimental work upon contemporary society might be carried out through a sober, narrative analysis of its inherent (and frequently comic) contradictions.

Consequently, the theory of the 'epic theatre' emphasizes rationality, and devices calculated to secure a suitable environment for its exercise. Brecht felt that to foster a state of relaxation in the theatre—an atmosphere in which reason and detachment, rather than passion and involvement, were to predominate—was to subvert the established theatre and the bankrupt 'culinary', 'Aristotelian' plays that were performed in it. He had in mind, essentially, the drama of bourgeois realism, with its roots in Lessing's neo-Aristotelian theory, and its aim of achieving empathetic identification between audiences and 'stars' who in turn identify themselves with their roles, and represent individual psychologies in emotionally charged styles of acting. One alternative model was cabaret, where drinks and smokes guarantee a laid-back, critical frame of mind: 'I even maintain' (wrote Brecht in a hyperbolic mood) 'that one man with a cigar in the stalls at a Shakespeare performance could bring about the downfall of western art'. In such an atmosphere, Brecht's plays are commonly introduced by narrators (sometimes cynics, like the compères of cabarets) who see through social façades and distance themselves from the events they recount; played by actors who do not identify with their rôles; and set in remote times and places—Chicago, China, medieval Georgia, and Victorian London—with which no spectator can identify her or himself.

The ensemble of these measures is to produce the famous *Verfremdungseffekt* or 'alienation effect'. This concept, with its formalist and idealist antecedents (the Russian FORMALIST *ostranenie* or 'making strange', and German Romantic 'romantic irony'), shifts critical attention from 'affekt' to 'effekt', to the perhaps idealized possibility of audience politicization through a process where cool detachment leads to correct and effective judgment and action. 'Alienation means historicizing, means representing persons and actions as historical, and therefore mutable', writes Brecht in the 1929 essay 'On experimental theatre', restating the Marxist equation of scientific and historical consciousness. The attainment of such consciousness means, for Brecht, the 'alienated' awareness that history's outcomes are never inevitable, always amenable to political intervention and transformation.

Consequently, the epic theatre's foregrounding of narratives and narrators does not imply any straightforward, unproblematical unfolding of chronological or other linear sequences. In a continual recapitulation, perhaps, of the frustrations of 1926, when he was forced to abandon plays that foundered upon the invisibility and unrepresentability of processes like the operation of the Chicago Grain Market, the emphasis of Brecht's work is upon discontinuity. No chain of events is held together by a natural or self-evident logic; the spectator is to experience the constant disruption of narrative structure, as one device undercuts another. Actors are continually abandoning speech for song, or taking off masks to become other characters, or to take part in other plays; scenes are shifted abruptly in time and space, with intervening chasms. The epic theatre asserts narrative in an unpropitious time (compare Benjamin's essay 'The story-teller', on the loss of narrative art), rather than takes it for granted.

Yet at this stage in the history of the reception of Brechtian theory, it may be possible to point to some of its *own* contradictions. It has created a new aesthetics, perhaps, but not a new politics of art. The ease and ubiquity of its absorption was foreshadowed by the instant worldwide success of *The Threepenny Opera* and 'Mack the Knife', a song whose basic propositions (1. that the equation of businessmen and sharks insults sharks; 2. that the upholders and subverters of bourgeois law are interchangeable) have seemed to offer little resistance to painless consumption. Whether or not Brecht can be held responsible for the dissemination of his work in versions that (to requisition a phrase of Clive James's) often have less of the atmosphere of poisonous old Berlin than of poisonous old Bournemouth, the fact remains that Brechtian techniques have now been universally domesticated all the way from *Grandstand* to *Sesame Street*.

Perceiving such problems, Brecht in his last years began to replace the theory of epic theatre with the theory of dialectical theatre, and to base it on the much more radical practice of the *Lehrstücke* (where the entire distinction between performers and audience was abolished, and the performance itself—with potential Nazi wreckers at the doors—became a political act). In Anglosaxony, where the critical working-through of Brechtian theory has been sluggish, such difficulties have surfaced only in recent years, but are thoroughly comprehended in (for instance) Fredric Jameson's 'Afterword' in *Aesthetics and Politics* (1978).

Cf. CONTRADICTION.

See also Walter Benjamin, *Understanding Brecht* (1973); John Willett (ed.), *Brecht on Theatre: The Development of an Aesthetic*

(1974); G. Bartram and A. Waine (eds), *Brecht in Perspective* (1982).

MAH

epistle
see VERSE EPISTLE

essay
Both the term and the form were invented by Montaigne (1533–92) and adopted soon afterwards into English by Bacon; literally the try-out in discursive prose of an idea, judgment or experience. Although the essay is by definition informal and even conversational in manner, the persuasive and rhetorical tradition of much Greek and Roman writing was familiar to Bacon and Montaigne and lies behind what they write. We therefore find in all essays a direct and even intimate appeal to the reader; sometimes, as in Swift's 'Modest proposal', this is complex and ambiguous in line with the ironic purpose of engaging the reader in the interpretative process; sometimes, as in George Orwell's most effective essays (e.g. 'Shooting an elephant'), the rhetoric is all the more influential for being muted and oblique. Usually, though, the essay is a polished and sophisticated form of fireside chat, a smooth way of putting over moral reflections, aphorisms and *obiter dicta* in a less rigorous and rebarbative manner than the treatise or ethical disquisition permits. It must appear relaxed but not flabby, nonchalant but not trivial. In France, Montaigne set the pattern of a fundamentally moral argument based on anecdotes and the lessons to be drawn from them—the gentle art of egotism, in fact, involving autobiography of a sort, if selective and intellectual in style rather than frankly confessional. In England William Hazlitt, Charles Lamb and others made it more sentimental and whimsical by playing down the serious aspect the French have kept to the fore. In America, Washington Irving, Emerson and Thoreau wrote in the genre, and the form flourishes today, particularly among black writers such as James Baldwin and Leroy Jones. In all cases, however, there is no formal structure of progression, and little attempt at a final synthesis: the play of the mind in free associations around a given topic is what counts. Essays are therefore not debates, but dialogues with an assumed reader; but in the finest examples of the art, this does not preclude a fruitful and stimulating tension between a frequent high seriousness in the theme and the almost casual informality of the way in which it is handled. An attempt has been made by Scholes and Klaus to subdivide the genre according to its analogies with the oration, the poem, the story and the play, but since even they admit that 'any essay may be a combination of the four basic forms', the most sensible approach is that which views the essay as a minor art-form in its own right.

See Robert Scholes and Carl H. Klaus, *Elements of the Essay* (1969).

JWJF

euphony
see TEXTURE

evaluation
When we engage critically with a literary work, we are not merely describing it, making it accessible to other readers; at the same time we *judge* it, explicitly or by implication (we would not generally write about a work unless we felt it deserved the effort). We can hardly avoid communicating some opinion of its merits. But the 'objectivity' of description is often felt to preclude evaluation, which is suspected of being a subjective, authoritarian action. T. S. Eliot testifies to the tension between the descriptive and evaluative roles of criticism by arguing for the primacy of both. In 1918 'Judgement and appreciation are merely tolerable avocations, no part of the critic's serious business' (*The Egoist*, V), while in 1923 the critic is urged to 'the common pursuit of true judgement' ('The function of criticism', *Selected Essays*, p. 25). Eliot's self-contradiction reflects the enduring tendency of criticism to define its ambitions in terms of one or the other of these ideally complementary activities. The alternative emphases have produced historically distinct traditions, and continue to propose sharply differentiated programmes.

The evaluative tradition is in England rooted in the neo-classic criticism of Dryden, Pope and Johnson. They saw themselves as arbiters of public taste, interpreting the works of the past and, in their light, judging the work of the present. Their concern was the preservation and assertion of traditional literary and cultural values; the commitment of such criticism to moral and aesthetic standards makes public judgment constantly necessary, and belief in them makes it possible. This tradition of public criticism, mediating between the past and the present, the artists and the public, is continued in the nineteenth century by major critics such as Matthew Arnold and Henry James, and survives in this century in the work of Leavis and the *Scrutiny* writers.

The challenge to this tradition, evident in Eliot's 1918 declaration, emerged from the aspirations of many academic disciplines at the beginning of this century to the attitudes and procedures of the fashionable sciences. The new enthusiasm for objectivity and disinterestedness, for precise analysis and comparison, implied the irrelevance of the public critic and his concern for judgment. Leslie Stephen urged that the critic 'should endeavour to classify the phenomena with which he is dealing as calmly as if he were ticketing a fossil in a museum'. The scientific analogies were ultimately false—literature is not, even for critics, fossilized, not so many value-free facts—and in practice the 'objective' criticism of Eliot and I. A. Richards is full of strident value-judgments. But the desire for objective procedures led to the development of a descriptive criticism whose end was not judgment but knowledge, which took the value of the works it examined for granted. Descriptive criticism assumes not that judgment is irrelevant but that it is implicit in description and analysis; the analysis of a work is a discovery of form, of order, and is thus a testimony to value. The public critic asserts and defines standards against which any work must be measured, but a descriptive critic like William Empson declares that 'you must rely on each particular poem to show you the way in which it is trying to be good; if it fails you cannot know its object' (*Seven Types of Ambiguity*, 1930). This lack of interest in bad literature and urbanity about problems of evaluation point to the critic's new role in the intellectual and cultural safety of the university: he is distanced from contemporary culture and the reading public, while the public critic's mantle is assumed by the weekly reviewer. The professionalization of academic criticism has ensured freedom from the need to rush to judgment; but every fine criticism is itself an assertion and a revelation of value. And hopefully this achievement should sustain public critic-ism as a force in contemporary culture, correcting its inherent tenden-cies to either reactionary or progressive prescriptivism.

See W. K. Wimsatt, Jr, 'Explication as criticism' and 'Poetry and morals' in *The Verbal Icon* (1954).

PM

existentialism

Literary and philosophical responses to the experience of nothingness, *anomie* and absurdity which attempt to discover meaning in and through this experience.

All Existentialist writers begin from a sense that an ontological dimension (Being; the Encompassing; Transcendence; the Thou) has been forced out of consciousness by the institutions and systems of a society which overvalues rationality, will-power, acquisitiveness, pro-ductivity and technological skill. Because this essential dimension properly constitutes the substantial unity between man and man, thing and thing, subject and object, past, present and future, its loss is said to cause men to feel that they have been thrown into a world of reified fragments which say nothing, into a world of men who talk past each other and into a time-stream of disconnected present moments without past or future (see Heidegger, *Being and Time*, 1927). Thus, human institutions, severed from the generative source, cease to be sign-structures of that source and become factitious structures which engage the surface levels of the personality and provide no home. Even language, the most self-evident institution, is felt to have become a complex of cerebralized structures which impede communication and give only limited control over the empirical world. Nietzsche called this total experience of forfeiture 'the death of God', and perhaps K.'s vision of the world in Kafka's *The Castle* (1926) forms its fullest literary expression: long conversations lead nowhere; shambling buildings are inhabited by beings going through meaningless motions like bees in a hive after the removal of the queen; and everything is permeated by a sense of groundlessness, futility and grey opacity. K. is therefore a menace because his wilfulness perpetually threatens to smash this fragile world and precipitate it into the nothingness that underlies almost everything.

At the same time, the *Angst* which haunts the Existentialist world is said—and this paradox is fundamental to Existentialist psychology—to point to the possibility of its own transcendence. Precisely because man can experience absurdity so intensely, there must, it is argued, be some inherent propensity to order and meaning within him. *Angst*, in other words, is seen as the by-product of the conflict between this propensity and the factitious forms which have been imposed upon it.

Existentialist writers and thinkers do not, however, share a unified understanding of this propensity. Sartre, the most consistently atheistic of the Existentialists, equates it with the human will shorn of all illusions and responsible only to itself. Camus, more of an agnostic, locates it below the will, in the spontaneous potential of the personality, but refuses to name it, pointing to it through a variety of metaphors. Heidegger, whose thinking is crypto-theistic, refers to it as *Sorge* (care) and Kierkegaard, an avowed Christian, identifies it with the soul. Nevertheless, it is this propensity which is said to save men from nihilism, despair or escape into the ready-made values of the fallen world.

Furthermore, Existentialist writers and thinkers draw radically different metaphysical conclusions from the existence of this propensity. Although, for Sartre, it points to nothing beyond itself and is not capable of overcoming the *néant* in any final sense, it does permit man to live with his 'unhappy consciousness', to tolerate his own *Angst*. For Camus, however, it enables man to find happiness and peace of mind in an absurd universe (Meursault and Sisyphe), engage in collective work against the forces of negation (Rieux and his friends) and, occasionally, to glimpse transcendent powers. For Jaspers, it enables men to alter their 'consciousness of Being' and 'inner attitude towards things' and to listen in an attitude of 'philosophical faith' for the silence of hidden Transcendence as it emanates into experience and overcomes fragmentation, isolation and encrustation (Jaspers, *The Perennial Scope of*

Philosophy, 1948). For Buber, the Jewish Existentialist, it indicates the possibility of attunement to and existence according to the timeless moments which are generated when the 'eternal Thou' breaks into time through the 'human Thou' (Buber, *I and Thou*, 1923). For Kierkegaard, a Christian Existentialist, it is the divinely motivated principle of 'subjectivity' which urges the individual to make the 'leap of faith' and discover the task and responsibility for that task which God has laid upon him even if that task ends in failure and absurdity (Kierkegaard, *Fear and Trembling*, 1843).

Consequently, Sartre's famous dictum 'existence precedes essence'—often considered to be the basic tenet of Existentialism—can mean one of two things. Either that existence is inherently meaningless so that man has, by the exercise of the will, to create his own values. Or that, for each individual, there is a hidden meaning embedded in existence which, by the exercise of his total personal resources, he has to discover and live by.

On the one hand then, theistic and crypto-theistic Existentialism moves towards an inner-worldly mysticism where the experience of the Transcendent is discovered within and not apart from the world of men. On the other hand, agnostic and atheistical Existentialism moves towards an attitude of defiance which can turn into a social or explicitly ideological commitment (Camus's Socialism and Sartre's Marxism).

In all cases then, a radically negative experience is seen to contain the embryo of a positive development—though the psychological and philosophical content of that development is extremely diverse.

See W. Barrett, *Irrational Man* (1961); J. Collins, *The Existentialists* (1977); C. Hanley, *Existentialism and Psychoanalysis* (1979); P. Roubiczek, *Existentialism* (1964); G. Rupp, *Beyond Existentialism and Zen* (1979); N. Scott, *Mirrors of Man in Existentialism* (1978); Mary Warnock, *Existentialism* (1977).

RWS

experimental

works break with the conventions of a dominant literary tradition; in our century primarily the conventions of mimesis designed to capture the illusion of surface reality characteristic of nineteenth-century realism. However, there may arise a secondary experimentation in reaction to the preceding wave of experiment.

Both types of experimental writing can derive much of their effect from contrast with the convention they are breaking, a form of artistic play. But many experimental techniques grow from the struggle to express new ways of looking at man and society. Experimental work based on revolutionary insight may found a new convention. Inner monologue techniques, though originally experimental—in Joyce and

Woolf uncovering scarcely explored areas of consciousness—are now the stock in trade of most novelists. In its own way, the new objectivity of the *nouveau roman* also rejects this now conventional inner vision. In the theatre, monologue expressing what in reality would go beyond the consciousness of a character is a once experimental device (see O'Casey's *The Silver Tassie*) now often used in otherwise non-experimental plays (e.g. Pinter's *The Birthday Party*). Traditional modes tend to re-emerge renewed by the assimilation of some experimental techniques which often gain in force when the truths they assert are also proved on the pulses through mimetic representation.

It is difficult to find common attributes in the succeeding waves of twentieth-century experimentalism. But perhaps most significant works are trying to express new concepts of the nature of reality. Consequently theme is elevated over mimesis: the need to express forcefully something about reality takes precedence over the creation of an illusory secondary reality in the work. Dream intrudes fantastically into waking life in SURREALIST works (e.g. the Buñuel-Dali films). Yet the apparent fantasy makes a point about the nature of reality, about how man is moved by subconscious urges more natural and 'real' than oppressive social conventions.

Much experimentalism was in part a reaction to intellectual tendencies—the growth of sociology, anthropology, theories of economic determinism, Freudian psychology, so that a realistic art based on mimetic representation of individual fates seemed inadequate. Hence the multi-layered identity of a character like Bloom in *Ulysses*. Vast social and economic changes played their part in this change of consciousness, and since then the accelerated pace of change is probably the main reason for the quickened succession of experimental movements. Recent adventures into throw-away art, happenings and anti-literate theatre no doubt reflect the stress of unassimilated change. See also CONVENTION, TRADITION.

See R. Brustein, *The Theatre of Revolt: An Approach to Modern Drama* (1965); Bamber Gascoigne, *Twentieth-century Drama* (1963); Allan Rodway, 'Modernism and forms in the esthetic of the novel', *The Truths of Fiction* (1970).

EJB

explication

see ANALYSIS

expressionism

A label applied to the *avant-garde* literature, graphics, architecture and cinema which appeared throughout the German-speaking world, 1910–c.1922, and of which Vorticism is the closest equivalent in England. First used of German painting in April 1911, and of literature in July 1911, the term gained rapid currency with reference to the visual arts but was probably established as a literary critical term only as late as mid-1913. Several important early Expressionists died without ever using the term; other important writers reacted negatively to it during the years in question; others now deny any validity to it or are unwilling to associate themselves with it.

At the most, Expressionism is a blanket term. It does not characterize a uniform movement propagating a neatly definable set of ideas or working towards well-defined and commonly accepted goals. The product of a generation which had been born into a pre-modern Germany, grown up during twenty-five years of unprecedentedly rapid social change and achieved maturity in a society which was extensively industrialized and urbanized, Expressionism stands between two worlds and is riven by inner conflict, contradiction and paradox. Thus, the classic early Expressionist poem, for example, is marked by a time-sense of imminent crisis, torn between a desire for stillness and an urge to lose itself in chaos, and characterized by a disjunction between a rigid verse form and images of rigidity and a violence which threatens to explode these. Correspondingly, the syntax of an early Expressionist poem involves a struggle for dominance between noun and verb, and its adjectives are used not to describe the surface of a static noun but to point metaphorically to a hidden dynamism at work below that surface. Expressionism is, however, not just a stylistic phenomenon but, in Bakhtin's sense, a meta-linguistic *Problematik* which can be resolved in a variety of ways.

The works of early Expressionism, 1910–14, are, typically, situated on the edge of the specifically modern context, the megalopolis of industrial Capitalism, and present this under two aspects: beneath a rigid asphalt crust, man-made and controlled by the authoritarian father-figure, chaotic forces, ungovernable by man, are destructively active. Furthermore, in the early Expressionist vision, the machine, ostensibly a tool for extending human dominance over Nature, turns back on itself, becoming a Frankenstein monster, a Golem which seeks to devour the beings that made it. Consequently, the inhabitants of the Expressionist city are presented as spectral, puppet-like beings, assailed by dark powers over which, despite their assumed and absurd self-confidence, they have no final control.

To this ambiguous and disturbing vision, various responses are possible: withdrawal into nostalgia for pre-modern forms (Ernst Blass's and Georg Trakl's poetry), cosmic pessimism (Georg Heym's poetry), irony (Jakob van Hoddis's and Alfred Lichtenstein's poetry), ecstatic irrationalism (Ernst Stadler's and Ernst Wilhelm Lotz's poetry; Ludwig Rubiner's manifesto *Der Dichter greift in die Politik*)—which may, as with *Ich-Dramen* like Reinhard Sorge's *Der Bettler* and Walter

Hasenclever's *Der Sohn*, involve a passionate wish to murder the father—or the Rimbaldian desire to find a saving, spiritual dimension beyond the sterile surface and demonic night-side of the modern city (Georg Heym's *Novellen*; Georg Trakl's last poems and Wassily Kandinsky's theoretical work *Über das Geistige in der Kunst*).

The outbreak of war reinforced the early Expressionist vision and gave urgency to some of the possible responses. Thus, the urban landscape seemed to the Expressionists to have prefigured the battlefields of the Great War whose mechanized slaughter was, in turn, seen as a horrendous extension of the Capitalist system of production, with men and material going in at one end and corpses coming out of the other. Correspondingly, although the War was greeted enthusiastically by some Expressionists for a few weeks or months as a means of overcoming everyday boredom and revitalizing a dead Society (Hugo Ball, Rudolf Leonhard, Hans Leybold, Ernst Wilhelm Lotz), the experience of trench warfare soon made it clear that something more than affective dynamism was necessary for social renewal. This realization accentuated in some Expressionists the temptation to withdraw from the modern world (Gottfried Benn) or surrender to cosmic pessimism (August Stramm).

At the same time, Autumn 1914 saw the emergence of Kurt Hiller's *Aktivismus*—a pacifist neo-humanism, shorn of idealist metaphysics, which attracted considerable support from among the Expressionists and which placed its hopes in the emergence of a new, spiritualized humanity and redeemed society out of the Purgatory of the War. These and similar millenarian aspirations intensified and spread as the War went on, merging by 1918 with a sterile revolutionary rhetoric of which the final scenes of Ernst Toller's *Die Wandlung* (1917–18) are an example and the whole of Toller's *Masse Mensch* (1920–21) a critique. When the German Revolution of 1918–19 failed to produce the hoped-for total revolution, a widespread disillusion set in among surviving Expressionists which frequently ended in suicide, exile, or a 'sell-out' to some totalitarian organization, and which is reflected in the drama of cultural and political despair such as Georg Kaiser's *Gas* trilogy (1916–19).

Expressionism issued into DADA, the Bauhaus and Constructivism. Where DADA continued the metaphysical investigations of early Expressionism, offering systematic folly and carnivalization both as a means of coming to terms with a many-layered and paradoxical vision of reality and as a political weapon, the Bauhaus and Constructivism, through the medium of architecture, investigated how the utopian neo-humanism of late Expressionism might be realized with the new techniques and materials provided by the twentieth century.

The latest and most comprehensive anthology on this subject is

Thomas Anz and Michael Stark (eds), *Expressionismus: Manifeste und Dokumente zur deutschen Literatur 1910–1920* (1982). Critical works include: R. F. Allen, *German Expressionist Poetry* (1979); R. S. Furness, *Expressionism* (1973); J. Ritchie, *German Expressionist Drama* (1976); K. L. Schneider, *Zerbrochene Formen* (1967); W. H. Sokel, *The Writer in Extremis* (1959); S. Vietta and H-G. Kemper, *Expressionismus* (1975); J. Willett, *Expressionism* (1970).

RWS

F

fable

A short moral tale, in verse or prose, in which human situations and behaviour are depicted through (chiefly) beasts and birds, or gods or inanimate objects. Human qualities are projected onto animals, according to certain conventions (e.g. malicious craftiness for the fox). Fables are ironic and realistic in tone, often satirical, their themes usually reflecting on the commonsense ethics of ordinary life: they dramatize the futility of relinquishing a small profit for the sake of larger (but hypothetical) future gains, of the weak attempting to take on the powerful on equal terms, the irony of falling into one's own traps, etc. Such themes are close to the advice of proverbs, and the moral point of a fable is usually announced epigrammatically by one of the characters at the end.

The beast fable is extremely ancient, evidenced from Egypt, Greece, India and presumably cognate with the development of a self-conscious folk-lore in primitive cultures. The Western tradition derives largely from the fables of Aesop, a Greek slave who lived in Asia Minor in the sixth century B.C. His work is not known directly, but has been transmitted through elaborations by such writers as Phaedrus and Babrius. Collections were extensively read in medieval schools; the tone of the genre became more frankly humorous. The most famous medieval example is Chaucer's 'Nun's Priest's Tale'. The fable achieved greater sophistication in the hands of Jean de la Fontaine (1621–95), whose verse fables revived the fashion throughout the Europe of the seventeenth and eighteenth centuries. England's representative in this mode was John Gay (1685–1732). In Germany, G. E. Lessing (1729–81) preferred the simpler model of Aesop to the refined modern version.

The fable has twentieth-century practitioners, too. George Orwell's *Animal Farm* (1945) employs the beast fable as the vehicle for an extended satire on the totalitarian state. In America, James Thurber has written *Fables for our Time* (1940).

RGF

fabula

see FORMALISM

fabulation
see FICTION

fancy
see CONCEIT, IMAGINATION, WIT

fantastic

Now commonly comprises a variety of fictional works which use the supernatural or apparently supernatural. Examples are found in German Romanticism (e.g. Tieck, Hoffman); in English GOTHIC fiction and ghost stories; in nineteenth-century French literature (e.g. Nodier, the later Maupassant); and in twentieth-century depictions of dream worlds (e.g. Carroll) or seemingly impossible worlds and events (e.g. Kafka, Borges).

Not all works in which the supernatural or eerie appears are classified as *fantastic*, however. Works of *fantasy*, such as Tolkien's fiction and C. S. Lewis's Narnia series, create their own coherently organized worlds and myths. References to familiar everyday activities render these worlds more homely and comprehensible. The everyday details are integrated into the other world, extending its range of reference; the combination of 'real' and 'supernatural' suggests a world of greater opportunity and fullness than one consisting of 'real' elements alone. If the 'real' world is also depicted separately (as in Lewis), movement between the two worlds happens at specific points in the text, so that any character is always in either one world or the other. The reader is invited to feel not bewilderment at but respect for the order of the 'supernatural' world, even awe and wonder.

It is characteristic of the *fantastic* text that the reader is made unsure how to interpret and respond to the events narrated. Critics have stated that the fantastic cannot exist without the notion of a clear dividing line (which the text transgresses) between things possible according to the laws of nature and things supernatural and impossible: for some, what defines the fantastic is a brutal intrusion of the mysterious into real life. But the reader's bewilderment is rarely confined to this shock effect. Are the ghosts in Henry James's *The Turn of the Screw* (1898) hallucinations created by the protagonist's repressed feelings, or are they external to her in some sense—and if so, what sense? Are we to read Kafka's *Metamorphosis* (1916) as a description of mental illness from the inside, a metaphor for some kind of alienation, or a literally true story (the protagonist turns into an insect, but the objective third-person narrative is remarkably matter-of-fact)? Are Poe's stories penetrating studies of human aspirations and limitations, or carefully contrived games which the narrator plays to keep the reader in suspense for as long as possible and maximize mystification and horror?

Frequently, the bewilderment is increased by the text's language. The STYLE is lucid, even crystalline, but poor in undertones, repetitive in its creation of ATMOSPHERE. The lucidity often resides in an over-general statement of the narrator's or protagonist's impressions: Poe's reference to 'the thrilling and enthralling eloquence' of Ligeia's 'low musical language' (*Ligeia*, 1838) leaves the reader unsure what kind of speech and auditory sensations to imagine, more aware of the intensity of the narrator's response than its quality. In Cortázar, a lucid, matter-of-fact style conveys bizarre and impossible meanings, the truth of which the narrator takes for granted. Lucidity and intensity, we may reflect, are compatible with some forms of insanity.

The confusion usually focuses on the narrator's or the protagonist's personality. The protagonist characteristically isolates himself from interaction and discussion. Family life, a steady career, friendship, even common everyday activities are either meaningless to him or highly problematical: Anselmus in Hoffmann's *Golden Pot* (1815), using a door knocker to gain admittance to a house, sees it turn suddenly into a snake. The protagonist's lack of conventionality and urge towards ideal perfection can take different forms. Frequently in Tieck and Hoffmann, he holds himself open to the unexpected, aware of both the spiritual opportunity and the spiritual risks of this, whereas in *The Turn of the Screw* and Maupassant's *Le Horla* (1887) attempts are made to create a stable world by leaving out worrying aspects of the self and its environment—repressing them, Freudians would say. The attempt to make life manageable yet satisfying thus becomes an attempt to transcend human limits: Stevenson's Dr Jekyll (*Dr. Jekyll and Mr. Hyde*, 1886) tries to resolve his tensions by neatly splitting his personality. But in thus pushing his own nature beyond its normal bounds, the protagonist sets up unconscious compensatory mechanisms and becomes decreasingly able to think straight. Rarely, however, are more restrained, socially conventional life styles presented favourably; the attempt to exceed one's limits invites in the reader a fascination which makes any condemnation ambiguous.

Recent criticism has stressed links between fantastic texts and the societies in which they appear. In industrial society, 'the individual comes to see himself at the mercy of forces which in fundamental ways elude his understanding' (David Punter, *The Literature of Terror* (1980), p. 128); the fantastic 'characteristically attempts to compensate for a lack resulting from cultural constraints' (Rosemary Jackson, *Fantasy: The Literature of Subversion* (1981), p. 3). The critic thus sees his task as a translation of the supernatural terrors of the text into the social ones which underlie it. The fantastic gives indirect expression to doubts about itself which society refuses to entertain if they are directly stated; the protagonist's confusion arises from the urge to express aspects of himself which society condemns and accordingly for which no adequate language is available.

See Irène Bessière, *Le Récit fantastique* (1974); David Punter, *The Literature of Terror* (1980); Eric S. Rabkin, *The Fantastic in Literature* (1976); Tzvetan Todorov, *The Fantastic* (English translation 1973).

MHP

farce

Interpolations in church liturgy; later, that 'forced' between the events of liturgical drama, usually comic. Farce is comedy involving physical humour, stock characters and unrealistic plotting. It combines elements from pantomime, music-hall and social comedy into a theatre of smut, snobbery and slapstick. English farce is broader and more physical, with dropped trousers and chamber-pots predominant. It stays close to circus and music-hall humour. French farce crudifies manner comedy (see MANNERS), balancing sexual innuendo and social humour, e.g. the plays of Georges Feydeau. More literate and polished, it reflects the elegant vulgarity of the *boulevardier*. English music-hall had its counterpart in American vaudeville, but this produced no distinctive American farce tradition. The American contribution is rather to be found in the visual and physical humour of silent films (Chaplin, Keaton) which in their turn provided models for the techniques of ABSURD drama.

Farce seeks to demonstrate the contiguity of the logical and the mad. It explores a closed world where belief is suspended because nothing has a real cause. Action is self-generated, once the ground-rules are accepted. These rules embody a mechanical, deterministic view of life which undermines pretensions to human dignity (free will): all women are predatory, all husbands are fools, all banisters rotten, all doors revelatory. This encapsulated universe encourages a comedy of cruelty since the audience is insulated from feeling by the absence of motive, and by the response being simultaneously more and less aggressive than real-life response, e.g. the custard pie routine.

Recent playwrights, such as the late Joe Orton (*Loot, What the Butler Saw*) have revived the farce conventions and used them to force us to rethink our concept of the normal and the abnormal. Called 'high-camp' comedy, it realizes its ideas through discarded fictions, involving its audience in the conscious manipulation of its own response. See also COMEDY.

See M. E. Coindreau, *La Farce est jouée* (1942); Leo Hughes, *A Century of English Farce* (1956).

GG

feeling

Accounts of how a work of literature is created, or of how it affects the reader, must touch on two areas of non-literary investigation. Epistemology, the theory of how we come to know, is an ancient philosophical puzzle. Since the late eighteenth century, psychology has also approached such problems. It is an axiom in epistemology that two processes are involved in knowing: traditionally, *reason* and *feeling*; philosophy has usually concentrated on the former, the latter being left to psychology. The two terms suffer from the woolliness of all traditional labels. *Feeling*, especially, has a wide and confusing range of meanings. It is partly synonymous with 'emotions'. Psychology has a similar axiomatic frame for discussion: the presentation of a mental event in terms of *thought* (cognition), *feeling* (the conscious character of the event) and *will* (conation, which may be conscious or unconscious). *Feeling* is a way of considering the general sensibility of the body.

Aesthetic theory has made use of such philosophical and psychological thought. In reaction to the Western belief that *reason* is dominant, it has been argued that feeling is itself formulation, that is, it prefigures thought or reasoning. Eliseo Vivas argues that literature is 'prior in the order of logic to all knowledge: constitutive of culture' (*Creation and Discovery*, 1955). The *gestalt*-psychologists are of this view, and some philosophers have followed their lead, arguing that feeling itself somehow participates in knowledge and understanding. Art is the area of creative activity in which organic sensation plays the strongest controlling part. I. A. Richards expounds a variant of this idea in his *Principles of Literary Criticism* (1924). He wants to restrict feeling to refer to pleasure/un-pleasure, to mean 'not another and vital way of apprehending' but a set of signs of personal attitudes. As well as people who neatly reason things out, there are, he suggests, some who can read these signs (feeling) particularly well, better than most of us. Such people are, when they create something which allows us to read some of the signs better, our great artists. Thus for Richards, it is not the *intensity* of the feeling that matters, but the *organization* of its impulses, the quality of the reading of the signs.

Another way in which *feeling* is used in aesthetic theory is illustrated in the work of the philosopher Susanne Langer: see *Philosophy in a New Key* (1942) and *Feeling and Form* (1953). She argues that feeling is expressed by ritual and attitude, which in turn are embodied by the artist in presentational symbolism. Music is the art which fits best with such ideas. Wagner argued that music is the representation and formulation of feeling itself. But literature has moral, social and rational dimensions that interfere with clear exemplification of any feeling-based aesthetic. See also EFFECT, PLEASURE, READER.

AMR

feminist criticism

is part of the discourse of the new feminism which emerged in Europe and America in the late 1960s to revive political and social issues associated with turn-of-the-century suffrage debates, and to question again the extent of women's actual participation in Western cultures. Both feminists and feminist literary critics are of course indebted to pre-twentieth-century writers, and to writers of the inter-war years, like Virginia Woolf—'if one is a woman, one is often surprised by a sudden splitting off of consciousness, say in walking down Whitehall, when from being the natural inheritor of that civilization, she becomes on the contrary outside of it, alien and critical' (*A Room of One's Own*, 1929). However, one of the fundamental observations, and difficulties, of feminist criticism is that the *continuous* traditions (including the anti-traditions) of literary studies have largely obscured women's work and women's perspectives. 'One serious cultural obstacle encountered by any feminist writer is that each feminist work has tended to be received as if it emerged from nowhere . . . women's work and thinking has been made to seem sporadic, erratic, orphaned of any tradition of its own' (Adrienne Rich, *On Lies, Secrets and Silence*, 1979).

Thus a major effort of feminist criticism has been to recover and re-read the work of women writers, as a problematic appendix to the existing corpus of literature, neither exactly 'a tradition of its own', nor yet part of a shared culture. Much of this re-writing of literary history is pragmatic, scholarly and anti-theoretical in its bias, devoted to rendering women's texts legible without foregrounding methodological issues. The 'feminism' involved sometimes recalls the late-romantic, vaguely androgynous individualism (intellectual and imaginative life as potentially neutral territory) which characterized Simone de Beauvoir's enormously influential retrospective survey of oppression in *The Second Sex* (1949). However, this is uneasily combined with the suspicion that, while society remains 'patriarchal' in its division of other kinds of labour, then neither access to, nor interpretation of, literature can be gender-free.

The most identifiable divergences in feminist criticism begin here: between a mainly Anglo-American emphasis on the recovery, reprinting and revaluation of works more-or-less admitted to belong to a minority culture (a defensive or recuperative strategy); and a more aggressive, mainly French stress on literary language (indeed, language itself) as a primary locus of the repression of 'otherness', of the radically disjunctive, of the female. The thinking of French feminist critics of the last decade is openly, if ironically, indebted to STRUCTURALISM and POST-STRUCTURALISM, and particularly to the revision of Freudian assumptions about creativity in the work of Lacan and Derrida. Whereas the work of reconstruction seeks to describe plural (if warring) cultures, the advocates of DECONSTRUCTION (in Derrida's term) argue that patriarchal culture continually subsumes 'otherness' by means of linguistic strategies still to be exposed and analysed. In its most extreme form the post-structuralist reading of patriarchy delineates a closed culture: the individual's entry into her/his own subjectivity is determined by the symbolic orders of language and family, in which

the phallus is the privileged signifier (Lacan); intellectual life and the world of letters constitute a hidden homosexual succession, a *logocentric* economy which has suppressed its own duplicitous origins (patricide) in imposing order and wholeness of meaning on its discourse (Derrida). Deconstruction opening up the relationship between what authors command and do not command of the language they use seeks to demystify the (phallic) Word, and authorise absence, disjunction, *différance*. Moves like these, concerned with subverting the authority of 'classical' traditions of thought and letters, have an obvious attraction for feminist thinkers, not least because they suggest an area of discourse in which 'Woman and artist, the feminine and the *avant-garde*, are elided. . . . Writing, the production of meaning, becomes the site of both challenge and Otherness; rather than (as in more traditional approaches) simply yielding the themes and representation of female oppression.' (Mary Jacobus, *Women Writing and Writing about Women*, (1979).

Feminist criticism which adopts such a position scrutinises its texts for fissures and cracks and signs of heterogeneity, re-examining 'the masculine imaginary, to interpret how it has reduced us to silence, to mutism . . . to find a possible space for the feminine imaginary' (Luce Irigaray). The 'feminine' is all that is repressed in a patriarchal linguistic structure: for example, the Oedipal phase of rhythmic, onomatopeic sound (unmediated, ecstatic) which precedes the symbolic order (Julia Kristeva).

Some current feminist critics seek for themselves a fluid and problematic language that will harmonise with the Babel/babble of the *avant-garde* (Hélène Cixous, Monique Wittig). Others' procedures are more traditional in style and method. All, however, subscribe to the thesis of women's continuing exclusion from full participation in the culture, while they differ widely on questions of the nature and extent of that exclusion, and on the centrality of 'language' (in the structuralist sense). To date, as well as extending the canon, and re-writing aspects of literary history, feminist criticism has brought new pressure to bear on the analysis of texts at many levels, from the structure of the sentence to the concept of 'character' and the composition of 'I', and has foregrounded certain literary 'kinds' (from diaries and journals to

GOTHIC, FANTASTIC and speculative fiction) as specially charged inter-
faces between masculine culture and female culture.

See Simone de Beauvoir, *The Second Sex* (1949); Mary Ellmann,
Thinking About Women (1968); Monique Wittig, *Les guérillères*
(1969); Kate Millett, *Sexual Politics* (1970); Julia Kristeva, *La révolu-
tion du langage poétique* (1974); Hélène Cixous, 'The Character of
"Character" ', *NLH* 5 (1978); Ellen Moers, *Literary Women* (1977);
Elaine Showalter, *A Literature of Their Own: British Women Novelists
from Brontë to Lessing* (1977); Angela Carter, *The Sadeian Woman*
(1979); Mary Jacobus (ed), *Women Writing and Writing About Women*
(1979); Marks and Courtivron (eds), *New French Feminisms* (1980).

LS and LSM

fiction

is a complex term with many overlapping uses. Although often used
synonymously with *novel*, it is a more generic and inclusive term.
NOVEL has a narrower historical and ideological content than *fiction*—
novels did not exist in Greek or Roman culture, but works of fiction in
prose did. Equally, allegories in prose (like *Pilgrim's Progress*) are
works of fiction, but not novels. 'Novel' is thus a genre term, while
'fiction' is a generic term. 'Fiction' can more easily designate hybrid
forms than 'novel'; it can include artistic intentions and formal characteristics in prose works (structures and devices borrowed from romance
or poetry, pastiche or dramatic forms, etc.) which indicate either
simple unawareness of novels (e.g. the *Satyricon*) or a deliberate
questioning of the assumptions of the novel-genre (e.g. *Tom Jones*).
Thus, by virtue of this high level of generality, 'fiction' can be opposed
to 'novel' by both writers and critics alike.

The two terms also diverge because 'novel' must refer to the *product*
of imaginative activity, whereas 'fiction' can be used to describe the
activity itself (it derives from the Latin *fingo*, to fashion or form).
Fiction thus has a transitive sense that implies a mental process; we
speak of works *of* fiction—an ambiguous phrase which suggests either
the category to which they belong or the activity by which they were
produced.

There has always existed a moral and intellectual distrust of fiction as
a mode of writing which leads people to believe in things which are not
'true' or which do not exist in nature. However hostile to each other's
definition of 'nature' (compare Plato's *Republic* with Bentham's *Theory
of Fictions*), the perennial opponents of fiction equate it with lies and
deception. The maker of literary fictions may be self-deceived, or he
may intend to deceive others. For a classic (and ironic) account of this
attitude, see George Herbert's platonic poem 'Jordan I' (beginning,
'Who says that fictions only and false hair/Become a verse?') and for an

explicit defence of fiction against the pressure of utilitarian 'fact', see Dickens's *Hard Times*. Traditional puritanism or moral scepticism is reflected in the pejorative epithet *fictitious* which derives from the sense of fiction as an unnecessary or undesirable deviation from truth; the adjective *fictional* does not normally have the same emotive content. Imaginative literature is of course the primary manifestation of this pernicious tendency, and attacks on fiction are usually attacks on literature, but clearly there is also a wider sense implied of fiction as an element in human thought and action.

A more positive use of *fiction* has recently been revived in literary criticism (see Hans Vaihinger, *The Philosophy of As If*, 1952 and Frank Kermode, *The Sense of an Ending*, 1967) which would appear to make both literature and what the critic wants to say about it more broadly relevant to other ways of writing and thinking and other educational disciplines. The assumption behind this use of the term is that all mental activity is to be construed on the analogy of imaginative creation. A fiction in this sense refers to any 'mental structure' as opposed to the formless flux existing outside our minds, the Pure Contingency which we call nature. Time, for example, is a fiction we impose on nature for the purposes of living. All mental activity, it is claimed, is fictional because it involves shaping material which is inherently shapeless. We can only make sense of things by imposing fictions (shapes or interpretations) on them. 'Fiction' thus becomes a kind of umbrella, sheltering many different kinds of mental activity and cultural institution. The term appears to have become the focus of a valuable relativism, an anti-positivistic, anti-empiricist *caveat*. The justification for such an extension is not so clear; the argument seems flawed and ultimately uninformative. If we can only make sense of things through fictions, how do we know of the existence of that which is non-fictional? By the same argument, the vitally necessary assumption of Pure Contingency is also a fiction. Equally, it is absurd to reduce whatever is true to whatever we cannot make sense of. In addition this extension of the term initiates a set of general conditions for the operation of fictions which makes it either impossible or unnecessary to distinguish between one fiction (say, poetry) and another (say, history).

Another aspect of the fashionable extension of this term needs justification. Fictions in general are like legal fictions—suppositions known to be false, but accepted as true for the purposes of practical or theoretical convenience. Where this usage extends to a description of mental processes, it overlaps with the preceding sense, but the stricter model gives a more explicit account of the role of belief implied in that sense. It is claimed that fictions are mental structures which we know to be false, but which we accept as true for the purposes of mental coherence and order. Thinking becomes a matter of simultaneous belief and disbelief in the truth of our ideas; we know that our interpretations of things are ultimately false, but we must go on relying at least in part on these fictions because we have no other way of making sense of things. The term seems relativistic because it sensitizes us to the limitations of our own and other people's viewpoints, but it also tends to imply such mental diffidence that it is hard to know how we could take the truth of any idea seriously enough to be sceptical about it. There is a danger that the unthinking use of the term could lead to a lack of intellectual commitment in criticism, because no fiction will need justification when it implies its own falsehood. On the other hand, the term is not really relativistic at all, if it implies that all our critical interpretations are ultimately invalid in the same way. It then becomes the banner of a naïve and reactionary fundamentalism, which measures the validity of all ideas by a single standard of truth (Pure Contingency or Chaos). Perhaps the most telling objection to the extension of this term is that it adds to our vocabulary without adding to our understanding: except where it can be shown to be false, according to conventional criteria, it makes no difference to an interpretation that we call it a 'fiction'.

Literary fictions may have various degrees of plausibility. The archaic adjective *fictive*, revived by the American poet Wallace Stevens, is used extensively in modern criticism to denote the making of fictions which do not suspend the reader's disbelief, but stimulate it, in order to establish particular kinds of rhetorical effect. Many novelists in the post-war period, such as Barth, Borges, Beckett, Genet and Nabokov, often depend for their effects on a consistent sense of implausibility, and such writers have forced the critics to distinguish shades of meaning in their terminology to account for varieties of literary self-consciousness. Hence the use of the cognate terms *fictiveness* and *fictionality*, which differ from *fiction* or *fiction-making* by their implication of authorial self-consciousness. Recently, critics have begun distinguishing between MODERNIST self-consciousness and the peculiar degree of self-consciousness in the post-war period which flaunts its own conditions of artiface. Hence the rise of such terms as *metafiction, surfiction* and *fabulation*, which purport to describe the mood of postmodernism. See R. Federman, *Surfiction* (1975); R. Scholes, *Fabulation and Metafiction* (1979); P. Waugh, *Metafiction* (1984). See also LITERATURE.

VRLS

figure

George Puttenham (*The Art of English Poesie*, 1589) defines 'figurative speech' as follows:

a novelty of language evidently (and yet not absurdly) estranged
from the ordinary habit and manner of our daily talk and writing,
and figure itself is a certain lively or good grace set upon words,
speeches, and sentences to some purpose and not in vain, giving
them ornament or efficacy by many manner of alterations in shape,
in sound, and also in sense, sometime by way of surplusage,
sometime by defect, sometime by disorder, or mutation, and also
by putting into our speeches more pith and substance, subtlety,
quickness, efficacy, or moderation, in this or that sort tuning and
tempering them, by amplification, abridgement, opening, closing,
enforcing, meekening, or otherwise disposing them to the best
purpose.

He then devotes a dozen chapters of his treatise to listing, classifying,
defining and exemplifying figures. In this enterprise he follows the
venerable tradition of RHETORIC, in which literary composition is
thought of as 'invention' (choosing a subject-matter) and 'amplification'
or as Puttenham calls it, 'exornation', of the subject by a decorous
choice from the figures. The hundreds of figures, schemes and tropes
available for this purpose were listed in many handbooks designed to
help budding and practising authors to regulate their style according to
received principles; this tradition of prescriptive rhetoric continued in
the school-books long after Puttenham's day. One must say that an
unrealistic and mechanical theory of composition is implied; and
authors within this tradition (e.g. Chaucer) achieved excellence largely
in spite of it, or by a self-consciously ironic use of figures. From a
critical point of view, very little is to be gained by memorizing lists of
names for figures, and much is to be lost in so far as the attitude
encourages students to view literature as theme plus ornament. True,
some terms have remained current and valuable in analysis (e.g.
chiasmus, hyperbole, metonymy, synecdoche, etc.). As mentioned in
the Preface, such terms may be looked up in the appropriate handbooks. See also RHETORIC, SCHEME.

RGF

foot
see METRE

foregrounding
(a free translation of the Czech term, *aktualisace*) is a concept evolved
by the pre-war Prague school of linguistics and poetics, under the
influence of Russian formalist doctrines, to represent the abnormal use
of a medium, its obtrusion against a background of 'automatic' responses, which is characteristic of much, if not all, artistic expression.

In literature, foregrounding may be most readily identified with linguistic *deviation*: the violation of rules and conventions, by which a poet transcends the normal communicative resources of the language, and awakens the reader, by freeing him from the grooves of cliché expression, to a new perceptivity. Poetic metaphor, a type of semantic deviation, is the most important instance of this type of foregrounding.

More generally, foregrounding may include all salient linguistic phenomena which in some way cause the reader's attention to shift from the paraphrasable content of a message ('what is said') to a focus on the message itself ('how it is said'). One may thus subsume under foregrounding the deliberate use of ambiguities (e.g. punning) and, more importantly, parallelism, in its widest sense of patterning over and above the normal degree of patterning which exists in language by virtue of linguistic rules.

Foregrounding is a useful, even crucial, concept in stylistics, providing a bridge between the relative objectivity of linguistic description and the relative subjectivity of literary judgment. It is a criterion by which we may select, from a mass of linguistic detail, those features relevant to literary effect. It is not, however, an entirely precise criterion: the contrast between foreground and background is a relative one, and only subjective response can ultimately decide what is and what is not foregrounded. Further unclearnesses are: Is the writer's intention a relevant indication of foregrounding? What is the psychological basis of foregrounding? (Foregrounded features can 'work' without coming to one's conscious attention.) Can foregrounding be equated with artistic significance?

One can answer the last question negatively, by pointing out two difficulties in the way of any attempt to make foregrounding the basis of a comprehensive theory of literary style. (1) Deviations and parallelisms often seem to have a background rather than a foreground function, and resist critical justification except in terms of vague principles such as euphony and VARIATION. (2) With prose, a probabilistic approach to style in terms of a 'set' towards certain linguistic choices rather than others is often more appropriate than an approach via foregrounding, since significance lies not so much in individual exceptional features of language as in the density of some features relative to others. Foregrounding in prose works applies rather at the levels of theme, character, plot, argument, etc. than at the level of linguistic choice. See also FORMALISM.

See V. Erlich, *Russian Formalism* (1965); Jan Mukařovský, 'Standard language and poetic language', in P. L. Garvin (ed.), *A Prague School Reader on Esthetics, Literary Structure and Style* (1964); G. N. Leech, 'Linguistics and the figures of rhetoric' in R. Fowler (ed.), *Essays on Style and Language* (1966).   GNL

form

is often used to refer to literary kinds or genres (e.g. 'the epic form'). But we prefer to take form as what contrasts with 'paraphrasable content', as the *way* something is said in contrast to *what* is said. The word 'paraphrasable' is important since the way of saying affects what is being said—imperceptibly in prose works of information, vitally at the other end of the spectrum in lyric poems. But since authors do in fact often revise their works to improve the STYLE rather than the matter, since synopses are written and found useful, since writers can turn prose versions of their work into verse (like Ben Jonson), and since it is evident that much the same point may be made in plain or figurative language, simple or complex sentences, it is clear that even though form and content may be inseparable for the 'full meaning' of a work, the paraphrasable content may nevertheless be used to enable the concept of *form* to be discussed (cf. PARAPHRASE).

Form in this sense is often felt to be either *organic* or *imposed*. Felt, because this is rather a psychological distinction than a technical one. In the one case, manner seems to fit matter like a velvet glove, form seems to spring from content; in the other case, the form seems an iron gauntlet that the content must accommodate itself to. In some short lyric poems where form and content are inseparable anyway, it may be difficult to decide whether, say, apparent oddities of metre and rhyme are flaws in an imposed form or examples of organic fluidity. In most of these cases, however, the difficulty of decision will itself suggest that the decision is irrelevant to a critical judgment. For the modern dogma that organic form is better hardly stands up to examination. All 'given patterns'—such as sonnet, rondeau, ballade—are imposed forms; and while it is true that the content must fit them effortlessly or be faulted, it is also true that the form took precedence. In some cases, too—particularly in large novels dealing with amorphous material—imposed form may seem a beneficial discipline even though the imposition is evident. Moreover, it is easier to encompass aesthetic effects of composition and complementarity (see AESTHETICS) by imposed form than by organic form. Organic form tends to emphasize what is said, imposed form how it is said. So where neither emphasis is evident other approaches to the work will clearly be more profitable.

Whether organic or imposed, form must be either *structural* or *textural*, the one being large-scale, a matter of arrangement, the other small-scale, a matter of impressionism. *Structure* at its most obvious (plot, story, argument) is the skeleton of a work, *texture* at its most obvious (metre, diction, syntax) is the skin. But certain elements are comparable to muscles. A *motif* for instance is structural in so far as the images making it up are seen as a chain, textural in so far as each is apprehended sensuously as it comes—and contentual, rather than formal, in so far as the chain carries a meaning that one link, an unrepeated image, would not. In the last analysis, structure is a matter of memory, texture of immediacy.

Since structure is a matter of arrangement, it includes the formal ordering of the content in time. *Temporal form* may be *linear* or *fugal*. Linear form is that of traditional literature, in which first things come first, last last, as in life. Fugal form is characteristic of modernist experimental writing, which takes liberties with chronology on the grounds that literature is not life, and need not resemble it. Linear works, of course, may give more or less reading-time to similar periods of narrative time, but fugal works, in addition, re-arrange temporal sequence so that first and last things come not in order but where they will make most impact (usually by standing in juxtaposition). Counterpoint takes over from melody, so to speak. Such structuring, used well, gains thematic and aesthetic benefits in return for the sacrifice of story-line and suspense. Such emphasis of temporal form tends to give greater importance to textural quality (since the reader is less distracted by an eagerness to see what happens next).

Works of this kind present themselves more concretely as objects in space than as abstract patterns of cause and effect, and it follows that the reader's attention will be directed towards their textural rather than their structural qualities. The elaboration of texture invariably has the effect of arresting movement—whether of thought or action—and substituting the opaque for the transparent in language. At its furthest extremes such developments lead to CONCRETE POETRY or Euphuistic Prose involving a progressive elimination of meaning, until a point is reached where the textural devices—dependent as they are on the meanings of words—become ineffective. In most works, however, where the marriage of sound and sense is not perfect, compromises are achieved between denotation and connotation, referent and reference. Texture, unlike structure, is an inherent (psychological) property of every part of language, and therefore less under the control of the artist. It follows that part of his task consists of eliminating or subduing indeterminate textural elements in the language he uses. More positively he strives to materialize his meanings, and if language were a more subtle medium, this imitative function could be classified according to the (various) sensory apparatus to which it appealed. As it is, it makes more sense to categorize textural qualities according to the known properties of language. They may be *musical* (onomatopoeia, alliteration, etc.); *lexical* (metaphor, synecdoche, etc.); *syntactic* (chiasmus, antithesis, etc.). See also ORGANIC, STRUCTURE, TEXTURE.

See Wayne C. Booth, *The Rhetoric of Fiction* (1961); Wallace C. Hiddick, *Thirteen Types of Narrative* (1968); Robie Macauley and George Laming, *Technique in Fiction* (1964); J. C. Ransom, *The*

World's Body (1938). For further reading, J. L.Calderwood and M. R. Toliver, *Forms of Poetry* (1968); Allan Rodway, *The Truths of Fiction* (1970); Elizabeth Boa and J. H. Reid, *Critical Strategies* (1972).

AER

Formalism

'Formalist' has long been a pejorative term in Soviet criticism, and it has been much abused. Properly it denotes a school of literary criticism that grew up in Russia in the experimental 1920s and erected on the foundations laid by the SYMBOLIST movement a critical method that posited the autonomy of the work of art and the discontinuity of the language of literature from other kinds of language. The Formalists outdid in purism the English and American NEW CRITICS, with whom they had much in common.

There were two groups of Formalist critics in the early days: the one in St Petersburg called itself *Opoyaz*, taking its name from the initial letters of the Russian words meaning *Society for the Study of Literary Language,* and was founded in 1916. The other, more linguistically oriented (though both derived their basic techniques from Saussure) was founded in 1915, and called itself the Moscow Linguistic Circle. The Formalists, impatient with the obscurantism that disfigured Symbolist poetics, set about the objective and 'scientific' examination of literary STYLE, defining it in terms of its departure from established norms by means of identifiable and analysable devices. One talented Formalist critic, Victor Shklovsky, in the early essay *Art as Device* (1917), emphasized that the deformation of reality, 'making strange' or 'defamiliarization' (*ostranenie*), was central to all art. He claims that the habitual nature of everyday experience makes perception stale and automatic, but

> art exists that one may recover the sensation of life; it exists to make one feel things, to make the stone *stony*. The purpose of art is to impart the sensation of things as they are perceived and not as they are known. The technique of art is to make objects 'unfamiliar', to make forms difficult, to increase the difficulty and length of perception because the process of perception is an aesthetic end in itself and must be prolonged. *Art is a way of experiencing the artfulness of an object; the object is not important.*

Plot in the novel was defined as consisting of the devices which defamiliarize the story, or 'make it strange' (hence the high regard of the Formalists for Sterne's *Tristram Shandy*). The terms *fabula* and *syuzhet* were introduced for, respectively, the raw story-material and the finished plot as presented through the formal devices of construction. An important set of devices drawing attention to the act of narration, the voice of the storyteller and therefore the artificiality of the fiction, are collectively known as *skaz*. In verse theory, one of the best early essays was Osip Brik's *Rhythm and Syntax* (1927), which attempted to describe all the significant linguistic elements in poetry, correcting earlier theorists who had established the primacy of metaphor and image. His concept of *zvukovoy povtor*, sound repetition, was notably fruitful. As the Formalists developed, they grew less iconoclastic, and often managed to assimilate their linguistic techniques to the study of literary history and biography (Eikhenbaum's work on Tolstoy is a notable example): but they took care always to go through the necessary adjustments and manoeuvres in passing from the literary text to its milieu and back. Through the influence in the West of Roman Jakobson, once a member of the Moscow group, Formalist aesthetics exerted a powerful influence on later STRUCTURALIST developments in linguistics and literary criticism. The history of the movement has been admirably described in Victor Erlich's book *Russian Formalism* (1965). See also Tony Bennett, *Formalism and Marxism* (1979), Fredric Jameson, *The Prison-House of Language* (1972), Ann Jefferson, 'Russian formalism' in Jefferson and David Robey (eds), *Modern Literary Theory'* (1982), L. M. O'Toole and Ann Shukman, 'A contextual glossary of formalist terminology', *Russian Poetics in Translation*, 4 (1977). English anthologies of the most important texts are Stephen Bann and John E. Bowlt (eds), *Russian Formalism* (1973), Lee T. Lemon and Marion J. Reis (eds), *Russian Formalist Criticism* (1965) and Ladislav Matejka and Krystyna Pomorska (eds), *Readings in Russian Poetics* (1971). See also LITERATURE, POETICS, STRUCTURALISM

GMH

free verse

For many, this is a misnomer not only because most free verse assimilates itself to at least one of the prosodies—syllable-stress (Eliot, 'Prufrock'), quantitative (Pound), pure-stress (Eliot, *Four Quartets*,) syllabic (Marianne Moore)—but also because as a term it is dated, too 'modernistic'. But some word is needed to describe speech still deliberate enough to be rhythmic, but not patterned enough to be a metre, to describe a poetry in which utterance is only an intermittent emergence from speech, and whose complexity derives more from multiplicity of tone than from multiplicity of meaning.

The origins of free verse are variously inferred: poetic prose, liberated blank verse (Browning), a specifically free verse tradition (Dryden, Milton, Arnold, Henley). There may be other factors. Versification re-articulates conventional syntax, releases unsuspected expressive dimensions; because we are so accustomed to the writtenness of poetry, typography alone can be relied upon to perform this function (hence a visual prosody). Alternatively, by using dislocated syntax (see OBSCURITY), the poet re-articulates language at the outset and versification is rendered in this sense otiose. And the new apparatus that has facilitated analysis of the recited poem, admits the vagaries of personal and regional reading as valid prosodic factors; once these are admitted free verse exists without anyone having to invent it.

The casting off of metres in favour of unopposed rhythms—particularly in the syntax- and cadence-centred prosodies of Whitman and the Imagists—is an attempt to fully develop the expressive function of the latter at the expense of the interpretative (*pace* Pound), discriminatory function of the former. It is also designed to more fully implicate the reader in the poem as a psychological or emotional event by withdrawing the substitute sensibility of an accepted prosody and by compelling him to create his own speeds, intonation patterns and emphases. In such verse a prosody is not to be disengaged from the linguistic material; in such verse the line is superseded by the strophe, the line itself (syntactic unit) becoming the measure, and variation in line-length the rhythmic play. What Amy Lowell means by cadence is a retrospectively perceived rhythmic totality, an overall balance, rather than the continuously disturbed and restored balance of regular verse.

Ironically the need to do away with rhyme as a worn-out convention coincided with the need to retain it as an inherent part of the psychology of creation, the new *'Muse Association-des-Idées'* (Valéry). Rhyme becomes the crucial ad-libbing mechanism, suited to capturing the miscellaneousness of modern experience. The irregular rhyme of free verse is a structuring rather than structural device and is a better guide to the tempo of memory, emotion, etc. than variation in line-length, which has no fixed relation to reading speed. Besides, with rhyme removed, a poem may be deprived of much of its magnetic compulsiveness; because nothing is anticipated, nothing is looked for. Without this inbuilt momentum, the free verse poet has often to fall back on the syntactic momentum of enjambment or the momentum of rhetoric (Whitman, D. H. Lawrence) and the concomitant dangers of overintensification and monotony of tone and intonation; the poet's energies may be too much concentrated on the mere sustaining of impetus, rather than on using language to explore mental states etc. In this sense at least, rhyme is liberating.

See T. S. Eliot, 'Reflections on vers libre' (1917) in *To Criticize the Critic* (1965); H. Gross, *Sound and Form in Modern Poetry* (1964); G. Hough, 'Free Verse' in *Image and Experience* (1960); G. Kahn, *'Preface sur le vers libre', Premiers Poèmes* (1897); C. O. Hartman, *Free Verse* (1980); D. Wesling, 'The prosodies of free verse', in R. A. Brower (ed.), *Twentieth Century Literature in Retrospect* (1971).

CS

G

generative poetics
see POETICS

genre

There is no agreed equivalent for this word in the vocabulary of English criticism—'kind', 'type', 'form' and 'genre' are variously used—and this fact alone indicates some of the confusions that surround the development of the theory of genres. The attempt to classify or describe literary works in terms of shared characteristics was begun by Aristotle in the *Poetics*, and the first sentence of his treatise suggests the two main directions genre theory was to follow:

> Our subject being poetry, I propose to speak not only of the art in general, but also of its species and their respective capacities; of the structure of plot required for a good poem; of the number and nature of the constituent parts of a poem; and likewise of any other matters on the same line of enquiry.

Classical genre theory is regulative and prescriptive, and is based upon certain fixed assumptions about psychological and social differentiation. Modern genre theory on the other hand tends to be purely descriptive, and to avoid any overt assumptions about generic hierarchies. In the present century, beginning with such Russian Formalists as Roman Jakobson there has been a continuing effort to link literary kinds to linguistic structures, but perhaps the most significant modern contribution to genre theory is that of Northrop Frye whose *Anatomy of Criticism* (1957) presents a comprehensive typology of myth and archetype. At the same time it is true, as W. K. Wimsatt and Cleanth Brooks point out in *Literary Criticism: A Short History* (1957), that history has produced at least four genre conceptions—dramatic, heroic, satiric, lyric—dominant enough in their own times to serve as compositional norms, and it follows that all attempts at objectivity have been severely affected by prevailing ideals: the dominance of a genre prejudices attempts to characterize it dispassionately (cf. current problems in the definition of the NOVEL).

The second major distinction is that between genres defined in terms of 'outer form' and 'inner form'. These terms are coined by René Wellek and Austin Warren in their *Theory of Literature* (3rd ed., 1963) to describe on the one hand specific metres and structures, and on the other, attitude, tone and purpose. These authors believe that genres ought to be based upon both inner and outer forms together: 'The ostensible basis may be one or the other (e.g. "pastoral" and "satire" for the inner form; dipodic verse and Pindaric ode for outer); but the critical problem will then be to find the *other* dimension, to complete the diagram.' It is only by adopting some such definition of genre that the confusions of neo-classical criticism can be avoided. In the seventeenth and eighteenth centuries no attempt was made to discriminate between the quite diverse criteria involved in differentiation by subject-matter, structure, language, tone, or audience. So not only was it impossible to make useful comparisons between particular works, it was not even possible to say what did or did not constitute a genre. The advantage of Wellek and Warren's definition is that it allows an important distinction between, for example, Novels of the Oxford Movement, which do not constitute a genre, and Gothic Novels, which do. See also CHICAGO CRITICS, FORMALISM, POETICS.

See Allan Rodway, 'Generic criticism: the approach through type, mode and kind', in Malcolm Bradbury and D. J. Palmer (eds), *Contemporary Criticism* (1970).

BCL

gothic

The gothic romance emerged in England when the novel form itself was only a few decades old. Thus when Horace Walpole published *The Castle of Otranto* in 1764, it was in part a reaction against limitations which the early novelists seemed to have accepted with equanimity. The novel of manners and the novel of didactic sensibility are exposed to the whole sub-world of the unconscious. Sensibility is shown under pressure. Sexuality, elemental passions and fear now moved to the centre of the novelist's stage.

The word 'gothic' initially conjured up visions of a medieval world, of dark passions enacted against the massive and sinister architecture of the gothic castle. By the end of the century it implied the whole paraphernalia of evil forces and ghostly apparitions. The gothic is characterized by a setting which consists of castles, monasteries, ruined houses or suitably picturesque surroundings, by characters who are, or seem to be, the quintessence of good or evil (though innocence often seems to possess a particular menace of its own); sanity and chastity are constantly threatened and over all there looms the suggestion, sometimes finally subverted, that irrational and evil forces threaten both individual integrity and the material order of society.

On one level the gothic novel was an attempt to stimulate jaded sensibilities and as such its descendants are the modern horror film and science fiction fantasy. Yet, as the Marquis de Sade detected at the time and as the surrealists were to assert later, the gothic mode was potentially both socially and artistically revolutionary. The iconography of decay and dissolution which filled such novels clearly has its social dimension (William Godwin in particular drawing political morals from his entropic setting) while the assertion of a non-material reality clearly stands as an implicit criticism of the literalism of the conventional novel as it does of the rational confidence of the age itself. The debate between rationalism and the imagination which came to characterize the age is contained within the gothic mode. Horace Walpole was content to leave his terrors irrational and unexplained; Ann Radcliffe, or, in America, Charles Brockden Brown, felt the need to rationalize the ineffable.

The 'classic' gothic novels spanned the years between 1764 and, approximately, 1820, which saw the publication of Maturin's *Melmoth the Wanderer*. Among the best known examples are: *The Mysteries of Udolpho* by Ann Radcliffe, 1794; *The Adventures of Caleb Williams* by William Godwin, 1794; *The Monk*, by M. G. Lewis, 1795; *Frankenstein* by Mary Shelley, 1818. The strain has continued in the nineteenth and twentieth centuries both in England (down to Iris Murdoch, *The Unicorn*, 1963 and David Storey, *Radcliffe*, 1963) and in America, where it has played an important role not merely in the work of such nineteenth-century gothicists as Charles Brockden Brown, Edgar Allan Poe and Ambrose Bierce or, less directly, Hawthorne, Melville, and James, but also in the work of modern authors such as James Purdy, John Hawkes, Kurt Vonnegut.

See Edith Birkhead, *The Tale of Terror* (1921, reprinted 1963); Leslie Fiedler, *Love and Death in the American Novel* (1960); Montague Summers, *The Gothic Quest* (New York, 1964).

There has been an enormous recent rise in the critical importance of the gothic; see for example G. St John Barclay, *Anatomy of Horror: The Masters of Occult Fiction* (1978); C. Brooke-Rose, *A Rhetoric of the Unreal* (1981); C. A. Howells, *Love, Mystery, and Misery: Feeling in Gothic Fiction* (1978); R. Jackson, *Fantasy: The Literature of Subversion* 1981); H. Kerr, J. W. Crowley, and C. L. Crow (eds), *The Haunted Dusk: American Supernatural Fiction, 1820–1920* (1983); P. B. Messent (ed.), *Literature of the Occult* (1981); D. G. Punter, *The Literature of Terror* (1980); Donald Ringe, *American Gothic* (1982); V. Sage, *Horror Fiction in the Protestant Tradition* (1986); T. Todorov, *The Fantastic* (1975).

grammar
see LANGUAGE, SYNTAX

grotesque

The grotesque, in works of art, usually makes us laugh. It does so by presenting the human figure in an exaggerated and distorted way; Bergson's theory of comedy as a whole as a deliberate dehumanization or mechanization of observed behaviour seems too limiting, but offers a stimulating approach to the grotesque. The grotesque exploits similarities between people and animals or things, and vice versa. There is a strong critical tendency to regard the grotesque as in opposition to REALISM. Grotesque art, such arguments run, is failed realism, its failure determined by social or personal inadequacies. Mark Spilka, in *Dickens and Kafka* (1963) puts forward the view that the grotesque is conditioned by 'oedipal arrest', an inability to realize the roundedness of personality because of a fixation with the mother; T. A. Jackson, in *Charles Dickens: The Progress of a Radical* (1938), argues that the flatness of Dickens's characters is determined by the dehumanizing forces of the society that Dickens lived in and depicted. But Wolfgang Kayser's book *The Grotesque in Art and Literature* (1963), even if it does little else but dilute the concept of the grotesque to include anything horrific, fantastic, or interesting to Kayser, at least reminds us of the origin of the term in the extravagant, whimsical representations of heads and faces that ornamented classical decorative friezes, rediscovered by Renaissance archaeologists and rapidly imitated by Mannerist artists. A definition of the grotesque that omits its unmotivated playfulness is likely to be defective.

The rhetorical strategy of the grotesque in literature is usually deadpan; the reader must not be allowed a perspective that permits him to explain or reflect upon its incongruity or preposterousness. So Kafka's 'Metamorphosis' opens with the matter-of-fact narration of Gregor Samsa's awakening into insecthood, a stratagem that enables him to pass off calmly the extraordinary state of mind in which the hero reflects that he has felt similarly before and it will pass—much more comic in intention than critics normally suggest. Likewise Pancks's breezy insinuation of grotesque comparison in *Little Dorrit*:

> A person who can't pay, gets another person who can't pay, to guarantee that he can pay. Like a person with two wooden legs getting another person with two wooden legs, to guarantee that he has got two natural ones. It doesn't make either of them able to do a walking match. And four wooden legs are more troublesome to you than two, when you don't want any.

Exaggeration and distortion—two separate doubly wooden-legged aspirants to walking honours is a bit much—gain their effect by being passed off in serious and woodenly correct prose.

See Arthur Clayborough, *The Grotesque in English Literature* (1965); Philip Thomson, *The Grotesque* (1972).

MAH

heresy of paraphrase
see PARAPHRASE

hermeneutics
Comprises the general theory and practice of interpretation. The term was first specifically applied in the seventeenth century; but hermeneutic practice is as old as the exegesis of texts. Many questions that are still current in contemporary interpretation can be traced through the history of Western hermeneutics, which typically handled two categories of text: Classical and Biblical. Each was obscured by cultural and historical distance, yet each held a meaning or value that the interpreter tried to reach. In theology, Origen produced a triple explication through grammatical, ethical and allegorical meanings, and Augustine added an 'anagogical' or mystical dimension. The Reformation intensified hermeneutic activity as Protestant theologians tried to form an autonomous interpretation of scripture; and later, Enlightenment rationalism made for codification of interpretive procedures. Early in the nineteenth century, Friedrich Schleiermacher proposed a general hermeneutics that would underlie all specific interpretations and provide them with a system of understanding. This programme has remained a hermeneutic ambition; as Paul Ricoeur points out, it echoes the Enlightenment and the Critical philosophy of Kant, but it also displays a Romantic element. Schleiermacher distinguished between 'grammatical' interpretation, based on the general discourse of a culture, and 'technical' interpretation, based on the individual subjectivity of an author. The interpreter seeks to reconstruct that subjectivity—indeed, he can understand an author better than he understood himself. Here an intuitive psychologism complements the comparatist approach of 'grammatical' method; and intuition is also evident in Schleiermacher's famous legacy, the hermeneutic circle. Trying to understand any hermeneutic object—a sentence, a text—we approach the parts by reference to the whole, yet cannot grasp the whole without reference to the parts. This 'circular' process also applies in approaching an unfamiliar author or period: some foreknowledge seems essential. For Schleiermacher, the problem was resolved intuitively, by a 'leap' into

the circle, like the leap of faith. This may sound suspiciously unscientific in an age of progress; and by the end of the nineteenth century Wilhelm Dilthey had to make room for hermeneutics in the face of the huge prestige of the natural sciences and their positive methods. He produced yet another division: between the explanation of external objects in the natural sciences, and the understanding of inner states in the human sciences. Hermeneutics applied to the latter; Dilthey thus follows Schleiermacher in his psychological emphasis. His concern is not so much to understand the text as to reconstruct the lived experience of its author. Such experience, says Dilthey, is intrinsically temporal, and interpretation must therefore itself assume a temporal or historical character. The role of history was to remain important for hermeneutics; and in the 'understanding of spiritual life and of history' Dilthey gave literature an 'immeasurable significance'; for 'in language alone the inner life of man finds its complete, exhaustive and objectively intelligible expression.' Literature is thus a privileged object for hermeneutic study.

Martin Heidegger moved twentieth-century hermeneutics away from psychologism towards ontology: the question of being, and of being in the world, a world whose strangeness demanded interpretation. The philosophical issues will not concern us here; but it is important to note Heidegger's reformulation of the hermeneutic circle, not as a problem to be resolved by an intuitive leap, but in terms of interplay between an interpreter and a tradition which is encountered, understood and remade in an open dialectic. As Heidegger's pupil Hans-Georg Gadamer describes it, 'There is a polarity of familiarity and strangeness on which hermeneutic work is based . . . that intermediate place between being an historically intended separate object and being part of a tradition.' This concept of tradition is crucial for Gadamer's dealings with history, and with what he calls an effective consciousness of history. Far from being neutral, the interpreter is always situated in relation to the tradition 'out of which the text speaks'. This situatedness (and its prejudices) must come to consciousness as the interpreter's 'horizon'. The text's horizon is of course different and distant; and though a fusion of horizons is sought, historical distance is not cancelled but recognized as itself productive of meaning. In this sense, and not in Schleiermacher's, the interpreter may understand more than the author.

The open dialectic and evolving tradition of Gadamer's hermeneutics act to prevent closure; meaning is understood but it is never final. A desire to avoid the 'Babel of interpretations' has prompted E. D. Hirsch Jr to seek a regulative principle for hermeneutics through another reconstruction of the author. He separates 'meaning' and 'significance'; significance is any relationship between meaning and something else—taste, period and so on. It is thus variable and the concern of criticism. Interpretation, on the other hand, deals with meaning; this does not change because it is intended by an author—though seen not as historically active, nor as unconsciously motivated, but as 'that "part" of the author which specifies or determines verbal meaning.' However, this specifying intention must itself be specified by the interpreter, and so its practical use for validation would seem to involve us in a really vicious circle. But the urgent controversy in contemporary hermeneutics does not stem from Hirsch, who has been subjected to devastating critique (see David Hoy, below). It rather concerns what could be called the optimism of Schleiermacher, Dilthey and Gadamer. Much as these hermeneuts differ, they do share an allegiance to universality, and to a common human nature which suggests a measure of co-operation and of shared discourse in the interpretive dialogue. Hermeneutic objects may differ, but they are credited as truths which await illumination. Ricoeur has distinguished between this 'hermeneutics of belief' and a contrary 'hermeneutics of suspicion' whose exemplary figures are Nietzsche, Marx and Freud. Such figures are concerned not just to clarify but to demystify; texts may be mistrusted rather than revered, and tradition may be a repository of false consciousness. Such attitudes are linked to oppositional practices for the READER, and to the concept of REFUNCTIONING. One noteworthy debate between belief and suspicion has concerned Gadamer and Jürgen Habermas, whose ideological approach derives from the Frankfurt School. For Habermas, a hermeneutics like Gadamer's offers knowledge which is 'sterilized', clear of the suppressed traces of special interest which critical reflection should uncover. But for Gadamer this task is not invariably necessary or primary; he resists the exclusive equation of understanding and unmasking, and the inevitable opposition of reason and authority.

Dilthey's distinction between natural and human sciences has also been challenged, and with it much arts-versus-science rhetoric. The distinction was still followed by Heidegger and Gadamer, prompting comments on the alienation of the detached scientific observer. But for much modern science the observer is not detached, the object is not passive, and investigation occurs within the horizon of a theoretical paradigm. An historian of science like Stephen Toulmin can now claim: 'Critical judgement in the natural sciences, then, is not geometrical, and critical interpretation in the humanities is not whimsical.' ('The Construal of Reality' in W. J. T. Mitchell (ed.), *The Politics of Interpretation*, 1983.) Both sides must abjure their myths; hermeneutics is no longer judged and delimited by 'hard' science, and its scope is implicitly increased. An even more far-reaching extension is described by Richard Rorty in *Philosophy and the Mirror of Nature*

(1980). Rorty proposes the abandonment of that quest for knowledge which seeks essential principles and tries to posit a meta-discourse that commands all others. He calls this ambition 'epistemology' and suggests hermeneutics as an alternative procedure: 'Hermeneutics . . . is what we get when we are no longer epistemological.' It is thus a polemical term which seeks to turn human inquiry away from envying some predictive sciences towards a pragmatic anti-essentialism which (following Gadamer in this respect) resists closure. Heidegger's open model of the hermeneutic circle applies, suggesting a 'notion of culture as a conversation rather than as a structure erected upon foundations.' This is arguably the widest scope yet proposed for hermeneutics: interpretation becomes a pervasive necessity, for as Stanley Fish remarked in another context 'interpretation is the only game in town'.

Richard E. Palmer, *Hermeneutics: Interpretation Theory in Schleiermacher, Dilthey, Heidegger, and Gadamer* (1969) is a thorough basis for study; David Couzens Hoy, *The Critical Circle: Literature and History in Contemporary Hermeneutics* (1978) has more recent material; and Paul Ricoeur, *Hermeneutics and the Human Sciences,* edited and translated by John B. Thompson (1981) is an acute commentary. *New Literary History* published a special issue on 'Literary Hermeneutics' in Autumn 1978: Vol. 10 no. 1. W. J. T. Mitchell (ed.), *Against Theory: Literary Studies and The New Pragmatism* (1985); despite its title, this book presents specific debates on interpretation. Kurt Mueller-Vollmer (ed.), *The Hermeneutics Reader: Texts of the German Tradition from the Enlightenment to the Present* (1986); an essential anthology.

EC

hero

In classical myth heroes had superhuman powers; they conversed with gods (sometimes, like Achilles or Theseus, they were demi-gods) and their courses were accompanied by prophecies and portents. But when these figures appear in the Homeric epics, their status, as Aristotle showed, is changed—they have become aspects of *literary* structure, and 'Unity of plot does not, as some people think, consist in the unity of the hero' (*Poetics*). Homer's heroes, for Aristotle, are elements in the unity of an action, not its sole origin and end as they had been in the loosely cumulative preliterary legends; in epic or tragedy heroes exist for the sake of the literary whole. But the hero is not easily demoted from his mythic status: Romantic criticism, culminating in A. C. Bradley's *Shakespearean Tragedy* (1904) is now notorious for the fallacy of considering heroes in artificial separation from their dramatic context (see L. C. Knights, *How Many Children had Lady Macbeth?*, 1933). Conversely, the New Critics who de-mythologized the hero stressed 'unity' to the point where plays became ritual re-enactments of order rather than actions. The concept of the hero seems inextricably involved with the discussion of dramatic structure. Though by an illusion they seem so, Shakespeare's heroes are rarely continuous creations. When the hero returns to the scene after an absence we do not take him up where we left off, or reconstruct some biographical fiction; we take him up from where the *play*, in the language and action of other characters, has got to. This is perhaps the clearest indication of the distinction (and the interaction) between dramatic structure and the structure of the hero's consciousness or career; we may in some works be more aware of one or the other, but neither can dominate without evaporating the drama.

The critical issues raised by the Protean forms of the hero in narrative poetry and novels are more complicated, and have been aired less. *Paradise Lost* provides an example: Milton established a distinctive 'heroic' diction, but initiated simultaneously a fertile debate about who (if anyone) was the 'hero'. Satan, as Dryden said, was *technically* the hero—but was the concept even relevant to a work claiming truth to universal moral and spiritual experience? Surely, Addison urged, Milton had *no* hero in the classical sense (though if we wanted one, it must be Christ)? When, in the romantic period, Blake and Shelley declared Milton *was* on the Devil's side, very different valuations of the heroic came into the open: on the one side radical individualism (represented diversely by Byron, the Brontës and Carlyle), on the other the communal values of restraint, civilization, maturity, first in Scott and Austen, later in the social novels of Mrs Gaskell and George Eliot. Thackeray, who subtitled *Vanity Fair* (1847–8) 'A Novel without a Hero', applied in *Henry Esmond* (1852) the searching perspective of domestic realism to the great men of the past. The eighteenth-century epigram, 'No man is a hero to his valet' encapsulated the kind of scrutiny that cut the hero down to size. Carlyle argued 'It is not the Hero's blame, but the Valet's: that his soul, namely, is a mean *valet*-soul!'—but his own version of 'the Hero' demonstrates grotesquely the vices of essentialism: 'For at bottom the Great Man, as he comes from the hand of Nature, is ever the same kind of thing: Odin, Luther, Johnson, Burns . . .'

Getting rid of 'the Hero' seemed a critical necessity: as wielded by Carlyle the concept was unmanageable, a barrier to the understanding of literary structures. Critics preferred the slippery term 'character', and analysed social and/or verbal detail; rhetoric, action, conventional motifs and large-scale effects were systematically played down. There were, however, many nineteenth-century novels where this obviously did not work (e.g. Emily Brontë's *Wuthering Heights*, 1847, Meredith's *The Egoist*, 1879) and recent fictional developments, like the absurd, villainous or insane narrator-heroes of Beckett or Nabokov, have produced the term 'anti-hero' to fill a much-felt gap. The hero has re-emerged, in complicity with the author against the norms of 'the whole'; he may be, as in Beckett's title, *The Unnameable* (1953), but this is of course a precise inversion, not a banishment, of his classical archetype. Dickens's *Our Mutual Friend* (1864–5) exemplifies a continuing ambivalence—the sinister yet patronizing attitude of the author introducing 'our hero'. We may agree with T. S. Eliot's debunking of 'Sir Philip Sidney/And other heroes of that kidney' but the concept seems inescapable despite its extra- or anti-literary overtones. The narrative without a hero remains a critical fiction. See also CHARACTER, EPIC, MYTH.

See Thomas Carlyle, *Heroes and Hero-Worship* (1840); Northrop Frye, *Anatomy of Criticism* (1957); R. W. B. Lewis, *The Picaresque Saint, Representative Figures in Contemporary fiction* (1959); Peter Mercer, 'Othello and heroic tragedy', *Critical Quarterly*, 11 (1969); Mario Praz, *The Hero in Eclipse in Victorian Fiction* (1956).

LS

heroic couplet
see COUPLET

historical novel
A term which refers to novels set in a period of time recognizably 'historical' in relation to the time of writing. The past tense may be employed in the narration, the account may purport to have been written in that past time, or in some intervening time. The subject-matter of the historical novel tends to encompass both public and private events, and the protagonist may be either an actual figure from the past or an invented figure whose destiny is involved with actual events. The major practitioners of this, the 'classic' form of the historical novel in English and American literature, were Sir Walter Scott and James Fenimore Cooper. The historical actions in Scott's 'Waverley' and Cooper's 'Leather-stocking' novels largely concerned social changes of great magnitude—the destruction of the Scottish clans, the impingement of the American settlers on the new land and their conflict with the Red man. The protagonist was often a man of mixed loyalties, and the diverse pressures which focused upon him mirrored in individual struggle the interplay of wider social forces.

In England, Thackeray carried forward the tradition of the genre, but reached back to connect it with the comic novels of Fielding and Smollett. Like Scott, Thackeray communicates a sense of momentous and irretrievable social change, but his dissatisfaction with that which prevailed in any given situation seems stronger than Scott's. On the

Continent, the successors to Scott included Manzoni, Pushkin, Gogol, Hugo, Merimée, Stendhal, Balzac and Tolstoy. Gradually the interests and techniques of the historical novel began to be applied to contemporary events and the genre merged with, even as it helped create, the great realistic novels of the nineteenth century. A double movement occurred in which the treatment of 'history' in fiction became progressively more exotic and archaeologically accurate—as in Flaubert's *Salammbô* (1862)—while treatment of the present became more 'naturalistic'.

The historical novel merges on one side with the realistic novel: on the other—as the historical substance generalizes—it merges with the national epic, and is perhaps the counter-phenomenon to Fielding's notion of the novel as a *comic* prose epic. The epic model is here Virgil's *Aeneid*, in so far as certain events can be seen as inaugurating and justifying (or failing to justify) the nation state.

The question of historical psychology—of the motives and feelings which can be attributed to people in the past—arises. Some historical novelists have attributed to characters in the past substantially the same inner lives as their contemporaries. This type of anachronism, which can be used to significant and to comic effect, is allied to other 'deteriorated' forms of the historical novel, including the 'historical romance', where only costume and not substance differentiates the period of the fiction from the present. See also *archaism*.

See Georg Lukács, trans. Hannah and Stanley Mitchell, *The Historical Novel* (1962).

AMG

historicism

Many branches of literary study involve the use of historical evidence: questions of textual transmission and authenticity, of archaic or obsolete language, of sources and literary borrowing, of relations between an author's life and work, are all in the strict sense 'historical'. But the term 'historicism' is usually reserved for that approach to literature which sets it in the context of the ideas, conventions and attitudes of the period in which it was written. Although good literature is 'not of an age, but for all time', the social and intellectual climate within which every writer has to work, and which his writing reflects in some degree, is subject to change. The uninformed modern reader is therefore likely to bring to the literature of the past assumptions and associations that may be quite alien to the frame of reference from which that literature derives its form and meaning. The aim of historicism is to make works of different periods more accessible to the modern reader by reconstructing the historically appropriate background as it affects an understanding and judgment of the work concerned.

The theory as well as the practice of historicism have not gone unchallenged. It has been argued, for instance, that a modern recon-struction of the cultural or ideological identity of a past age must still be essentially modern in its point of view. Historicism cannot transform a twentieth-century mind; it may only be transferring modern precon-ceptions from the critical to the historical plane of thought. Moreover, historicism must inevitably be selective and interpretative in treating what evidence there is concerning standards and habits of mind that differ from our own; it may tend to impose a falsifying uniformity and immobility upon its conception of a literary 'period', and its findings are themselves demonstrably subject to change from generation to genera-tion. Much of the historicism of thirty years ago is now as obsolete as other kinds of literary interpretation which were merely of their age. In addition, there is a tendency in historicism to interpret and measure the work of great and original imagination by the commonplaces of its time, reducing the uniqueness and subtlety of genius to the lowest common denominator of a reconstructed idea of 'period'. If, for instance, a knowledge of Elizabethan ideas about kingship, or of their dramatic conventions, helps us to understand Shakespeare's history plays, we must still remember that Shakespeare is hardly to be circumscribed by an abstraction of the average mentality of his contemporaries. Conven-tions that have been obliterated by time may be recovered for us by historicism, but the great writers of the past are more than convention-al.

Historicism, therefore, cannot provide us with an absolute or objec-tive measure of literary meaning or value. It is not a substitute for the act of intelligent imagination which we call criticism; but it is, properly used, one of the critic's most valuable tools. Provided its limitations are one of the critic's most valuable tools. Provided its limitations are recognized, it can extend and refine our understanding of the literature we most admire. The validity of historicism rests not upon an anti-quarian curiosity about how a writer was influenced or interpreted by the world he lived in, but upon the endeavour to enrich modern sensibilities by comprehending and transmitting those ideas and values which preserve the continuity of our civilization. Cf. MARXIST CRITICISM.

See Helen Gardner, *The Business of Criticism* (1960); René Wellek, *Concepts of Criticism* (1963); W. K. Wimsatt, Jr, *The Verbal Icon* (1954).

DJP

homophony
see AMBIGUITY

humours
In medieval medicine the four humours were the fluids whose domi-

nance determined the nature ('complexion') of men: Blood (sanguine); Phlegm (phlegmatic); Choler (choleric); Black Choler or Bile (melancholic). These are used by Ben Jonson to construct an idea of character obsession. A humour may 'so possess a man, that it doth draw / All his affects, his spirits and his power, / In their confluctions, all to run one way' (Prologue to *Every Man Out of His Humour*, 1600). The obsessional humour riding the character is the source of the 'comedy'. In the early plays the humour is 'spent' in the course of the action, freeing the character, in a literal use of the medical analogy. Later the humours are developed as symbolic stances through which the characters are seen to react to the values of the world they inhabit, rather than as simple flaws or biases in their nature. Thus Morose's silence (phlegmatic melancholy) is simultaneously a cause and a product of his relationship with his society. This sophistication of the theory culminates in a humour character like Overreach (sanguine/choleric?) where the bias is a complex symbol of the general and social values of the world of the Fair in *Bartholomew Fair* (1614? folio 1631) and man's response to them.

Restoration dramatists continue to insist in their critical responses that humour theory is central to comic effect but in practice the increased interest in the presence or absence of the *acceptable response* by which society judges the wit and worth of its members makes humour characterization seem too inflexible. Attempts are made to distinguish Affectation, with its conscious, social overtones, from Humour, where the stress is individual and pathological. As Congreve says, 'what is *Humour* in one, may be *Affectation* in another; and nothing is more common, than for some to affect particular ways of saying, and doing things, peculiar to others, whom they admire and imitate' (*Concerning Humour in Comedy*, 1696). But though he seems determined to defend the humour concept he rings its knell when he admits in the same work 'that a continued Affectation may in time become a Habit'. For in the world which he inhabits and describes it becomes impossible effectively to distinguish continued affectation from reality (witness the marriage contract in *The Way of the World*). Humour remains an influence in the figures of the Tunbellys and Clumsys of Restoration plays but they no longer have the distinction of being vessels of disruptive forces who must be freed if others are to escape the shadow of their obsessions: they have become mere butts to provoke the humour of those who have learned the correct manner to suit the mood of the world. See also MANNERS.

See Alain C. Dessen, *Jonson's Moral Comedy* (1971); Paul Lauter, *Theories of Comedy* (1964); Kenneth Muir, *The Comedy of Manners* (1970).

GG

hyperbole
see CONCEIT

I

illocutionary act
see DISCOURSE

image
In the eighteenth century, one theory of 'imagination' was that it was a faculty for visualization, so literature was often regarded as a medium which promoted visual responses in the reader: that is to say, 'images'. Descriptive poetry flourished. One basic meaning for 'image' is provided by that context, but other, looser and more treacherous, meanings have accreted: any sensuous effect provoked by literary language; any striking language; metaphor; symbol; any figure. 'Image' and 'imagery' have also come to be vaguely laudatory terms, lazily gesturing a taste for concreteness, richness of texture, in verse. Finally, NEW CRITICAL poetics, encouraging us to view poems as virtually concrete artefacts, allows whole poems to be regarded as 'images'. Though used apparently without polemical intent, as if it is universally accepted currency, the term 'image' frequently determines the direction of critical thinking, proving that the metaphor involved in talking about literary works or verbal effects as 'images' is not dead at all, but inconveniently alive.

The great advantage of 'image' to lazy criticism, and hence danger to serious criticism, is its shifting application: in *Macbeth*, for example, the following might be called 'images' or 'imagery':

(1) metaphors, similes, figurative language: 'Pity like a naked newborn babe . . .'
(2) Lady Macbeth's children: 'I have given suck . . .'
(3) Macduff's son, who is a flesh-and-blood character
(4) The vision 'Who wears upon his baby brow . . .' whom the witches show to Macbeth
(5) All of these, as 'iterative imagery', a play-within-the-play where distinctions between language, action and character lapse (see Cleanth Brooks, *The Well Wrought Urn*, 1947, ch. 2).

The point of having one word to do all these jobs is clear: the whole play becomes one symbolic utterance, a 'dramatic poem' (or, of course, an 'image'), its central preoccupations iterated at every level. This New Critical treatment of imagery congratulated itself for avoiding the damaging assumption that verbal texture was incidental ornament, for having found a way of integrating the critical response.

The effect of over-reliance on the word image is to encourage a focus on literature which makes syntax, argument, plot, temporal and relational structures recede into invisibility, while description and figurative language become foregrounded to a distorted degree. The whole thus isolated becomes a static 'spatial' experience, imagined as a 'cluster' of 'images'. The very use of the term encourages the critic to project his own desire for pattern, while sounding reassuringly objective. It is easy to move on to assertions that poems are revelatory, symbolic, 'icons', that the process they enshrine is 'miraculism' or 'incarnation', the Word made flesh. What starts as a gesture of respect for the TEXTURE of literature ends by importing a sub- or supra-literary structure. The rejection of the work's overt order (dismissed as abstraction) leads to the search for some more esoteric 'hidden' pattern. Studies of imagery tend almost irresistibly towards the assumption that images are not the expression of the artist's purpose, but of a greater force working through him (the Great Mind etc.).

'Image' has not got much to do with verbal analysis, and the most persuasive analysts, e.g. Empson, hardly use it. It has become associated with the demand that we respect what is 'there' in the work, but the connection is tenuous, and the empiricism fake. As Richards has shown, 'image' blurs the verbal facts about metaphor, by obscuring the *relations* that are being made (between 'tenor' and 'vehicle') and suggesting that a free-floating 'emblem' is being offered. The real connection of 'image' is with a group of assumptions which 'place' poetry, more or less frankly, in relation to some 'deeper' structure—depth psychology, Baroque Christianity, etc. This may seem to dignify literature, but in the long run it impoverishes, since it substitutes for the diversity and fluidity of the literary medium a shadow-play of 'images' whose resolution lies elsewhere.

See P. N. Furbank, *Reflections on the Word 'Image'* (1970); Frank Kermode, *Romantic Image* (1957); I. A. Richards, *The Philosophy of Rhetoric* (1936).

LS

imagination

(like 'tragedy') leads a double life. In common usage it has a very equivocal sense, more often than not trivial, even derogatory—'it's all in your imagination'. But as soon as it is associated with any form of art it becomes one of the highest, probably *the* highest indication of value. The extremes meet in the distrust of Art as the enemy of common sense, decency, reason, good government or sound business. But the decadent West in the later twentieth century seems to live for Art almost as hectically as our damned Victorian ancestors did a hundred years ago.

This ambivalence is ancient, if not universal. In theory, the Renaissance assigned Reason and Imagination to different faculties, and reason was certainly the higher. Imagination co-ordinated the physical senses on which alone it depended, and was therefore shared by all animals; reason was angelic, free of the body, even god-like and therefore peculiar (beneath the moon) to man. Such a simplistic version of experience was not really accepted, but the problems of over-valuing imagination were illuminated by Theseus in *A Midsummer Night's Dream*:

> The lunatic, the lover, and the poet
> Are of imagination all compact.

The same trinity bedevilled William Blake in his espousal of Hell. Behind him was not only the superb rationalism of the eighteenth century, but also its terror of lunacy. Samuel Johnson knew no difference between 'imagination' and 'fancy' and defined them as the power of representing things absent from oneself or others; but he found no power in either to distinguish the tangibly real from dangerous hallucination. It had therefore both the power and the danger of mescalin or its synthetic derivatives. Yet Johnson also recognized Imagination as one the three constituents of genius in Pope: 'He had *Imagination*, which strongly impresses on the writer's mind, and enables him to convey to the reader, the various forms of nature, incidents of life, and energies of passion . . .' Pope had likewise Good Sense, but Johnson did not discover any principle to reconcile the two. Nor did Blake, who found subservience to reason as idiotic as the belief in general truths, and both hostile to the energy of particular imaginative experience.

Coleridge's early reflections on the problem produced the image of an Aeolian harp: the chance play of the wind over a mechanical device. It was an old idea, and has been revived since. Automatic writing and SURREALIST theory came close to it, but were usually sustained by a Freudian faith in their origins in a subconscious mind which offered a concept, but not an explanation, of ultimate meaning. A stricter application of the idea is in the forms of self-generating art that have followed the mobiles of thirty years ago; the closest literary equivalent is probably the random association of cut-outs. For Coleridge the image served to relate the internal unity of an individual human mind to the external multeity of the random collection of objects it perceives; and it made a proper (if disturbing) allowance for chance. But it allowed of only a very limited relation to reason, and none at all to the energy of creative power. His efforts to modify the image in revising the poem only produced confusion, and he moved towards a fresh epistemology assisted by reading German transcendentalists (Kant and others). The eighteenth-century propositions that the mind merely received impressions from objects (Locke), and that objects could not be *known* to exist except when contacted by our senses (Berkeley) gave way to the proposition that perception depends on an active mind perceiving an object which nevertheless exists without us.

The peculiar achievement here is to re-define *all* perception as imaginative, a *creative* act of the subjective self; but simultaneously the sanity of a perception is guaranteed by the reality of the object perceived. Subject and object coalesce; objects are only known subjectively, but equally one's self is only known in objects. A bush may burn in a visionary blaze; but it is not a bear: it is a bush perceived in a certain way dependent on one's imaginative predisposition. The position is reassuring, even if paradoxical. Blake placed less confidence in the solidity of objects, far more in subjective vision: he, too, was sane, and knew that a flower was a flower; but he might, in contemplating it, see an old man or an angel, and the validity of the vision was assured solely by the fact that he *saw* it. For Coleridge, a major difficulty remained in distinguishing art from normal perception, which is presumably what he intended by dividing 'secondary' from 'primary' imagination (although nothing he says about secondary imagination is peculiar to art).

Coleridge effectively reconciled imagination with Reason, without apparently diminishing either. The lighter values of poetry were relegated to 'fancy'; imagination was essential to all knowledge, and poetry therefore became a serious form of knowledge. Matthew Arnold expected it to replace discredited religion. The study of literature eventually became a central discipline in universities. 'Object' was ambiguous: strictly, it meant anything, tangible or intangible, regarded objectively; but Coleridge was deeply involved with Wordsworth's poetry, so that his discussion often seems to imply rocks and stones and trees. IMAGISM was therefore a direct derivative and through that, T. S. Eliot's insistence that emotion in art can only be expressed through objects, the OBJECTIVE CORRELATIVE. Wallace Stevens's poetry could fairly be described as a set of variations on a theme by Coleridge. In Eliot and Stevens the association with reason remained dominant; their sanity was never in doubt. Yeats was far more ambiguous: teasing rationalists by flirting with all forms of the esoteric, including blatant charlatanry, yet retaining an ostentatious sanity as well. But Yeats saw imagination as essentially hostile to reason, and their relationship rather as fruitful tension than reconciliation; his study of Blake was early and lasting, and it was supplemented by intense interest in his wife's automatic writing.

The *status* of Imagination as a concept owes far more to Coleridge than to Blake; but its use nowadays often owes more to Blake. His celebration of vision has been closely linked (by Ginsberg, for instance) with exposure to drugs, in which he is not known to have been involved; whereas Coleridge, notoriously, was.

See J.A. Appleyard, *Coleridge's Philosophy of Literature* (1965); R. L. Brett, *Fancy and Imagination* (1969); C. C. Clarke, *Romantic Paradox* (1962); S. T. Coleridge, *Biographia Literaria* (1817), G. Watson (ed.) (1956).

NSB

Imagism

The term was coined by Ezra Pound to denote the principles agreed on by himself and the other members of a literary group he formed in London in 1912. As a broad movement, Imagism signals the beginning of English and American MODERNISM, and a definite break with the Romantic-Victorian tradition. As a stylistic programme, it manifests the desire of the post-Symbolist, pre-war generation for a harder, more precise and objective medium. As a particular school, *Les Imagistes* are the heirs of T. E. Hulme's 1909 group of Impressionist poets who experimented with brief visual poems in the Oriental manner. Finally, Imagism shares with Gautier and the Parnassians the penchant for sculptural hardness and immaculate craftsmanship; with the SYMBOLISTS—the accent on pure poetry to the exclusion of all extra-poetic content, as well as the practice of irregular, 'free' verse; with REALISM—the resolve to remain close to the outlines of concrete reality. The poem projected by Imagism is a laconic complex in which 'painting or sculpture seems as if it were just coming over into speech'. As a model, Pound chose the 'Oread' by H. D. (Hilda Doolittle), commonly considered the most representative of his group:

> Whirl up, sea—
> whirl your pointed pines,
> splash your great pines
> on our rocks
> hurl your green over us,
> cover us with your pools of fir.

The poetics of Imagism may best be considered as three interlocking entities: Hulme's prognosis of a classical revival, the stylistic or work-shop prescriptions formulated by Pound and upheld by the school even after his departure from it, and Pound's full-blown Doctrine of the Image. Hulme's brilliant if inconsistent case is argued in the few articles and short pieces published during his lifetime and, more elaborately, in his posthumously published work. It consists of a repudiation of

Romanticism and its aesthetics of the Beyond. The new poetry was going to be that of 'small, dry things' conveyed by concrete visual metaphor. Rejecting infinity, mystery and an indulgence in emotions, he called for a poetry of self-imposed limitation, corresponding to a metaphysical attitude which regards man as an 'extraordinarily fixed and limited animal', and reality as something that may only be apprehended in isolated glimpses.

The stylistic canon of Pound's school comprises the three principles agreed on by its three original members, Pound, H. D. and Richard Aldington:

(1) Direct treatment of the 'thing' whether subjective or objective.
(2) To use absolutely no word that does not contribute to the presentation.
(3) As regarding rhythm: to compose in the sequence of the musical phrase, not in sequence of a metronome.

These are augmented by Pound's list of 'Don'ts', chiefly intended for the apprentice poet. They vary in substance from general advice (the avoidance of abstraction, rhetoric and non-functional ornament) to suggestions of a more technical nature (the practice of enjambment to diversify the rhythmical 'waves'). Central is the emphasis on poetry as an acquired art, the mastery of which demands the labours of a lifetime. The modern aspect of the programme is reflected in Pound's dictum that 'no good poetry is ever written in a manner twenty years old'. But the Imagist is given a free choice of subject-matter, not excluding classical themes, and is counselled to study a vast and disparate 'tradition' so as 'to find out what has been done, once for all, better than it can ever be done again'.

Pound's Doctrine of the Image centres around his successive definitions of the term. His earliest attempt—'an "Image" is that which presents an intellectual and emotional complex in an instant of time'—yields its full meaning when read in conjunction with later pronouncements in which the Image is described as the poet's 'primary pigment', the hard core of poetry wherein it reveals itself as distinct from, and yet basically parallel to, other arts. Only with the Image, the 'word beyond formulated language', is the poet given the medium that is specifically his. The Image may comprise traditional metaphor, when the latter can be said to be 'interpretative' of reality, i.e. when it posits a relationship based on inherent, not merely fanciful, qualities. Commonly, however, it connotes in Pound such modern procedures as juxtaposition and superposition. Pound's illustration is his own haiku-like 'In a Station of the Metro':

The apparition of these faces in the crowd;
Petals on a wet, black bough.

Here 'one idea is set on top of another' to produce the synthetic complex, also described as language's 'point of maximum energy'. The two (or more) components of the Image remain faithful to objective reality, representing two distinct acts of sense-perceptions, yet their fusion is expected to form a higher, governing reality, untainted with photographic realism. In actual Imagist writing, stringent conformity is the exception. A shorthand notation of impressionistic glimpses, concise metaphoric miniatures and 'hard', asymmetrical treatments of Hellenic and other motifs constitutes the bulk of a poetry compatible with, but not necessarily occasioned by, the theory.

Assessments of the significance of Imagism vary greatly. Eliot's opinion was that its accomplishment in verse had been 'critical rather than creative, and as criticism very important'. Leavis, another early critic, considered that 'in itself it amounted to little more than a recognition that something was wrong with poetry'. But the formidable influence Imagism exercised, and continues to exert, suggests that such a judgment is untenable. Other critics consider it of importance chiefly as a stage in Pound's development towards his *Cantos*. Wallace Stevens reproaches Imagism with its belief that all objects are equally suited for poetry, and its equation of meaning with bare surface. As a critical movement, Imagism's main significance probably resides in its revaluation of Romanticism and of the nineteenth century which, with few exceptions, it dismissed as a sentimental, blurry, manneristic period. No less significant was its insistence on the functional, rather than the merely ornamental, potentiality of the poetic image, and the latter's capacity for conveying the concrete and definite. In this, it 'isolated the basic unit of the modern poem', as Stephen Spender suggested. But in overstating its case, it was ignoring other, no less effective, poetic energies, as well as dangerously limiting its own scope.

See D. Davie, *Ezra Pound—Poet as Sculptor* (1965); G. Hough, *Image and Experience* (1960); G. Hughes, *Imagism and the Imagists* (1931); A. R. Jones, *The Life and Opinions of Thomas Ernest Hulme* (1960); H. Kenner, *The Poetry of Ezra Pound* (1951); H. Kenner, *The Pound Era* (1972); F. Kermode, *Romantic Image* (1957); M. Roberts, *T. E. Hulme* (1938); C. K. Stead, *The New Poetic* (1964); R. Taupin, *L'Influence du symbolisme français sur la poésie américaine* (1929); A. Kingsley Weatherhead, *The Edge of the Image* (1967).

NZ

imitation

The first recorded use of 'imitation' (*mimesis*) as an aesthetic term is Plato's: in the *Republic* it is a derogatory way of describing the poet's counterfeit 'creations', which reflect and mimic the transient appearances of this world (see PLATONISM). Aristotle in his *Poetics* stretches the term to give it a radically different and more complex application: the poet 'imitates' not the accidental features of character in action, but the universal type, 'clothed with generic attributes' (Coleridge). Aristotle is not arguing for a symbolic or emblematic function for literature (only that would have satisfied Plato) but for a concrete manifestation of the 'natural' order he asserted was present (though obscured) in ordinary experience.

Aristotle's 'imitation' combines a sense of the literary work as the representation of some pre-existent reality, with a sense of the work itself as an object, not merely a reflecting surface. The poet is not subservient to the irrationality of the actual: his play or poem has its own natural form and objective status. In the *Poetics* tragedy is like an organism—it grows, achieves its prime (with Sophocles) and decays. The form has an imperative logic whereby (e.g.) the poet chooses a 'probable impossibility' rather than an event which though possible (even historical) does not follow 'naturally' in context. The poet 'imitates' best by allowing his work to achieve its own fitting formal excellence.

This stress on the imitative function of formal harmony (Aristotle says music is the most 'mimetic' art) connects with the second major use of the term in classical and neo-classical criticism—the 'imitation' of one writer by another (Homer by Virgil, both by Milton, all three by Pope). If Homer's epics are the fullest realization of the laws of epic (and involve therefore the fullest correspondence with the laws of reason and nature) then to imitate heroic action and to imitate the form and style of the *Iliad* is one complex process of mimesis. Hence Pope's snappy line on Virgil:

> Nature and Homer were, he found, the same.

Theoretically there is no conflict between formal imitation and representation, but neither 'nature' nor language stay 'the same', and in practice there is tension, issuing in the characteristic neo-classical forms of MOCK-EPIC and PARODY.

For the concept of imitation to retain its precision and range, social, moral and psychological values must seem self-evident: there has to be consensus about what is 'natural' and 'probable', or at least agreement about the value of such generalizations. In the eighteenth century an anti-theoretical realism, reflecting a more fluid, fragmentary and individual reality (see Ian Watt, *The Rise of the Novel*, 1957; and REALISM) began to erode the assumptions behind imitation. The term lost its great virtue of referring to both form and content and was used almost synonymously with 'representation'. Deliberate efforts to resurrect Aristotelian usage (see CHICAGO CRITICS) have foundered in stilted and questionable generalization, while more fluent use of the term (e.g.

Auerbach's *Mimesis*) has had to accommodate shifting definitions of reality.

See Erich Auerbach, trans. W. Trask, *Mimesis* (1953); S. H. Butcher, *Aristotle's Theory of Poetry and Fine Art* (1907) with an introduction by John Gassner (1951); R. S. Crane (ed.), *Critics and Criticism* (1957); G. F. Else, *Aristotle's 'Poetics': the Argument* (1957); Raymond Williams, *The Long Revolution* (1961).

LS

implied author
see AUTHOR, PERSONA

intention
In their influential essay 'The intentional fallacy' (in *The Verbal Icon*, 1954) W. K. Wimsatt, Jr, and Monroe C. Beardsley argued that the author's intentions were not the proper concern of the critic. Their argument has produced many misconceptions about descriptive criticism—that poems are autonomous, or autotelic, that they are discontinuous from language and each other, that any external evidence is critically inadmissible. Essentially the essay disputed the formulae and terminology of expressive criticism with its Romantic concentration on the poet and his inspired utterances, and asserted the existence of the poem as a fact in the public language. The characteristic vocabulary of expressive or intentionalist criticism, its criteria of sincerity, fidelity, spontaneity, originality, pointed to a misconception about the mode of existence of a literary work. It was not a practical message, a real statement, which could be measured for its sincerity against a known context, but a fictional utterance by a dramatic speaker; so it was more properly judged in terms of coherence, profundity, beauty. Consequently, the essay argued, the meaning of a work was better discovered by attention to 'internal' evidence, the language of the poem, which paradoxically, because it *was* language, was public, than to external evidence—the private disclosures of poets, their friends or biographers. This advice has often been understood to mean the irrelevance to critical enquiry of all information that is not derived from the linguistic characteristics of the text. Of course it is nonsense to suppose that we approach any literature in this kind of vacuum, as if we had no literary or cultural experience. We bring to any reading information about the period, the poet, the poetic tradition, the language, and from our critical experience we have a sense of the work's intentions, of what kind of thing it is doing. But Wimsatt and Beardsley do not dispute this; the core of their argument is that our ability to *use* this information depends upon our sense of its relevance, and that relevance can be established only in relation to the poem as a fact in

language. In proposing that the only *public* existence a work of literature has is its existence in language, they were stating an axiom of descriptive criticism. See also ANALYSIS, AUTHOR, DISCOURSE, EFFECT, NEW CRITICISM.

PM

interior monologue
see STREAM OF CONSCIOUSNESS

interpretant
see SEMIOTICS

interpretation
see ANALYSIS, HERMENEUTICS

intertextuality
see CREATION

irony
is a mode of discourse for conveying meanings different from—and usually opposite to—the professed or ostensible ones. There are several kinds of irony, though they fall into two major categories: situational and verbal. All irony, however, depends for its success on the exploitation of the distance between words or events and their CONTEXTS. Since the contexts of situational irony may be primarily social, moral, or metaphysical, irony can be further classified as comic or tragic, though these adjectives are in a sense inaccurate. In tragic irony the ostensible reasons for the hero's downfall, whether it be the anger of the gods or his own relentless pursuit of an ideal, are undercut by psychological explanations of a more mundane sort. Conrad's *Lord Jim* is a good example of this. Comic irony uses similar kinds of juxtaposition to describe and deflate the social aspirations of its protagonists. In both forms the pivotal character tends to be the *eiron* himself, a dissembler who brings two conflicting and contrasting worlds in sharp focus. Examples of such characters are Conrad's Marlow and P. G. Wodehouse's Jeeves. Without such characters there is a danger that an author's ironies will be completely missed, for, unlike the satirist, he tends to suppress any direct attitudes to his subject, and to rely on a shared set of assumptions or prejudices, for the establishment of a context.

It is, however, possible to introduce structural ironies without the use of an *eiron*. Typically, this is the form situational irony takes in plays, where narrators—concealed or otherwise—are more difficult to employ; hence the term *dramatic irony*. Here the *eiron* is replaced by the members of the audience who have been apprised of a character's real situation before he knows it himself, and who can therefore anticipate and enjoy the frustration of the ideal by the actual. Sophocles's *Oedipus Rex* uses multiple dramatic ironies to criticize naïve rationalism, by reversing all the protagonist's normal expectations. Oedipus in attempting to avoid his fate, acts in such a way as to seal it inexorably. Within this large irony many others operate both to reinforce Sophocles's view of life and to express it with maximum dramatic force. Dramatic irony can take many forms. For a more extended discussion see William Empson's *Seven Types of Ambiguity* (2nd ed., 1947), 38–47.

Verbal irony usually operates by exploiting deviations from syntactic or semantic norms, and the ability to recognize such irony depends upon an appreciation of the particular linguistic, or sometimes more general social or moral, context. In speech it is possible to indicate by tone of voice, that the word 'clever' in the sentence 'He's a clever chap' is to be understood to mean 'stupid', but as this cannot be said to be any of the meanings of the word 'clever', the writer has to convey his sense obliquely. Irony is thus an art of indirection and juxtaposition, relying for its success on such techniques as understatement, paradox, puns and other forms of wit in the expression of incongruities. In the following lines from Pope's *Rape of the Lock* the contrasts between heroic style and banal content reflect the opposition within the lines between the spiritual and the physical:

> Whether the nymph shall break Diana's law,
> Or some frail china jar receive a flaw;
> Or stain her honour, or her new brocade;
> Forget her prayers, or miss a masquerade.

Modern criticism has seen, in the ambiguities of the ironic mode, a response to experience particularly sympathetic. Like symbolism, allegory and metaphor, irony provides a means for unifying the apparent contradictions of experience, but is also uniquely able to assert the world's diversity. Cleanth Brooks's *The Well Wrought Urn* (1947) is one of the more influential modern studies which makes large claims for the prevalence and persistence of the ironic mode.

See William Empson, 'Tom Jones', *Kenyon Review*, 20 (1958) on double irony; Northrop Frye, *Anatomy of Criticism* (1957) on the *eiron* figure (adapted from Aristotle's *Ethics*); D. C. Muecke, *Irony* (1970).

BCL

K & L

katharsis
see CATHARSIS

kinetic
see LITERATURE

lament
see ELEGY

language
is, strictly speaking, not a critical term; but it is a concept which is central to one of the major disputes of modern criticism: does literature consist of language, or is language simply one component of literature? In Aristotle's enumeration of the six parts of tragedy, *lexis* (diction) is merely one component. The CHICAGO CRITICS extended this analysis to poetry, detecting four 'parts' in the lyric, among which 'diction' (= language) was said to be the least important. Elder Olson ('An outline of poetic theory' in R. S. Crane (ed.), *Critics and Criticism*, 1957) speaks of 'such embellishments as rhythm, ornamental language'—other examples of 'ornaments' are masques, pageants, progresses, in drama. Language may be decorative, but it is essentially a means, a medium: 'the words are the least important, in that they are governed and determined by every other element in the poem'.

It is curious that Olson gives unobservable elements such as 'choice', 'thought' and 'character' priority over language. He does grant that our access to these elements is through language, but he seems not to realize the implications of this concession: that our apprehension of the abstract structure and meaning of a piece of literature is determined by linguistic arrangements. An intentionalist view of literature might claim that the author's poetic decisions control choice of appropriate language, but this neglects the fact that language, once chosen, is out of the control of the author—it is public property and elicits public responses and perceptions: a word in a poem is not simply the *poem's* word, but the *language's* word also—it imports senses and connotations from contexts external to the poem. Thus, as psycholinguists and semanticists would agree, language controls conceptualization and hence apprehension of poetic structure. This has been the standpoint of the NEW CRITICS: in poetry, 'content' is inaccessible except in the terms laid down by 'form'. And as David Lodge has argued (*Language of Fiction*, 1966), there is no good reason to propose a different kind of theory for prose fiction. Language may exercise a particularly stringent control over our responses to lyric poetry because of the FOREGROUND-ING of surface structure, but this control, even if less powerful in fiction, cannot be qualitatively different: if language governs meaning, it does so in all its usages.

Although many modern critics have asserted the prime importance of language in literature, they have not wholly agreed on this question of different 'uses' of language. I. A. Richards, setting up a Romantic, affective theory of literature, distinguished two uses of language, the 'scientific' or 'referential' versus the 'poetic' or 'emotive'. His claim that only scientific language is used 'for the sake of the *reference*, true or false, that it causes' is an essential preliminary to any theory of the 'fictionality' of literature—truth conditions must be suspended (cf. BELIEF). Another influential literary-theoretical account of 'uses of language' is that propounded by the late Roman Jakobson. Jakobson distinguishes six uses of language—*emotive* (better, *expressive*), *conative, phatic, referential, metalingual* and *poetic*—according to the degree of importance of different constitutive factors of the communicative event: the referential function, for example, lays stress on the non-linguistic context (the 'world') referred to in communication, minimizing other factors such as the characteristics of speaker and addressee, and the actual structural form of the utterance. The 'poetic' function, on the other hand, invests attention precisely in the formal linguistic construction; and Jakobson offers a very illuminating formula (too complex to detail here) to explain the structural principle of poetic form. The validity of Jakobson's 'poetic principle' is not at issue here; what is questionable is the classification of 'functions'. A partition of functions of language which sets off the 'poetic' or 'literary' as a separate category can lead to neglect of linguistic features which do not fall under the criterion; and thus to an incomplete apprehension of the literary text (see R. Fowler, *Literature as Social Discourse*, 1981, Chs 9 and 10).

Fortunately, contemporary theorists of literature are increasingly ready to recognize the continuity of linguistic processes within and outside literature. Certainly, there are no *linguistic* criteria for distinguishing literature and non-literature (cf. LITERATURE). The consequence of these decisions—to grant priority to language and to see language in literature as not essentially different from the language of other texts—is that we may feed into literary criticism whatever insights we gain about language at large. Such insights, in the last fifty years, and particularly the last twenty-five, have been very considerable, resulting in a refined and rich debate over the theory of language; a detailed understanding of the principles of linguistic construction at different levels, particularly syntax and phonology; great strides in our empirical knowledge of different languages; massive advances in the understanding of the relations between language and thought, and language and society; and a sophisticated discussion of the relationships between linguistics and adjacent disciplines—education, psychology, sociology, anthropology, politics, artificial intelligence, literary theory, literary criticism. A small selection of good textbooks to give a flavour of various parts of contemporary linguistics might include N. Smith and D. Wilson, *Modern Linguistics: The Results of Chomsky's Revolution* (1979); J. Aitchison, *The Articulate Mammal* (2nd edn., 1983); W. Downes, *Language and Society* (1984); J. Lyons, *Semantics* (1977); M. A. K. Halliday, *Language as Social Semiotic* (1978).

The linguistic study of literature, known as 'stylistics' (often inappropriately; cf. STYLE) or 'linguistic criticism', has advanced in several ways over the last twenty years or so. It has built on the work of Mukařovský and of Jakobson to make powerful contributions to literary theory (cf. FORMALISM, STRUCTURALISM). It has added substantially to our knowledge of some aspects of literary structure which are manifestly linguistic in character (e.g. METAPHOR, METRE); and some less obvious topics such as SYNTAX have been made more salient to the critic. The best way to sample these diverse contributions would be to browse in some of the collections of specialized papers which have been published, e.g. T. A. Sebeok (ed.), *Style in Language* (1960), especially the seminal paper 'Linguistics and poetics' by Jakobson; D. C. Freeman (ed.), *Linguistics and Literary Style* (1970) and *Essays in Modern Stylistics* (1981); S. Chatman (ed.), *Literary Style: A Symposium* (1971); R. Fowler (ed.), *Style and Structure in Literature* (1975); R. Carter (ed.), *Language and Literature* (1982); M. K. L. Ching, M. C. Haley and R. F. Lunsford (eds.), *Linguistic Perspectives on Literature* (1980). See also E. C. Traugott and M. L. Pratt, *Linguistics for Students of Literature* (1980).

Linguistic studies have also focused on specific genres of literary writing. For poetry, see G. N. Leech, *A Linguistic Guide to English Poetry* (1969); M. Riffaterre, *Semiotics of Poetry* (1978). For the novel, see R. Fowler, *Linguistics and the Novel* (2nd ed., 1983); G. N. Leech and M. H. Short, *Style in Fiction* (1981). For drama see D. Burton, *Dialogue and Discourse* (1980).

Finally, the most promising development, as far as linguistic criticism is concerned, has been the recent willingness to theorize literature as DISCOURSE. In this approach language is regarded as far more than formal structure and communicated ideas: it is seen as an interpersonal practice with causes and effects in social structure, and ideological implications. The Linguistic criticism on discourse premisses is a historically grounded practice of analysis, seeking to interpret texts with reference to their and our cultural contexts and ideological systems. In this approach the analysis of linguistic form, and reference to context, are integrated rather than divorced as in most modern criticism. See R. Fowler, *Literature as Social Discourse* (1981); *Linguistic Criticism* (1986). Also M. L. Pratt, *Toward a Speech Act Theory of Literary Discourse* (1977); A. Easthope, *Poetry as Discourse* (1983).

RGF

lexis
see DICTION, LANGUAGE

lisible
see PLEASURE

literary mode of production
The concept of a 'literary mode of production' has been developed by modern MARXIST CRITICISM to explain the ways in which all literary writing depends upon social institutions and relations. Any form of production draws upon certain material forces (in the case of writing, paper, printing, publishing technology and so on), but these material forces are themselves part of a set of social relations between producers, intermediaries and consumers. The social relations between a tribal bard, his chief and his audience will differ from those between an eighteenth-century poet, his aristocratic patron and his readers; and these in turn are contrastable with the often isolated literary producer of our own day, who produces his work as a market commodity for an audience whom he does not meet. Any society may contain a set of different, even conflicting, literary modes of production: the social relations between the popular modern novelist, his publishers and his readers contrast with those between the writers, directors, actors and audiences of a political theatre group. Certain literary modes of production may be merely sub-sectors of what we might term the 'general' mode of economic production in society as a whole: modern-day writing is largely part of the capitalist publishing industry. But other literary modes of production may represent survivals from earlier societies, or may try to prefigure new kinds of social relations in society as a whole.

The concept of a 'literary mode of production' does not merely belong to what is termed the 'sociology of literature'. It is not a purely external fact about literary writing, as the colour of a dust-jacket may be. On the contrary, it is part of the critical analysis of literature itself. For every work of literature, in however indirect a fashion, implies how and by whom it was written, and how and by whom it is to be read. Every work posits an 'implied author' and an 'implied reader', establishes tacit contracts and alliances between itself and its audience. In order to be accepted as 'literature' at all, the work must be a certain kind of product within certain social institutions; most critics would not regard graffiti, which is indubitably a mode of writing (often of considerable interest and value) produced for an audience, as an acceptable literary topic for academic study. What counts as 'literature', in other words, is already a matter of social (and ideological) definition; a piece of writing may be 'literary' for one age and not for another. 'Non-literary' writing may be treated in a 'literary' way, or *vice versa*.

The very definitions and criteria of 'literature', then, belong to a set of values and ideas embedded in a literary mode of production. In turn, the values and social relations of that mode of production will leave their imprint on the works it produces. It is thus very difficult to distinguish an 'external', historical study of literary works from an 'internal', critical one. See also CREATION, CRITICISM, LITERATURE.

See T. Eagleton, *Criticism and Ideology* (1976); P. Macherey, *A Theory of Literary Production* (1978).

TE

literature

Editors of literary dictionaries have often failed to offer a definition of the central collective term (though definitions sometimes slip in under 'fiction' or 'poetry', in the generalized senses of those words). This diffidence is not surprising, since the greatest literary theorists, from Plato down, have failed to find agreement on the nature of their subject-matter. But even though no complete definition may present itself, there are some criteria which provide interesting insights into the way 'literature' as a cultural phenomenon is regarded.

I will restrict myself to the generally current usage of the term 'literature': that is to say, imaginative compositions, nowadays mainly printed but earlier (and still, in some cultures) oral, whether dramatic, metrical or prose in form. This is a relatively recent usage, having general acceptance in the European languages only from the nineteenth century. Earlier senses have been less restricted: e.g. the body of writings in a language, artistic or not; and particularly, the *study* of such a corpus of written materials. For an account of the history of the term, see René Wellek, 'The name and nature of comparative literature' in *Discriminations* (1970), especially pp. 3–13.

No 'discovery procedure' is needed for literature. Usually, the corpus of literature in any particular community is recognized by that culture.

We are much less likely to ask 'is this literature?' than 'why do I call this "literature"? what holds the category together?'. Borderline cases are easier to resolve than at first appears, and their manner of resolution is instructive. William McGonagall may be a bad poet, but he is clearly a poet: there is craftsmanship, a sense of tradition, even if both qualities are precariously fulfilled in his work. (We can say he is a poor artist, but that is not the same as asserting that he is not an artist: EVALUATION is quite independent of identification as literature.) But the telephone book, though highly structured, fails to be literature because it is 'real': a list of people, addresses, numerical codes for calling these actual people. Contrast Scott Fitzgerald's list of Gatsby's visitors in *The Great Gatsby* (1925), a parodic manipulation in art of a form from mundane life. So the criteria seem to be of different kinds, some formal and some existential; but they apply fairly clearly in individual cases.

We may seek the nature of literature from many points of view, some intrinsic and some extrinsic. Extrinsically, we will certainly want to regard it as a definite cultural institution, an interrelated set of SEMIOTIC systems. We can note the values a society assigns to its literature: these vary from society to society and from age to age, ranging from serious-ness, ritual, to frivolity, verbal play (and different GENRES have different expectations). Literature is commonly distinguished from linguistic ephemera, effort being expended to preserve it in script or oral tradition; it is regarded as timeless ('not for an age . . .') or at least as a potent tool in the transmission and preservation of traditional values; it is often associated with an élite, either conservative or revolutionary, or with an influential and self-esteeming bourgeoisie. Cultural attitudes towards literature such as these are empirical: they may be derived from anthropological and sociological observations. A different series of extrinsic criteria involves speculation about the relationship between literature and individuals. In relation to authors, works have been claimed to be either *expressive*, gestures from the writer's personal character and perceptions, (Longinus, Wordsworth) or, contrariwise, *impersonal*, creations which efface their creators as individuals (Yeats, Eliot, NEW CRITICS). In relation to the reader, literature has been supposed to have many different functions and effects. Theorists who assume impersonality in respect to origin generally assume *stasis* in respect to effect: if the audience is 'moved' by the aesthetic experience, it is not moved to action (so propaganda, PORNOGRAPHY, etc. are not art because *kinetic*); the experience is of a contained, 'unreal' sort, irrelevant to personal behaviour. On the quality of stasis, the aesthet-ician would generally concur with the law courts: that which pumps our adrenalin is not art. (Cf. AUTHOR, READER, ART.)

More specific theories of literary EFFECT have been proposed: the various sophistications of a concept of PLEASURE, or I. A. Richards's belief that literature causes stability, harmonization of impulses, in a successful reader (*Principles of Literary Criticism*, 1924), or the doctrine of CATHARSIS, the essentially *harmless* release of emotions. Such theories proliferate, and escalate: pressed to the extreme, they lead to a belief that literature can cleanse and save society (Arnold, Leavis)—but here the theory has undermined itself, since on that interpretation literature hardly differs from propaganda or sermons. If literature is a form of persuasion (as the RHETORICAL tradition claims) there must be supplementary criteria specifying exactly what kind of persuasion it is—e.g. persuasion to adopt a certain 'world-view' but not persuasion literally to *fight* to change the world.

Fictionality is one such criterion (see FICTION, IMITATION). Evidently literature 'imitates', 'depicts', 'represents', 'presents', 'embodies' people, objects, societies, ideas: Mr Micawber, Middlemarch, Howards End, Camus's plague. Literature is not alone in this respect— the telephone book, an inventory of the contents of my house, the service manual for my car, are also representational. But my neighbours listed in the directory enjoy spatio-temporal existence, Mr Micawber does not; thus the concept of imitation is different for *David Copperfield* and for the Norwich Area telephone directory. Fiction is *creative*: its creations are felt to be real, but are actually abstract and therefore cannot impinge on one's worldly experience (despite the beliefs and lusts of naïve readers). Literature is irresponsible in the sense of amoral. Abstractions wrought of words stand at a decent aesthetic distance from the reader: he can 'love' Mrs Wilcox or Molly Bloom or Lolita, but never make love to her, for he can never get around the prohibitive sign which reads 'this road does not go through to action; fictitious' (J. C. Ransom). Compare Archibald Macleish's dictum that a poem must be 'equal to: not true' (*Ars Poetica*). Considerations of truth and reality are not relevant to literature; but my car handbook *must* be true, since it is designed to guide actions.

On the basis of such observations, literature is traditionally distinguished from science, history, philosophy, etc. The distinction can be made with regard to non-literary arts, too: ART is opposed to non-art. Literature is at the same time like the other arts (in terms of FORM or STRUCTURE) and unlike them (in terms of LANGUAGE). Now we appeal to intrinsic criteria, and 'poem' creeps in as the general term, inviting us to substitute a focus on the individual literary construct for the 'extrinsic' focus on literature as a cultural institution or as an influence on the psyche. 'Poem' retains its etymological connotations (Greek *poesis*, 'making') and evokes the literary work as a 'made thing', an artefact, a single, unique, construct; a hard enduring object (and not a pale reflection of something else). As soon as we have achieved a definite conception of the poem as a single, coherent, aesthetic object, we are instantly involved in ontological speculations: what mode of being does a literary work enjoy? Is it, in fact, an independent entity, or is it located in, for example, the writer's or reader's consciousness? (see EFFECT, INTENTION, LANGUAGE). If it has a mode of separate being, what are its 'internal' characteristics? Various styles of criteria have found fashion in attempts at the intrinsic definition of literature or of particular kinds of literature. The CHICAGO CRITICS avoided an overall definition, but erected a scheme of 'parts', abstract structural components (CHARAC-TER, DICTION, PLOT, etc.); a particular selection from this set of components, in an appropriate order of importance, serving to define the nature of each GENRE. Thus the complete field of literature is, allegedly, mapped out by a set of characterizations of the genres. The intrinsic quality (if it exists) remains undefined. A quite different approach, though dependent on equally abstract notions, results from assuming that any literary work is literary by virtue of possessing certain qualities which are common to the arts as a whole (cf. AESTHE-TICS, and the recommended reading below): 'balance', 'composition', 'structure' and so on. My reading of general aesthetics leads me to suspect that such properties are inevitably, and regrettably, general and mystical by virtue of simplification away from the inexorable con-straints of the different art media. A definition of literature derived from general aesthetics would certainly have to be augmented by criteria which make reference to the linguistic medium.

The search for intrinsic linguistic criteria for the essence of literature intensified in Russian, Czech and French Formalism and Structur-alism, with writers such as Jakobson, Mukařovský, Todorov and Culler making strong, illuminating claims. This has been the most important and influential development in modern theory of literature, and I hope that my brief mention here does not suggest inadequate recognition. The ideas are dealt with fully in the articles on FORMALISM, STRUCTUR-ALISM, and particularly POETICS, which also list major titles for further reading.

For the older traditions see M. C. Beardsley, *Aesthetics: Problems in the Philosophy of Criticism* (1958); M. Bradbury and D. J. Palmer (eds), *Contemporary Criticism* (1970); E. Vivas and M. Krieger (eds), *The Problems of Aesthetics* (1953); M. Weitz (ed.), *Problems in Aesthe-tics* (2nd ed., 1970); R. Wellek and A. Warren, *Theory of Literature* (3rd ed., 1963); W. K. Wimsatt, Jr, and C. Brooks, *Literary Criticism: A Short History* (1957).

RGF

logocentrism
see DECONSTRUCTION, FEMINIST CRITICISM

lyric

That the lyric was originally a song set to the lyre, and later to other
musical instruments, is worth remembering now only because the
post-Renaissance lyric, or lyrical passage, though not often intended to
be sung, nevertheless tends to be relatively mellifluous in sound and
rhythm and to have a flowingly repetitious syntax that lends itself to
expansive, often exclamatory, expressions of intense personal joy,
sorrow or contemplative insight. A sixteenth-century English example
is Thomas Wyatt's 'Fforget not yet', from which these two verses are
taken:

> Fforget not yet the gret assays,
> The cruell wrong, the skornfull ways,
> The paynfull pacyence in denays.
> > Fforget not yet!
>
> Fforget not yet, forget not thys,
> How long ago hathe ben and ys
> The mynd, that neuer ment amys,
> > Fforget not yet.

The lyric poem, usually short, was often constructed on a single mood.
But the twentieth-century lyric is frequently more complex, allowing
for contrastive themes and for changes, even ambivalences, of attitude,
though remaining in an emotional rather than intellectual mode. A
contemporary example, by the Irish poet Richard Weber, shows a
technical relationship with Wyatt's song but greater complexity:

> As my eyes moved thoughtfully
> Over your face
> And your eyes moved thoughtlessly
> Into place
> I knew that all I could not say
> Had been said before
> And left no trace.

British poetry has on the whole developed in the direction Pater
suggested (favourable to lyricism) rather than in that which Arnold
suggested (favourable to the long poem). Life seen as a sequence of
intensely-felt moments, rather than a structure of interrelated and
assessed experiences, tends to encourage the use of the first person,
vivid images and 'local life' at the expense of architectonics, anecdotal
narrative and intellectual abstraction. The effect on criticism (on, say,
Leavis's criteria for evaluating Milton) or on poetry (even our longest
modern poems tend to be fragmentary, like 'The Waste Land', or built
out of poem-sequences, like Ted Hughes's 'Crow') makes it desirable to

redress the balance by suggesting that the pressure of feeling *and* intellect which the long poem accommodates has considerable human value, and is due to the fact that, while it can avail itself of all the devices of lyricism, the long poem builds up, in addition, a larger structure of controlling tensions and so may achieve a more inclusive intensity than that afforded by isolated 'peak moments'.

See H. J. C. Grierson, *Lyrical Poetry of the Nineteenth Century* (1929); C. M. Ing, *Elizabethan Lyrics* (1951); J. L. Kinneavy, *A Study of Three Contemporary Theories of Lyric Poetry* (1957); Norman Maclean, 'From action to image: theories of the lyric in the eighteenth century' in R. S. Crane (ed.), *Critics and Criticism* (1952); Edwin Muir, *The Estate of Poetry* (1962); Gilbert Murray, *The Classical Tradition in Poetry* (1930).

AAAC

M

mannerism

has three different, but related usages: as a fairly narrow stylistic term; as a historical period; as a broad literary mode.

A mannered style is marked by obtrusive 'mannerisms' or peculiarities: often an elaborate syntax and elevated diction, remote from a colloquial register. Since the manner remains the same irrespective of the matter, the twin dangers of monotony and bathos threaten. Mannered writers such as Sir Thomas Browne or Walter Pater are better taken in small doses. But a mannered style, in drawing attention to presentation as distinct from representation, may bring aesthetic gains. A test-case is perhaps the late work of Henry James: boring, brilliant—or both?

By analogy with the mannerist painting of the late sixteenth and early seventeenth centuries, mannerism may, as a term for a 'period', designate the transition between Renaissance and Baroque literature. The widespread mannered styles of the period such as Euphuism and Gongorism might be called mannerist, rather than just mannered.

As a literary mode rather than a period, mannerism largely overlaps with BAROQUE. Indeed Curtis substitutes mannerism for baroque altogether, but extends its reference to mean the dialectical antithesis of classicism, in whatever period. He defines mode in terms of style. Mannerist style is hermetic and ingenious, full of paradox and puns, asyndeton, hyperbole and pleonasm. For other critics mannerism means, more dubiously, a style reflecting a psychological type or sociological pressures. The mannerist spirit is calculating yet passionate, disharmonious and modern. In English literature the META-PHYSICAL poets are the archetypal mannerists and parallels are drawn or denied between seventeenth- and twentieth-century mannerism, as, for example, in Joyce. The term suffers from the reductive tendency of all such vast generalizations.

See E. R. Curtius, trans. W. Trask, *European Literature and the Latin Middle Ages* (1953); Giorgio Melchiori, 'The tightrope-walkers', *Studies in Mannerism in Modern English Literature* (1967); W. E. Yuill, 'Literary potholing' in *German Life and Letters*, 14 (1966).

EJB

manners

Literature has always sought to define the relationship between character and environment. The social context of behaviour makes visible the inner conflicts of men. Thus Hamlet's antic posturing is defined not only against his soliloquizing but also against the *manners* of the court. This becomes of more central importance when the society represented is *aware* of the rules by which it exists; when they have attained the status of social conventions. Societies create patterns of behaviour by which success or failure can be measured, and the writer, too, must react to these either by conforming to them or by attacking and exposing them. These conventions are most revered in periods of high social mobility, when outward behaviour becomes the 'sign' of personal success and social respectability. In such periods literature may become over-preoccupied with the recording of mannerisms and behaviour patterns, e.g. in some Victorian novels, such as those of Mrs Gaskell.

The term *manners* is most frequently employed in the phrase 'comedy of manners', usually referring to Restoration comedy (Etherege, Wycherley, Congreve) and sometimes by analogy to the work of writers like Oscar Wilde. These plays explore a universe where all values are bound up with appearances, where honour is synonymous with reputation and truth identified with a glib tongue and a steady eye. The veil of conventions shields the action from anarchy and despair. By their success or failure at life's intricate play characters separate into true wits or gulls. They, and we, learn to live with the precarious balance of forces which govern the way of the world. See also CULTURE, SOCIETY.

GG

Marxist criticism

is distinguished from all forms of idealist, FORMALIST and aestheticist criticism by its belief that 'Literature' is a social and material practice, related to other social practices, and finally explicable only in these terms. It differs from other historical or sociological approaches to literature mainly in its view of the nature of history itself. For Marxism, 'history' does not form a single category or seamless whole: it is grasped, rather, as a field of conflicting interests and forces (cf. CONTRADICTION). Dominant among those conflicts is the epochal struggle between social classes—between those who, by virtue of controlling a society's economic production, can usually dominate its cultural and intellectual production as well, and those exploited classes whose labour makes this privileged situation possible in the first place.

In such class societies, all intellectual production is likely to bear the indelible print of these fundamental material struggles; and in so far as it does, it can be said to be 'ideological'. 'Literature' is for Marxism a particular kind of signifying practice, which together with other such practices goes to make up what may be termed an ideological formation. Such a formation is always complex and contradictory, but it is never innocent. Its impulse is to stabilize and unify the various meanings, values and representations in which a society lives out its own experience, in ways which help to secure and reproduce the power of its ruling class. 'Literature', then, might be said to represent the classstruggle at a specific level; in writing, reading, interpreting and evaluating we are already, consciously or not, engaged in a struggle over linguistic meanings which is intimately related to systems of power.

'Vulgar Marxist' criticism has accepted this conclusion with a vengeance, reducing literary texts to a mere reflex or symptom of history, content to determine the political 'tendency' of the work. The major traditions of Marxist criticism, however, while firmly locating literature in its historical context, have nevertheless granted it a high degree of 'relative autonomy'. It is never merely a 'reflection' or 'expression' of historical forces, but a specific, highly codified social practice with its own conditions of material production and reception (cf. LITERARY MODE OF PRODUCTION), its own conventions, devices and histories (cf. CREATION). Its ideological significance is to be sought not merely in its abstractable political content, but more rewardingly in its *forms*—in its narrative structures and generic rules, its habits of language and characterization, its modes of imagery and technical mechanisms. 'History' and 'ideology' are not merely the extraneous outworks of a literary text: as the intimately informing pressures at work within its very capacity to signify, they are constitutive of its very being.

Historically speaking, Marxist criticism might be roughly if conveniently divided into two main types. On the one hand has been what one might broadly term a *genetic* criticism, concerned to relate the literary work to its historical and ideological conditions of possibility. The scattered literary writings of Marx and Engels themselves, drawing as they do on the aesthetics of Hegel, fall into this category, as do Lenin's well-known articles on Leo Tolstoy, or Trotsky's superbly sensitive accounts of his Russian poetic contemporaries. The Hungarian Georg Lukács, perhaps the most eminent Marxist critic of all, also belongs to this lineage: his work aims to identify the complex relations between certain historical epochs and the rise and fall of certain literary forms such as REALISM. The great bourgeois realists, still able to 'totalize' history into a complex significance by deploying characters and events at once sharply individuated and historically 'typical', give way at a point of political crisis to the disturbed, private, more fragmentary forms of MODERNISM. In the work of Lukács's disciple Lucien Goldmann, Marxist and STRUCTURALIST themes are interwoven to provide a similarly genetic account of the flourishing of French seventeenth-century tragedy.

Lukács and Goldmann inhabit an Hegelian, 'humanistic' current of Marxism for which many of the traditional categories of bourgeois aesthetics (unity, truth, beauty and so on) are still valid. The later work of Louis Althusser, Pierre Macherey and others has interrogated these assumptions, grasping the literary text as divided, uneven and contradictory, forced by its complicities with ideology into certain revealing gaps, silences and absences whereby it 'deconstructs' itself and betrays its ideological hand. Such critics have also been more concerned with literature as a form of analysable 'production' than as a mysterious, author-centred 'creation'.

But for both Lukács and Althusser, 'Literature' itself remains a largely unproblematic term—as it does indeed for the Hegelian Marxists of the German Frankfurt School (notably Theodor Adorno and Herbert Marcuse), who find in the very forms of art a spiritual transcendence of a sordidly class-bound society. They differ thus from the second major Marxist cultural heritage, which concerns itself less with the genesis of the art-work than with its political uses and effects, less with the literary product itself than with the social relations and cultural institutions from which it emerges. The aim of this tradition is to transform or dismantle the very meaning of the term 'literature' by transforming the material means of cultural production in society as a whole. Prominent among such revolutionary cultural workers were the Bolshevik avant-garde artists (Futurists, Formalists, Constructivists, etc.) of the 1920s, who sought not merely a new meaning *in* art but a new meaning *of* art, fashioning new social relations between artists and audiences, collapsing the barriers between art and social life, and insisting on new media of cultural communication. Crushed by Stalinism, their great inheritors were the revolutionary artists and critics of Weimar Germany (Erwin Piscator, Bertolt Brecht, Walter Benjamin), and to some degree the Marxist SURREALISTS of France gathered around André Breton.

Contemporary Marxist criticism has revived or sustained these influences, rejecting some timeless notion of the 'literary' for an insistence that what counts as 'literary' in the first place is always a matter of ideological and institutional definition. The 'para-Marxist' work of Raymond Williams in England has been central in this respect. But other influences have been at work too: PSYCHOANALYSIS (how are readers constituted as collective or individual subjects by the unconscious meanings of literary texts, and in what political direction?); 'reception theory' in a political context; and SEMIOTICS and sociolinguistics (the understanding of literary works as social codes and DISCOURSES, inseparable from ideological modes of perception). For contemporary Marxist criticism, there is no isolated 'literature' to be ideologically examined; what we have instead is a set of LITERARY MODES OF PRODUCTION, embedded in the dominant social relations of capitalism, which may themselves be transformed by political practice to produce new meanings of 'literature' and new audiences. The literary works of the past must be studied in their historical conditions; but, more importantly, they must be constantly rewritten, in order to be put to different kinds of political use.

See further H. Arvon, *Marxist Esthetics* (1973); L. Baxandall and S. Morawski, (eds), *Marx and Engels on Literature and Art* (1973); W. Benjamin, *Illuminations* (1973), *One-Way Street and Other Essays* (1979), *Understanding Brecht* (1973); T. Bennett, *Formalism and Marxism* (1979); P. Demetz, *Marx, Engels and the Poets* (1967); T. Eagleton, *Marxism and Literary Criticism* (1976); F. Jameson, *Marxism and Form* (1971); M. Jay, *The Dialectical Imagination* (1973); G. Lukács, *The Historical Novel* (1962), *The Meaning of Contemporary Realism* (1963); R. Taylor (ed.), *Aesthetics and Politics* (1977); V. N. Voloshinov, *Marxism and the Philosophy of Language* (1973); R. Williams, *Marxism and Literature* (1977).

TE

mask
see PERSONA

metafiction
see FICTION

metaphor
and simile are easier to illustrate than to define. In the phrase

The barge she sat in, like a burnish'd throne
Burn'd on the water

as well as much else, there is both a metaphor, 'the barge . . . burn'd on the water', and a simile, 'the barge . . . like a burnish'd throne'.

In general, a metaphor ascribes to some thing or action X a property Y which it could not literally possess in that context. Responding to this anomaly, the hearer or reader infers that what is meant is that X is Z, where Z is some property suggested by Y, X or the interaction of the two, that can be literally true of X in some context. A simile, using one of several possible syntactic devices of comparison (. . . as . . . as, . . . like . . ., etc.) states explicitly that there is a similarity (Z) between X and Y though it usually does not state explicitly what this similarity is, and thus the hearer is likewise forced to infer what Z might be in that context.

The study of metaphor generates a great deal of terminology, often itself metaphorical. The most firmly established terms for describing a metaphor are perhaps those of I. A. Richards (*The Philosophy of Rhetoric*, 1936) and Max Black (*Models and Metaphors*, 1962). Richards describes a metaphor as resulting from the interaction of a 'vehicle' and a 'tenor . . . the underlying idea or principal subject which the vehicle or figure means'. 'Tenor' seems to be used by Richards (as Black points out) to mean either X, or the proposition that X is Z, while 'vehicle' seems to correspond to Y. Black himself uses 'principal subject' (X) and 'subsidiary subject' (Y); more recently, 'primary' and 'secondary' subject ('More about metaphor', 1979).

Metaphors as elliptical comparisons

There is a tradition, traceable to Aristotle, which maintains that there is no important logical difference between metaphors and similes, and that metaphors can be regarded as either similes or literal comparisons with the explicit comparative particles suppressed. Against this view many people feel that, in the first place, metaphors are usually more effective than similes or comparisons, suggesting that there is a real difference between them (Black, 'More about metaphor'), or further, that there is a distinction to be drawn between them in terms of their truth conditions (and thus a difference of meaning). Thus J. R. Searle argues that a sentence like 'Richard is a gorilla' might say something true about Richard (viz. that he is coarse and brutal) whereas in reality, gorillas could be charming and gentle in their behaviour, making 'Richard resembles a gorilla in his behavior' false (Searle, 'Metaphor').

The paraphrasability of metaphors

We usually find no difficulty in paraphrasing dead metaphors (those which have become wholly or partly lexicalized, like 'tying up a few loose ends' or 'swim like a fish'), but the consensus seems to be that fully satisfactory paraphrase of a live and effective metaphor is not generally possible (see especially Davidson, 'What metaphors mean'). This is often taken to argue against the 'truncated simile' view, and Davidson, in particular, claims that metaphors have not just an elusive or incomplete literal meaning, but no meaning at all, over and above their false or anomalous one. To the extent that this view rests on the difficulty of satisfactory paraphrase, it would, of course, be more convincing if our experience was not that paraphrase of ordinary literal sentences is often difficult to achieve to everyone's satisfaction.

Creativity and interaction

The view that metaphors work by a process of 'interaction' between X and Y is a popular one, and surely true, though the precise nature of this interaction needs further clarification. There is a stronger thesis, argued for by Black, that metaphors are 'creative', by which he means that rather than just drawing our attention to some similarity already existing, they 'create' a new similarity (a possibility which, ironically, his own theory finds it difficult to accommodate; cf. P. Ricoeur, 'The metaphorical process as cognition, imagination and feeling'). It is certainly the case that people can often find some aspect to the interpretation of a word in a metaphor that they may not be able to find in the word in isolation. But as we have no very good way of delimiting what counts as part of the 'meaning' of a word, it is difficult to know whether this is evidence for the creativity thesis, or for the view that there is no sharp distinction between word meaning and factual belief. This is complicated by the fact that people are inclined to say retrospectively that the aspect of meaning focused on in the metaphor may well have been an unnoticed regular part of the meaning of the word. If there are cases where the meaning of a metaphor is not derivable from the meanings of the words in it, it may well be that the meaning is derived from the mechanisms of conversational implicature (see H. P. Grice, 'Logic and conversation' in P. Cole and J. L. Morgan (eds), *Syntax and Semantics* Vol. 3, *Speech Acts* (1975).

The literature on metaphor is massive. T. Hawkes, *Metaphor* (1972), oriented towards literary approaches, is a useful starting point. The books by Richards and by Black cited above are modern classics, which have each generated a large secondary literature. Useful recent collections are A. Ortony (ed.), *Metaphor and Thought* (1979) and S. Sacks (ed.), *On Metaphor* (1979). The articles in Ortony (which has a large bibliography) are views from Anglo-American linguistics, philosophy, and psychology; included are the papers by Black and by Searle cited above. Sacks represents a variety of literary and philosophical standpoints, and includes Davidson's and Ricoeur's papers. C. Brooke-Rose, *A Grammar of Metaphor* (1958) is a useful work on the syntax of metaphorical expressions in literature. See also SIMILE.

SGP

metaphysical

Dr Johnson's observation in *The Life of Cowley* (1779) that 'about the beginning of the seventeenth century appeared a race of writers that may be termed the metaphysical poets' gave currency to a label that is convenient though imprecise. Before Johnson, Dryden had remarked in 1693 that Donne's love poetry 'affects the metaphysics', and in Donne's own lifetime William Drummond of Hawthornden complained of a new poetical fashion for 'Metaphysical Ideas and Scholastical Quiddities'. The twentieth-century interest in this 'race of writers', which after Donne includes Herbert, Crashaw, Vaughan and Marvell, was promoted chiefly by H. J. C. Grierson's anthology, *Metaphysical Lyrics and Poems of the Seventeenth Century* (1921) and by T. S. Eliot's essay, 'The Metaphysical Poets', originally a review of that anthology. Modern admiration for the intellectual agility and stylistic complexity of this poetry, for its analytical and ironic modes, makes a curious contrast with the disparaging overtones originally attached to the term 'metaphysical'. But the modern rediscovery of the metaphysicals was part of a reaction to the Romantic tradition of nineteenth-century poetry, and T. S. Eliot's critical interest was closely related to the 'modern' qualities of his own poetry in that period.

As Grierson pointed out, 'to call these poets "the school of Donne" or "metaphysical" poets may easily mislead if one takes either phrase in too full a sense'. Direct imitation of Donne is not the main feature of most metaphysical poetry, nor is it 'metaphysical' in the sense of being philosophical. It is essentially the poetry of 'wit', in the seventeenth-century sense of wit as the capacity to recognize similarity in disparity, and to combine playfulness with seriousness. Thus the metaphysical CONCEIT, of which the best known example is Donne's comparison of two lovers to a pair of compasses (in 'A Valediction Forbidding Mourning') turns upon a surprising and ingenious analogy between apparently unrelated areas of experience. It is produced not by the arbitrariness of free association or the irrational process of the unconscious mind, but by the alertness of a mind accustomed to think in terms of correspondences and to reason by analogy. In this respect the 'metaphysic' underlying metaphysical poetry is a traditional but by then obsolescent conception of an ordered universe in which correspondences were held to exist between all planes of being. The metaphysical conceit, of which Dr Johnson said that 'the most heterogeneous ideas are yoked by violence together', characteristically forms part of an ingeniously paradoxical argument in which immediacy of feeling is apprehended through conceptual analogies rather than in sensory images.

Other notable features of metaphysical poetry include a dramatic sense of situation, a plain rather than ornate diction, an elliptical and condensed syntax, a strong tension between the symmetries of metrical form and the asymmetrical rhythms of speech and thought, and a capacity for abrupt shifts of tone. Not all metaphysical poetry possesses these qualities in the same degree; on the other hand, they are also found in the Jacobean drama, and in the prose of the period. The attempt to produce a consistent or exclusive definition of metaphysical poetry is therefore less profitable than a flexible understanding which obscures neither the distinctions between individual poets nor the properties of 'wit' common to the period as a whole. See also CONCEIT, WIT.

See T. S. Eliot, 'The Metaphysical Poets', *Selected Essays* (1961); F. R. Leavis, *Revaluation* (1962); J. A. Mazzeo, *Renaissance and Seventeenth-Century Studies* (1964); R. Tuve, *Elizabethan and Metaphysical Imagery* (1961); G. Williamson, *The Donne Tradition* (1961).

DJP

metre

If we are presented with a sequence of events, we tend to perceive them *rhythmically*: they seem to fall into patterns, whatever their actual temporal relationships might be. This is true of linguistic experiences. Hearing English sentences, we feel that the most prominent syllables recur at about the same time-interval, regardless of the number of intervening light syllables. VERSE is metered as well as rhythmical: there is a metrical superstructure over the rhythm. An additional level of phonetic organization gathers the rhythmical groups into metrical units—lines. In prose, the rhythm continues sequentially as long as the text lasts, but verse is chopped up into regularly repeated metrical units. (It is a nice question whether there can be a one-line poem.)

Metre emerges from the numerical control of rhythm: it entails counting. Classical French verse counts syllables; typically, twelve define the line. Anglo-Saxon counts stresses, four to a line, ignoring the number of light syllables. Modern English measures are based on syllabic *and* stress patterning: the paradigm iambic pentameter has five strong stresses—the even syllables out of a total of ten, with the odd ones light. Classical metres were equally complex—syllables were either long or short, and both were counted. In principle, any phonological feature of a language may provide the basis for metre; but the features available vary from language to language. Length of syllable is phonologically inactive in English, so it makes no sense to talk about long and short syllables in English metres; in fact, conventional prosodic analysis is meaningless in so far as it relies on such terms.

Scansion is analysis of verse lines by stating the distribution of the metrically significant features; it displays the design the poet works to, and a set of idealized expectations by the reader:

```
x    /    x   /  x /  x   /    x  /
```
The Sylphs/thro' mys/tic maz/es, guide/ their way.

(Pope)

For a line like this, the reader expects five pairs ('feet') of light and heavy syllables. Actually, his experience is much more complex than this neat up-and-down model suggests. Compare:

Before, behind, between, above, below
(Donne)
Unfolded transitory qualities
(Wordsworth)

both instances of the same verse design, but radically different in texture. In the first, the natural stress-patterns of the words fulfil exactly the reader's prosodic expectations, his 'metrical set'; in the second, the word- and phrase-stresses run against the expected pattern, smoothing out the stress-contrasts of the verse design so that there are only three dominant accents. The Pope line presents a middle stage, a delicate syncopation of the prose rhythm against the verse design. Note the way the words *mystic* and *mazes* run across the foot boundaries, bridging the junctures between the second and third, and third and fourth, feet. The interest of metre, it seems, lies in just this tension of the rhythm of prose played against the more stylized norms of metre. We cannot neglect the normal stress-patterns of speech without destroying meaning; at the same time, we throw our prose experience into fruitful conflict with the regularizing metre. Since the stress-patterns of language are infinitely variable, so is the experience of metrical tension. The complexity of the verse experience demands a proportionately discriminating analytic apparatus. The abstract metrical patterns described and classified by the older historians of metre (G. Sainsbury, *History of English Prosody*, 1906–10; T. S. Osmond, *English Metrists*, 1921) give too little information, failing to capture the intricate interplay between the reader's expectations of verse accents or 'beats' and the linguistic realities of ordinary stress. Very few of the older prosodists managed to convey the 'feel' of verse (Robert Bridges, *Milton's Prosody*, 1921, is a brilliant exception). At the other extreme, pure phonetic expositions of verse performances tell us too much—in the physical detail, we lose the abstract scheme which orders the phonetic facts (see Wilbur Schramm, *Approaches to a Science of Verse*, 1935). Contemporary techniques of *phonemic* metrical analysis concentrate on a display which seeks to show the tension between prose rhythm and ideal metre. The aim is to present an account of the internal structure of lines as selections from the infinite repertoire of rhythm/verse design juxtapositions which a language affords.

See Seymour Chatman, *A Theory of Meter* (1965); Roger Fowler, ' "Prose rhythm" and metre', *Essays on Style and Language* (1966); Roger Fowler, 'What is metrical analysis?', *The Languages of Literature* (1971); Donald C. Freeman (ed.), *Linguistics and Literary Style* (1970) (the last three essays); Morris Halle and Samuel Jay Keyser, *English Stress* (1971); John Thompson, *The Founding of English Metre* (1961); W. K. Wimsatt and Monroe C. Beardsley, 'The Concept of Meter', *PMLA*, 74 (1959); W. K. Wimsatt (ed.), *Versification* (1972).

RGF

mimesis

see IMITATION, REALISM, TYPICALITY

mock-epic

In heroic epic, the extraordinary and the trivial can coexist and can be respected as part of one another; the trivial has a reassuring, integrative, anchoring function. However, in mock-epic (e.g. Butler's *Hudibras* 1662–78; Boileau's *Le Lutrin*, 1674; Pope's *Dunciad*, 1728; Zachariae's *Der Renommist*, 1744) the poet is less interested in an open-minded and discursive treatment than in the delights of intellectual penetration and dismissive speed; he leavens the even-paced equanimity of epic narration with the unmerciful self-assurance of personal satire. In the society he portrays, the trivial attempts to usurp the position of the extraordinary but manages only to make its pretensions and unrelieved concern with itself extraordinary; in mock-epic the ritualistic becomes the fussy, dignity becomes pomposity, and respect turns out to be veiled but exasperated familiarity.

Groups are parodied by mock-epic because they suffer from that immaturity and falsity which come from self-satisfaction and from the use of criteria of evaluation peculiar to an essentially parochial society; an obsession with behavioural patterns comes to predominate over any broader, more humane understanding of social activity. The characters are not enlarged by encountering resistance to their wishes—actions have the ease and versatility of game and the gods, unlike Homer's, connive with humanity to the point of subservience (see especially Pope's *The Rape of the Lock*, 1712 and 1714). But in the poet's attitude, too, the satirist's contempt gives way to the virtuoso's unfailingly apt and delightfully varied development of his initial stance; the subject, while never ceasing to be a target, is exploited as an instrument of a self-consciously formal and decorative achievement which, through its own game-like quality, its refusal to impoverish a spade by calling it a spade, becomes itself increasingly exhilarating and life-affirming. Mock-epic is a developed form not so much of sarcasm as of euphemism: it has a paradoxical willingness to 'extract from contemporary life its epic dimension, showing us . . . how grand and poetic we are in our cravats and highly-polished boots' (Baudelaire).

More recently, mock-epic has functioned less as a generical concept and has instead been limited to the area of language, where it covers most grandiloquent modes. Here it is a *defensive* posture and a necessary guarantee of the poet's desire to establish a plausible relationship between language and a contemporary environment; the image is no longer enhanced by being embedded in a rhetorical syntax allegedly equal to it, but rather is given 'epic' finality by being set *against* voracious and self-perpetuating dictions. This may account for a cyclical mock-epic like Ted Hughes's 'Crow' (1970), a mock-epic of short and complete utterances. Other poets have won through to an easy and incessant intercourse with the small coinage of civilization or to a belief that all cultural coinage is small (e.g. Pound in his *Cantos*); here the epic is in the amount and the mockery not in the pretensions but in the lack of them.

See R. P. Bond, *English Burlesque Poetry, 1700–1750* (1932); J. Dixon Hunt (ed.), *Pope—The Rape of the Lock* (1968); Ian Jack, *Augustan Satire* (1952); L. Rochon, 'Lautréamont et le style homérique', *Archives des lettres modernes*, 123 (1971); K. Schmidt, *Vorstudien zu einer Geschichte des komischen Epos* (1953).

MHP and CS

modernism

Though sometimes loosely used as a label for the dominant tendency of the twentieth-century arts, as 'neo-classicism' is for eighteenth- and 'romanticism' for nineteenth-century arts, 'modernism' raises problems crucial to the character and destiny of those arts. Not only is much modern writing not modernist—so Stephen Spender distinguishes between 'modern' and 'contemporary' writers (*The Struggle of the Modern*, 1963)—but it resists the thesis that modernist style and sensibility are inevitable in our age. For modernism tends to propose special opportunities and difficulties for the arts. Modernist art is, in most critical usage, reckoned to be the art of what Harold Rosenburg calls 'the tradition of the new'. It is experimental, formally complex, elliptical, contains elements of decreation as well as creation, and tends to associate notions of the artist's freedom from realism, materialism, traditional genre and form, with notions of cultural apocalypse and disaster. Its social content is characteristically *avant-garde* or bohemian; hence specialized. Its notion of the artist is of a futurist, not the conserver of culture but its onward creator; its notion of the audience is that it is foolish if potentially redeemable: 'Artists are the antennae of the race, but the bullet-headed many will never learn to trust their great artists' is Ezra Pound's definition. Beyond art's specialized enclave, conditions of crisis are evident: language awry, cultural cohesion lost, perception pluralized.

Further than this, there are several modernisms: an intensifying sequence of movements from Symbolism on (Post-impressionism, Expressionism, Futurism, Imagism, Vorticism, Dadaism, Surrealism) often radically at odds, and sharp differences of cultural interpretation coming from writers apparently stylistically analogous (e.g. T. S. Eliot and William Carlos Williams). A like technique can be very differently used (e.g. the use of STREAM OF CONSCIOUSNESS in Virginia Woolf, James Joyce and William Faulkner) according to different notions of underlying order in life or art. The post-symbolist stress on the 'hard' or impersonal image (see IMAGISM) can dissolve into the fluidity of Dada or Surrealism or into romantic personalization: while the famous 'classical' element in modernism, emanating particularly from Eliot, its stress on the luminous symbol outside time, can be qualified by a wide variety of political attitudes and forms of historicism.

Modernism means the ruffling of the realistic surface of literature by underlying forces; the disturbance may arise, though, from logics solely aesthetic or highly social. Hence, even if we distinguish 'moderns' from 'contemporaries', modernism still remains a loose label. We can dispute about when it starts (French symbolism; decadence; the break-up of naturalism) and whether it has ended (Kermode distinguishes 'paleo-modernism' and 'neo-modernism' and hence a degree of continuity through to post-war art). We can regard it as a timebound concept (say 1890 to 1930) or a timeless one (including Sterne, Donne, Villon, Ronsard). The best focus remains a body of major writers (James, Conrad, Proust, Mann, Gide, Kafka, Svevo, Joyce, Musil, Faulkner in fiction; Strindberg, Pirandello, Wedekind, Brecht in drama; Mallarmé, Yeats, Eliot, Pound, Rilke, Apollinaire, Stevens in poetry) whose works are aesthetically radical, contain striking technical innovation, emphasize spatial or 'fugal' as opposed to chronological form, tend toward ironic modes, and involve a certain 'dehumanization of art' (Ortega y Gasset). Yet they finally manifest not so much one modern style as a perpetual pursuit of modern styles for the given creative occasion, in a context in which style is presumed absent. Clearly such writers are of the highest importance; but we cannot regard them as proof of the inevitability and necessity of modernist style, as the true art of a century of modernization, though that issue is still being fought in creation as well as in criticism. See also CLASSICISM, DADA, EXPRESSIONISM, IMAGISM, SYMBOL, SURREALISM.

See B. Bergonzi (ed.), *Innovations* (1968); M. Bradbury, *The Social Context of Modern English Literature* (1971); M. Bradbury and J. Macfarlane (eds), *Modernism* (1976); R. Ellman and C. Fiedelson (eds), *The Modern Tradition* (1965); I. Howe (ed.), *The Idea of the Modern in Literature and the Arts* (1967); F. Kermode, *Modern Essays* (1971); D. Lodge, *The Modes of Modern Writing* (1977).

MSB

monody
see ELEGY

motif
see FORM, THEME

myth

'Myth' and 'mythical' have long been commonly used in contexts opposing them to 'truth' or 'reality', a situation that is now considerably altered, in literary criticism at least, for one of two reasons: either because the truth content of the insights of myth is valued, or because the status of words like 'truth' and 'reality' is considered problematic. Both tendencies ultimately derive from ROMANTICISM, and its revaluation of primitive and non-Christian religions.

Myths are stories of unascertainable origin or authorship accompanying or helping to explain religious beliefs. Often (though not necessarily) their subject is the exploits of a god or hero, which may be of a fabulous or superhuman nature, and which may have instituted a change in the workings of the universe or in the conditions of social life. Critics value myth positively because of its apparent spontaneity and collectivity, expressing some lastingly and generally satisfying account of the experience of man. Equally attractive is the apparent universality and timelessness of myth. The tantalizing recurrence of the mythic hero and his exploits, or of natural or animal motifs (the moon or water or serpents or horses) have activated many 'Keys to All Mythologies', of which Frazer's and Jung's have gained most favour with literary critics. The work of Northrop Frye, for instance, reflects the influence of Frazer's attempt to explain myths by reference to rituals designed to ensure the continuing fertility of animal and vegetable life; Frye assigns all myths to an appropriate place in the cycle of seasons, with their alternation of barrenness, growth and fruitfulness. Their ubiquitous hero is the corn-god, who passes through stages of growth, decline and death in harmony with the turning year. Literature derives from myth, and literary history recapitulates the process, as it moves through a seasonal cycle in which appropriate modes and genres are dominant— comedy belongs to summer, tragedy to autumn, and so on. We are now in winter, and the weather is ironic.

Jung and Frazer have nowadays little standing with professional students of mythology and comparative religion; indeed, the relations between literary criticism and anthropology practised as a social science have been meagre. Though the tendency of social anthropologists to explain myths in relation to the social and economic conditions from which they allegedly spring may often rest on sociological hypotheses as unsatisfying (though not as unverifiable) as Jung's 'collective unconscious' or Frazer's theory of magic, the perspective of ethnography at least allows us to perceive how much 'myth' there is in many of the attempts to explain myth swallowed by literary critics. Frazer's beliefs that primitive societies have literal faith in the efficacy of magic, or adopt totems because they regard themselves as blood relations of the totemic animal, or are ignorant of the connection between sexual relations and birth (wittily exploded by Edmund Leach), are checked by ethnographic work, and betray the obvious mental furniture of an apologist for Christianity, evolution and progress. Frazer's ethnocentrism is paralleled by Frye's; his cyclical system to contain all myths and all literary works as a simultaneous order of the mind projects proclivities for autonomy and timelessness derived from SYMBOLISM or perhaps, in their enthusiastic embrace of universal identical duplication, from the optimism of capitalist technology.

Critics would do well to take account of more up-to-date and less 'literary' approaches to myth, and the work of Lévi-Strauss certainly offers possibilities to criticism only marginally explored as yet in this country. STRUCTURALISM itself undoubtedly falls foul of the pitfalls of ethnocentrism which it only partially negotiates by declaring itself as 'the myth of the mythologies'; Lévi-Strauss's sophisticated savages meditating on raw and cooked food bear a suspicious resemblance to French intellectuals of discriminating palate. But its approach to mythic universals is superior to (say) Jung's in accounting for differences as well as for similarities; it does not seek a constant significance for the same motif, but rather a variable meaning dependent on its relation to other symbolic elements within a mythology.

The assumption operating here is that myth is a language designed to communicate thought, amenable to a reconverted form of linguistic analysis; the properties common to all myths are not to be sought at the level of content but at the level of a structure necessary to all forms of communication. Mythic thought is about insoluble paradoxes of experience, which appear as 'gaps'; the elements of a mythic message are so arranged as to attempt to mediate the gaps. The essential gap is between nature and culture—nature felt as an undifferentiated continuity and culture as the institution of difference upon which communication (which utilizes it to construct binary pairs) rests; the project of myth is therefore an impossibility. The primary mythic theme is thus a Rousseauistic version of the Fall.

Myth as a language, an abstract, 'contentless' systems of signs, thus becomes closer to literature in a different way; in the words of Geoffrey Hartman, 'literature and myth are both mediators rather than media', presupposing an *absence*—nature, reality, God, eternity. The structuralist approach to myth gives strong impetus to fresh thought about the relations between language and 'the thing itself' in imaginative writing. Myth itself may fruitfully be approached as an *absence* in literature, all the more potent for being so; Romanticism in particular thrives on making poetry out of the longed-for return of the lost gods and myths of the childhood of the race or the childhood of the individual (the poetry of Hölderlin is its major expression). *Ulysses*, 'The Waste Land' and similar works of the same generation also exploit (in a different spirit) the gap between primeval myth and its contemporary parodies and urge a more complex approach than the critical tendency to see the presence of a myth as a sign of its reincarnation, regardless of context.

The structural approach to myth as a form of language also makes manageable the analysis of secular myth—about race or foreignness or 'them' or dirt—as a schematic ordering of otherwise unintelligible experience similar in its functioning to language. But literary criticism is only beginning to cope with this overlapping of disciplines. See also SEMIOTICS, STRUCTURALISM.

See J. G. Frazer, *The Golden Bough* (1923); Northrop Frye, *Anatomy of Criticism* (1957); Geoffrey Hartman, 'Structuralism: the Anglo-American adventure' in Jacques Ehrmann (ed.), *Structuralism* (1970), 137–58; E. Nelson Hayes and Tanya Hayes (eds), *Claude Lévi-Strauss: The Anthropologist as Hero* (1970); C. G. Jung, *Archetypes of the Collective Unconscious* (1934; trans. R. F. C. Hull, 1959); Edmund Leach, *Genesis as Myth* (1969); Edmund Leach, *Lévi-Strauss* (1970); Claude Lévi-Strauss, *The Savage Mind* (1966), *The Raw and the Cooked* (1970); Octavio Paz, *Claude Lévi-Strauss* (1971); Thomas A. Sebeok (ed.), *Myth: A Symposium* (1955: reprinted 1958 and 1968); P. Maranda (ed.), *Mytholgoy* (1972); K. K. Ruthven, *Myth* (1976).

MAH

mythos
see PLOT

N

narrative

is the recounting of a series of facts or events and the establishing of some connection between them. The word is commonly restricted to fiction, ancient epics and romances or modern novels and short stories. In imaginative literature the nature of the link between the reader and the text is crucial, and here the *narrator* becomes important. This may be the author speaking in his 'own voice'; the author adopting some role towards the reader such as an honest friend, a joking companion or a contemptuous enemy; or a 'character' or 'characters' introduced to 'tell the story'. Narrative thus has two overlapping aspects. One is a question of content, the assemblage of material, the nature of the connections implied. The other is rhetorical, how the narrative is presented to the audience. Such questions are in literary criticism apt to be considered exclusively in terms of 'imaginative' literature, but an examination of some non-fictional narratives may illuminate the profound and far-reaching power of this art. The word is used in Scots law for the recital of facts at the beginning of a deed or agreement. The connection between them is their relevance to some declaration of intent. There are no complex rhetorical considerations apart from the legal solemnity of the document which claims demonstrable truth for some state of affairs. Similar kinds of narrative, in which convention suppresses the power of the narrator, are found in accounts of scientific experiments or in do-it-yourself books. When we come to 'scientific' eye-witness reports of journeys or travels, the narrator becomes of great importance, a fact recognized by early travel writers like Captain Dampier who commonly establish their credentials in an Introduction. This key role of the travel-narrator has been exploited by satirists and expert rhetorical writers like Lucian, or Swift in *Gulliver's Travels*. Narrative is also of crucial importance in the writing of history: the selection of incidents for recording, the treatment of time and its effects, and the kind of connection which the historian establishes between events. The latter is a mark of the cultural context of the writer and is to a degree outside his conscious control.

All historical narrative seems to take up some position at a point in the scale between the demonstration of limited relationships between discrete events, and the implication of some vast, non-human design. Psychological determinism and Marxist apocalypse are only two of the many narrative styles. The rhetorical aspect of historical narrative is important, for instance the epigrammatic fastidiousness of Tacitus:

Ubi solitudinem faciunt, pacem appellant:
When they make a desert, they call it peace:

or Churchill's ring-masterly flourishes. In English literature, one of the most fascinating instances of historical narrative, in its content, selection, discussion of time and rhetorical skill, is Gibbon's *Decline and Fall of the Roman Empire* (1776–88). Perhaps the particular characteristic of the mid-eighteenth-century world is the chaotic flux of time and experience. In Gibbon's vast panorama of fifteen centuries, the most lasting imaginative effect on the reader is a sense of the way in which the historian's own mind imposes a pattern on the bewildering uncertainties of events. Poets and writers of fiction have long exploited these characteristics of narrative. A sophisticated example of such expertise, pre-dating the novel, is found at the beginning of Chaucer's 'Troilus and Criseyde':

> For I, that god of Loves servaunts serve,
> Ne dar to Love, for myn unlyklinesse,
> Preyen for speed, al sholde I therefor sterve . . .[*help . . . even if . . . I die*]

If this poem was read out by Chaucer to a courtly audience, the distinction between the poet, a man of worldly accomplishment, and this narrator who does not 'dar to Love' must have been a witty gesture, and of importance to the narrative. There is an added complication in the tone, since Chaucer ironically makes the narrator describe himself in the same terms as the Pope did in a papal bull, 'the servant of the servants of God'. Defoe's *Robinson Crusoe* (1719) is archetypal both in the fictional development of the narrative, and in the rhetoric of the employment of a narrator, Crusoe himself. A shadowy 'editor' appears in the introduction, and the book is thus an early example of the framework of 'journals' found in drawers and desks, a popular 'realistic' device in the next century. As far as *Moll Flanders* (1722) is concerned, controversy has long raged about whether the moral doctrine which Moll as narrator expounds is ironically intended or whether Defoe is actually speaking through his character. Richardson's novels are rhetorically more complex. The employment of a series of 'narrators' in letters to rehearse accounts of the same events from different points of view enriches Richardson's embodiment of moral imagination, and intensifies the reader's appreciation of the force and ubiquity of obsessional states. Sterne's *Tristram Shandy* (1760–7) questions the nature of the assumed connections between narrated events. Our assumptions about cause and effect, or the relation between thought and action, are attacked. Sterne explores another feature of narrative, the fact that there is a time-scale of events and a time-scheme of narration itself, which are not the same. Each of the characters has his own interior cinematograph of events and 'explanations' for the connection between them. Tristram Shandy himself, the narrator, has a more complicated picture, but still presents an 'omniscient' view.

The narrator or narrators in a novel may be made puzzled, unreliable or misleading. The early years of this century, in the work of Freud and others, saw the swift development of certain lines of speculation about the self which have fragmented irretrievably the certainty which had prevailed that men's perceptions were pretty much the same everywhere. Novelists like Conrad, Ford Madox Ford, Virginia Woolf, Joyce and Faulkner strained the rhetorical technique of fiction to present a refracted picture of experience in all its complexity as unique mental pictures. The reader was increasingly required to interpret a difficult text, to inspect his own responses as he read. There has been a similar strain on the choice of events in the narrative and the identification of the connection between them. Why does the novelist choose bizarre acts of violence, the 'seamy side of life', 'eccentric' mental lives such as *voyeurs* or other deviants? A discussion of the nature of a narrative and the mode of narration can carry us to the heart of the 'meaning' of a work of fiction, and properly managed to an understanding of the culture and context in which it was created. See also CHARACTER, NARRATIVE STRUCTURE, STRUCTURALISM.

See Erich Auerbach, trans. W. Trask, *Mimesis* (1953) which gives one kind of analysis of *narrative*; Wayne C. Booth, *The Rhetoric of Fiction* (1961) provides an exhaustive discussion of modes of *narration*. See also Robert Scholes and Robert Kellogg, *The Nature of Narrative* (1966).

AMR

narrative structure

The shape of a story's trajectory. Every story is projected from a state of rest by a force of some kind in an arc of rising tension until it reaches the apogee where it begins to fall towards a point of impact. This trajectory represents the 'unity of action' proclaimed by Aristotle to be the essential principle of tragedy, but also applicable to related genres such as the epic.

Poeticians and students of dramatic and narrative forms have tended to take for granted Aristotle's division of the action into 'complication' and 'dénouement' (or 'unravelling') around a central 'peripeteia' or turning-point. Modern literary theorists, strongly influenced by Russian Formalism, have often ignored this unifying structural principle, either following Propp in focusing on the mere chaining of narrative functions, or distinguishing (after Shklovsky) between the underlying material of the story, *fabula*, and its compositional form, *syuzhet* or 'plot'. This distinction usually only highlights the sequential relations between episodes and neglects the essential relations of 'complication' and 'dénouement' such as their mirror-like opposition in intensity and result, a patterning which is preserved in the traditional 'trajectory' metaphor.

The central point around which the narrative structure pivots is the *peripeteia,* and the nature, placing and stylistic marking of this turning-point determines the nature of the conflict, whether on a physical, psychological or moral level. As Petrovsky showed in 1925, the central phases of narrative structure are normally framed by elements of 'prologue' and 'epilogue', both of these having a general phase (i.e. the total social scene out of which the world of the story arises and to which it reverts) and a specific phase (i.e. essential prior and subsequent information about the lives of the main protagonists).

Most models of narrative structure start by assuming a previous state of rest or equilibrium or normality which is disturbed by an outside force of some kind. The condition initiated by this force gets worse until it reaches an extreme degree. At this point another force comes to bear which reverses the process and allows for the gradual resumption of normality or the establishment of a new equilibrium. This homeostatic pattern may have either a social or a psychological function, or both. Myths in both primitive and modern societies tend to come into being as highly formalized, even formulaic, structures which resolve the society's deepest tensions. These may concern social conflicts, ritual taboos or man's struggle to come to terms with his physical environment. The narrative structure of the myth allows the real conflict to be projected in dramatized form and resolved via the *peripeteia* and *dénouement*, thus providing both a ritual enactment and a magical relief for the society in question. On the individual level a similar process may be at work: tensions are produced by narrative in the reader/listener which will match in their variety and diffusion his residual psychological tensions, but which are specific enough to be resolved within the context of the art experience, thus channelling the residual tensions into a manageable framework and allowing for their vicarious relief.

Whatever the social or psychological functions of narrative structure, it must be accorded a major role in establishing the aesthetic unity which creates pleasure through the contemplation and enjoyment of purely formal patterning in narrative art. See also DENOUEMENT, FORMALISM, MYTH, NARRATIVE, PLOT, STRUCTURALISM.

See G. F. Else, *Aristotle's 'Poetics': The Argument* (1957); L. M. O'Toole, *Style, Structure and Interpretation in the Russian Short Story* (1982); M. Petrovsky, 'Morphology of the novella', *Russian Poetics in Translation*, 10 (1983).

MO'T

naturalism
see REALISM

neo-Aristotelianism
see CHICAGO CRITICS

neo-classicism
see CLASSIC, DECORUM, IMITATION

neo-Platonism
see PLATONISM

new criticism

The term *new criticism*, originally coined by J. E. Spingarn in 1910 in protest against the brutal pedantry of the American academic scene (see *Creative Criticism*, 1917) is now used to refer specifically to the work of the American critics associated with the programme announced in John Crowe Ransom's book *The New Criticism* (1941), notably Cleanth Brooks (*The Well Wrought Urn*, 1947), R. P. Blackmur (*Language as Gesture*, 1952), Allen Tate (*Collected Essays*, 1959) and Robert Penn Warren (*Selected Essays,* 1964). Ransom discovers the stimulus for this movement in T. S. Eliot's urging of a new spirit of objectivity in criticism, and in I. A. Richards's attempt to provide a scientific terminology for describing poetic effect. The fundamental effort was to free criticism from the impressionism and emotionalism of the amateur tradition and the intentionalism of literary-historical scholarship (see EFFECT and INTENTION), and to propose an aesthetic that would consider poetry 'primarily as poetry and not another thing' (Eliot). Richards's development of Romantic theories of form as the systemiza-tion and harmonizing of elements in poetry, with its idea of the poem as a complex activity of meaning, inspired many of the key terms and concepts of the new criticism: ambiguity, irony, paradox, tension, gesture, etc. However, Richards's attempt to locate this complexity in the psychological *effects* of poetry, rather than in the linguistic struc-ture of the work, had failed to produce immediately useful descriptive attitudes and terminology. The major stimulus here probably came from his pupil William Empson, whose determination to prove poetry capable of explanation led to a brilliantly imaginative account of its verbal complexity (see ANALYSIS). His demonstration that poetic effect often arose from a rich exploitation of the references and relationships inherent in language lies behind the new critical disposition to regard all literary works as structures of language, and to be relatively indifferent to concepts like GENRE, CHARACTER or PLOT.

However, much of the American new criticism took its ideas about language not from Empson but from the semantic work of Richards himself. His identification of poetry as an example of the *emotive* use of language, in contrast to the *scientific* use, perpetuated Romantic thought/feeling dualisms, and encouraged 'new critics' to conceive of poetry as a special *kind* of language. This fallacy, attacked by the CHICAGO CRITICS, often led to a narrowly prescriptive view of poetic form—such as Brooks's *paradox*—and a concentration on the rhetorical features of certain kinds of complex, highly concentrated poetry. One consequence was a re-writing of literary history; the poetry of the early seventeenth century replaced that of the nineteenth in critical popularity. Another was a narrowing of descriptive procedures; the axiom that the poem as an organization of language was the only determinant of the critical relevance of external evidence was sometimes modified into meaningless assertions of the 'autonomy' of poems, their explicability without any external reference or knowledge.

The larger tradition of descriptive criticism in England and America derives its assumptions about language in literature from the later Richards of *Philosophy of Rhetoric* (1936), and Empson. It identifies poetry not as a kind of language but as a *use* of language, and therefore declares its essential continuity with all language and with culture; it rejects distinctions of language function along emotive/descriptive lines, and asserts a concept of 'meaning' as the result of the total linguistic activity of words in a context (see ANALYSIS). And it rests on the conviction that true descriptive criticism must be ultimately a criticism of literature as organized language, because it is only *as* language that the work has an objective existence at all.

See Roger Fowler and Peter Mercer, 'Criticism and the language of literature', *Style* 3 (1969), 45–72; reprinted in Fowler, *The Languages of Literature* (1971); Stanley Edgar Hyman, *The Armed Vision* (1947, revised ed., 1955); Murray Krieger, *The New Apologists for Poetry* (1956); Brian Lee, 'The New Criticism and the language of poetry', in Roger Fowler (ed.), *Essays on Style and Language* (1966); Walter Sutton, *Modern American Criticism* (1963); W. K. Wimsatt, Jr, and Cleanth Brooks, *Literary Criticism, A Short History* (1957); D. Robey, 'Anglo-American New Criticism', in A. Jefferson and D. Robey (eds), *Modern Literary Theory* (1982); T. Eagleton, *Literary Theory: An Introduction* (1983).

PM

novel

Of the three main kinds of literature (poetry, drama, novel), the novel is the last to evolve and the hardest to define, for reasons suggested in the name. 'A fiction in prose of a certain extent': this economical definition by a French critic begs more questions than it answers. There are many such fictions predating the emergence of the species as a recognizable type: that we usually date from *Don Quixote* (1605–15), and in England from the early eighteenth century (Defoe, Richardson, Fielding, Sterne), and associate with the rise of prose as an empirical, sceptical instrument for probing familiar environments. This links the novel with realism and a-genericism; Fielding set it up as a mock-species in calling it a 'comic epic poem in prose', intending to suggest its low (or else mock-heroic) style, its width of social range and bagginess of structure, its contingency and episodic design. The self-sceptical element is reinforced by Fielding's willingness to parody Richardson, and then Sterne's to flout the emergent conventions of the species in *Tristram Shandy* (1760–7), which mocks beginnings, middles, and ends; chronicity; and reliable narrators. The circumstantial and specific elements, and the engrained scepticism (Ian Watt's 'realism of presentation' and 'realism of assessment', *The Rise of the Novel*, 1957), easily merge here into self-conscious fictiveness, constituents of the novel ever since. Though touching on reportage and history at one extreme, taking structure from non-fictional prose forms (journalism, history, sociology), the novel touches on high literary formalism at its other extreme, taking structure from myth, and symbolic or linguistic coherence. Many classic debates about fiction (novel versus romance in the nineteenth century; life-novel versus art-novel at the turn of the century; 'journalistic' versus 'crystalline' novels today) cover this spectrum. So does every individual novel. Lacking the metrical-typographical and generic conventions of most poetry, and the theatre-audience presentation of most drama, and using the most familiar, open and deconventionalized form of written language, prose novels are open to a wide variety of registers, structures, typologies. This range an adequate critical definition must cover too.

The fascination of the novel is that, because of its representational dimension, it raises the problem of the nature of a fiction at a point very near to familiar, *un*fictionalized versions of reality. The propensity of novels towards 'giving to the imaginary the formal guarantee of the real', their dependence on recognition and their relative formal contingency, are essential features; though clearly 'reality' is not a stable object. These features have often led critics to see it as a basically referential or mimetic species; sometimes (though not today) to doubt its critical respectability. The 'livingness' of fiction—its capacity to give us 'felt life', its social density and range, its following of loose and lifelike sequences—are valid objects of critical attention, so long as we remember that realism is an imaginative creation and that the term itself encourages confusion (cf. REALISM). One consequence of the term was the growth of a critical method based on 'plot', 'character', 'description', etc. (i.e. mimetic assumptions); against this, there has been a critical tradition of post-Jamesian fictional theory, stressing other essential structuring features: 'point of view', 'paradox', 'symbol', 'tension', and what Mark Schorer calls 'technique as discovery', a poetic emphasizing means of presentation rather than objects of imitation. What seems apparent is that, though both approaches stress primary features of novels, each often best serves discussion of the kind of fiction contemporary with it: the former tends to get us closer to nineteenth-century realistic fiction, the latter to twentieth-century neo-symbolist fiction. The latter is the more sophisticated, reminding us that all fictions are makings, *verbal* constructs; its weakness is that it tends to ascribe *all* primary structure in fiction to rhetorical and linguistic features, rather than to the unfolding of orders perceived in psychology, experience or society (cf. STRUCTURE). Synthesis is still needed. Some recent criticism (e.g. Frank Kermode, *The Sense of an Ending*, 1967) has sought this through the idea of analogical structure, resemblance between fictional orders and structures in other species of writing (e.g. history-writing), while stressing that all writings are implicit plots and hence fictions in some sense.

The novel, being an 'institution' of modern society particularly exposed to the contingency of life and prevailing structures of perception (Harry Levin, *The Gates of Horn,* 1963), has passed through marked stages of development; this has encouraged historicist criticism. It has been called the 'burgher epic'; identified with the social eminence of its main reading public, the bourgeoisie; seen as a manifestation of its perception of reality, the secular, material but moralized reality of a particular class; linked with its view of the rounded, individuated human character in sequential moral growth; tied in with particular notions of cause-and-effect and chronological sequence in character and society, a 'progressive' view of self and history. Such criticism tends to assume that MODERNISM constitutes a crisis of the species; hence it often concludes in prophecies of the imminent death of the novel. This helps demonstrate that versions of reality change over time, and helps explain certain features of novel-development: the dominance of the form at its most realistic in the nineteenth century, and the later emergence of naturalism, certain types of fictional modernism, the anti-novel. It tends, however, to encourage the view that the novel of morals-and-manners (see Lionel Trilling, 'Manners, morals, and the novel', *The Liberal Imagination*, 1961) is the prototypical novel, hardly accurate if we take a broad international perspective; to see 'fabulation' as either aberrant or a crisis-symptom (cf. FICTION); often to undervalue contemporary production. Reminding us that realism is a convention, it gives that convention a historic-cultural rather than a creative explanation. Like much stylistic history, it assumes inevitability and undervalues the startling plurality of the novel-form, its remarkable endurance in many different cultural circumstances.

While an effective novel-criticism is likely to attend to such matters of historical variation in order to identify the broad species, it needs an adequate discourse in order to encounter particular works. This will have to retain certain distinctive and inherent features of the novel as it conventionally exists: as a species given to neo-comic scepticism; as a species in prose and therefore open to plurality of languages; as a species normally involving interaction of persons in social, often familiar, milieux; as a species of extended length and therefore involving large actions and what Conrad called 'long logics'. In considering such matters, criticism still has a long way to go; though the present emphasis on novels as objects of critical study suggests the effort is intensifying. See also CHARACTER, FICTION, NARRATIVE, PLOT.

See Miriam Allott (ed.), *Novelists on the Novel* (1959); Erich Auerbach, trans. W. Trask, *Mimesis* (1953); Wayne C. Booth, *The Rhetoric of Fiction* (1961); Malcolm Bradbury, *What is a Novel?* (1969); Henry James in R. P. Blackmur (ed.), *The Art of the Novel* (1934); Harry Levin, *The Gates of Horn* (1963); David Lodge, *Language of Fiction* (1966); Mark Schorer, *The World We Imagine* (1969); Philip Stevick (ed.), *The Theory of the Novel* (1967); Ian Watt, *The Rise of the Novel* (1957); R. Scholes and R. Kellogg, *The Nature of Narrative* (1966).

Theoretical discussions of various aspects of the novel have proliferated greatly in recent years. See, for example, M. Bloomfield, (ed.), *The Interpretation of Narrative* (1970); D. Cohn, *Transparent Minds: Narrative Modes for Presenting Consciousness in Fiction* (1978); U. Eco, *The Role of the Reader* (1979); R. Fowler, *Linguistics and the Novel* (2nd ed., 1983); G. Genette, *Narrative Discourse* (1980); J. Halperin (ed.), *The Theory of the Novel: New Essays* (1974); W. Iser, *The Implied Reader* (1974), *The Act of Reading* (1978); F. Jameson, *The Political Unconscious: Narrative as a Socially Symbolic Act* (1981); S. S. Lanser, *The Narrative Act: Point of View in Prose Fiction* (1981); G. Prince, *Narratology: The Form and Functioning of Narrative* (1982); H. Ruthrof, *The Reader's Construction of Narrative* (1981); F. Stanzel, *Narrative Situations in the Novel* (1969).

MSB

O

objective correlative

Popularized by T. S. Eliot (who later admitted his astonishment at its success) in 1919 to explain his dissatisfaction with *Hamlet*:

> The only way of expressing emotion in the form of art is by finding an 'objective correlative'; in other words, a set of objects, a situation, a chain of events which shall be the formula of that *particular* emotion; such that when the external facts . . . are given, the emotion is immediately evoked.

The application to *Hamlet* now seems fanciful, but as the technical procedure in 'pure poetry' the general formula is plausible. The most serious omission is the creative contribution of the unconscious mind. Eliseo Vivas criticizes the concept in detail in *Creation and Discovery* (1955), pointing out that a writer only discovers the particular emotion he wishes to express in the act of composition.

See T. S. Eliot, *'Hamlet'* (1919) in *Selected Essays* (3rd ed., 1951), 145.

FWB

obscurity

Before we completely understand a poem or a style of poetry, we often call it 'obscure'; the label is a stop-gap reaction until critical ingenuity catches up with the poet's ingenuity. As the reader has grown accustomed to extremely 'wide-angled' metaphors, so his own ability to metaphorize has increased; somewhere, though it be at imaginative infinity itself, any two words or collections of words can strike up a meaningful relationship. Anything in any way organized is intelligible. Poems may be intelligible in a purely prosodic sense and for this reason one should be wary of calling any regular verse obscure. The peculiar charm of nonsense verse is that despite its meaninglessness it carries on as if it were meaningful; its sheer prosodic regularity endows it with a patentness, a proof of its own comprehensibility.

The Symbolist poem is obscure because its meaning is so total, so fully and continuously busies all its constituents, that it never settles; as Valéry puts it, its obscurity lies in its refractive capacity. In a situation like this, the poem can be rationalized only in terms of the formal demands it makes on itself. Much modern poetry is obscure because it never has more than a general sense, compounded of intermittent intuitions and experiential shocks valuable in themselves and for which the general sense is merely a pretext. It can be argued that much modern poetry has not really outgrown the 'symphonies' and 'nocturnes' of the later nineteenth century, it has merely augmented their tendentiousness by discouraging language from ever being fully literal, a trend that alarmed the IMAGISTS. If the obscure poet commits a crime, it is not against reason but, paradoxically, against the inconsequentiality of the world. The poem can no longer provide a processional for the rich mereness of existence, the patterns run too deep.

But in both cases, it is exegesis that most obscures; it cannot help but separate out those incompatibilities which are the very cohesive forces of the composite, cannot but make enumeration out of apposition.

It is perhaps most profitable to think of obscurity as a term descriptive of a modern poetic rhetoric of ellipsis, metaphor, typographic enterprise, as a convention for accuracy and authenticity; not a classical accuracy derived from a constant correction and reapplication of ready-authenticated material, but an accuracy of the unimaginable, authentic because unchallengeable; not 'nobody else has thought this therefore I must have thought it' but 'nobody else could have thought this therefore I must have thought it'. For two comprehensive and opposing views of the problem see: J. Press, *The Chequer'd Shade* (1958); J. Sparrow, *Sense and Poetry* (1934); see also G. Steiner, 'On difficulty' in his *On Difficulty and Other Essays* (1978).

CS

ode

In English, a much-practised form of lyric poetry from the time of Ben Jonson to that of Tennyson, with sporadic modern revivals. The most elevated and complicated species of lyric, the ode was often written to celebrate notable public occasions or lofty universal themes. It attracted an exalted diction and free metrical experimentation, highly formalized stanza-types rather removed from the main currents of English versification. The exponents of this genre were usually explicitly conscious of their classical models, hence the strangeness of the verse forms: many poets attempted to render in English metrical patterns which were natural only in terms of the sound-structure of Greek.

The classical models are Pindar (522–442? B.C.) in Greek and Horace (65–8 B.C.) in Latin. Although Horace was much more familiar to the English, the Pindaric ode interested poets more, because it was metrically highly distinctive. Pindar's odes (derived from choral lyrics in drama) were composed to be chanted to music by a dancing chorus.

The demands of music and dance resulted in a highly elaborate stanzaic structure: this type of ode was built on a sequence of sections called *strophe, antistrophe* and *epode*, the sections constructed from lines of varying length. Such a complicated verse-form provided a stimulating challenge to English metrists. The Pindaric ode was 'occasional', that is to say, composed for a specific and important public event (e.g. to honour the victors in Greek athletic games). The Horatian ode, though sometimes public, was frequently personal and reflective. It shared the solemnity and dignity of the Pindaric ode, but was less of a metrist's virtuoso-piece. Its contribution to English poetry was a matter of tone and feeling rather than of technical design.

The English ode begins with Ben Jonson and rises in esteem through the period of neo-classicism, culminating in some of the more exalted poems of the Romantics and then surviving in public Victorian verse. In 1629 appeared Jonson's 'Ode to Sir Lucius Cary and Sir H. Morison', a conscious attempt to provide an exact English equivalent for the complicated stanza forms of Pindar; Milton's 'On the Morning of Christ's Nativity', written in the same year, though not Pindaric in the same way, exercises an extremely complex metrical pattern. The Horatian model is represented in the 'Horatian Ode upon Cromwell's Return from Ireland' by Milton's younger contemporary Andrew Marvell. In 1656 Abraham Cowley's collection *Miscellanies* made available a number of adaptations as well as imitations of Pindar, and set a fashion for a type of free Pindaric ode which was to become pleasing to the Augustans. Three odes of Dryden were also influential: two of them, odes for St Cecilia's Day (1687 and 1697, the second entitled 'Alexander's Feast'), honoured the patron saint of music and returned to Pindar at the same time, for they were designed to be set to music. William Collins (1721–59) and Thomas Gray (1716–71) continued the Pindaric fashion; William Cowper (1731–1800) favoured the less spectacular, more quietly serious, Horatian manner. Towards the end of the eighteenth century burlesques of the ode began to appear, but the genre was taken over by the Romantics and employed in several great lyric poems on political, emotional and aesthetic themes: Wordsworth's elaborate ode, 'Intimations of Immortality' (1803, published 1807) and the great odes of Keats published in 1820 ('Nightingale', 'Psyche', 'Grecian Urn', 'Autumn', 'Melancholy') are the best-remembered examples in this period: highly philosophical, intense, yet controlled. Coleridge ('France', 'Dejection') and Shelley ('West Wind', 'Liberty', 'Naples'—the last employing an extraordinarily complicated metrical arrangement with some claims to Greek heritage) also practised the form.

Although exceptionally diverse in its structural patterns, the ode was sustained as a poetic ideal for over two centuries of English verse. Its dignity, classical pedigree and technical potentialities endeared it to the Augustans; its intensity and philosophical pretensions made it suitable for the most exalted Romantic verse. Since the Romantic era it has declined in fortune, become the prerogative of poets laureate and of other writers given to ceremonious public utterance. It was the vehicle for high seriousness, and could not survive the increasingly cynical modern age; so easy to deflate that no great pleasure was to be derived from writing parodies. It used to be the mode for metrical experimentation (the classical models warranting departure from established English prosodies) but the radical experimentalism of Europe and America in this century has no need for such an outmoded excuse for metrical licence.

See John Heath-Stubbs, *The Ode* (1969); Norman Maclean, 'From action to image: theories of the lyric in the eighteenth century' in R. S. Crane, *Critics and Criticism* (1952); Carol Maddison, *Apollo and the Nine, A History of the Ode* (1960); Robert Shafter, *The English Ode to 1660* (1918); George N. Shuster, *The English Ode from Milton to Keats* (1940, repr. 1964).

RGF

onomatopoeia
see TEXTURE

oral composition
see EPIC

organic
The notion of organic form in literature (bequeathed to Modern Anglo-American criticism by Coleridge, who referred to it constantly) appeals to a biological analogy which can be misleading as well as revealing. Its revealing aspect is the emphasis it places on the overall structure of the work and, consequently, on the *relationship* of the parts and aspects to each other and to the whole. The whole is thought of as being 'more than the sum of its parts' in the sense that the whole provides impressions which cannot be traced back to the parts in isolation. The validity of this notion, as applied to the non-biological world of art, receives support from modern perceptual psychology. Visual impressions of length, colour, texture, prominence and so forth can be altered not by altering the parts that appear to produce them, but merely the context in which those parts function. A simple example is provided by the four equal straight lines below:

It seems likely that similar effects occur in the medium of language. The greater the amount of formal and semantic detail we are able to describe, as linguists, the more we stand in need, as literary critics, of criteria for selecting and organizing those details in ways relevant to their role in the individual work. At the time of writing, this is undoubtedly the chief problem of stylistics. Until we have discovered more about the way language works, we can at least be guided by the aim of providing in our descriptions of literary works the maximum differentiation of parts and aspects compatible with a synthetic view of the whole—and therefore of the true role played by its aspects and parts.

A misleading aspect of the biological analogy is the implication that the critic must 'murder to dissect'. A work may be a *gestalt* (a form open to modification by the creative perceptual dispositions of the reader), but it is not a living organism.

A distinct use of 'organic form' opposes organic (irregular, unique) forms to inorganic (regular, traditional) forms. Little harm would result if the opposition were merely descriptive. But it generally involves an evaluative preference for organic (living, natural) as against inorganic (mechanical, artificial), the central assumption being that organic forms grow from the meaning and embody it while inorganic forms pre-exist and therefore act as a strait-jacket to meanings (which are, after all, unique). This use of the term ignores the fact that both 'organic' and 'inorganic' forms can be relevantly or irrelevantly used. Perhaps a more neutral term, such as 'structure' will come to replace it, since it has all the advantages and none of the disadvantages of the older, Romantic term. See also FORM, LANGUAGE, STRUCTURE.

See George Rousseau, *Organic Form* (1972). On organic doctrine in criticism, see Murray Krieger, *The New Apologists for Poetry* (1956). See also Anne Cluysenaar, *Introduction to Literary Stylistics* (1976).

AAAC

originality

'An *Original* may be said to be of a vegetable nature; it rises spontaneously from the vital root of Genius; it grows, it is not made: *Imitations* are often a sort of *Manufacture* wrought up by those *Mechanics, Art* and *Labour*, out of pre-existent materials not their own' (Edward Young). The eighteenth-century notion of originality rests on an analogy between artistic and natural creation, on a cult of individualism and self-expression and, later, a realization that nature, indeed all creativity, is evolutionary. Art may then follow nature without being unoriginal; may be original without being eccentric. What man discovers on looking into himself will be original, not just because each individual is both a part of nature and a unique being, but also because the nature and the culture to which he belongs are constantly changing.

These historical connotations still affect current usage. Three distinct, though often conflated, senses of 'originality' are present in this complex of ideas: a psychological theory about the creative act; a theory concerning the proper function of art in society; an aesthetic theory.

That the original work is the product of a creative act of self-expression is either unprovable or a truism. Unfortunately self-expression is often conceived in oversimplified terms. A work apparently imbued with the *furor poeticus* may be the product of infinite labour and well-assimilated literary influence. A Petrarchan sonnet may be ultimately self-expressive, and indeed original, within its convention. Of course the psychological notion of originality cannot be a literary criterion; many original productions of immense sincerity, uninfluenced by any model, are none the less appalling.

Should a work be original by treating new issues, expressing contemporary sensibility? Would one accept a good Shakespearean sonnet written in 1970? On aesthetic grounds, yes. But one might for other than aesthetic reasons, attach greater value to a more 'original' work. But even here, if originality is equated with simple 'relevant' newness of material, it is not an all-important criterion of social worth. The new material may be trivial, or a writer may treat with original insight material by no means new.

The third, aesthetic, sense of originality is the most important for the critic. If an original work is so because each aspect contributes to the internal economy of the whole and is not there only for external reasons, then 'original' is virtually synonymous with 'good'. Such a work is original irrespective of whether it is conventional or not. If, however, a work is original because it breaks with convention or, more radically, with tradition, originality in this sense is not an evaluative but a descriptive term. See also AUTHOR, CREATION.

See Ezra Pound, *Make It New* (1934); Edward Young, *Conjectures of Original Composition* (1759, repr. 1966).

EJB

ostranenie

see FORMALISM

P

paradox

An apparently self-contradictory statement, though one which is essentially true. Two examples of paradox may help to demonstrate its special significance in modern thought (Schopenhauer, Shaw):

> The more unintelligent a man is, the less mysterious existence seems to him.

> The man who listens to reason is lost: reason enslaves all whose minds are not strong enough to master her.

The movement of twentieth-century philosophy away from causal modes of thought towards an acceptance of contrarieties and oppositions, seems to be reflected accurately in the present critical preoccupation with paradox in literature. An acceptance of the radical discontinuity between thought and existence prompts both Shaw and Schopenhauer to point to the futility of searching for solutions within the unity of thought. Modern criticism, beginning with the rehabilitation of the Metaphysical poets and continuing with the rediscovery of the Augustans, has gradually progressed from the exploration of simple intellectual paradox associated with irony and satire, to a discovery of the paradox of wonder in the existential poetry of the Romantics. As Cleanth Brooks has shown (*The Well Wrought Urn*, 1947) the paradoxes upon which such poems as Wordsworth's 'Immortality Ode' are built represent the basic structure of Romantic thought and are far removed from a trivial verbal exercise.

BCL

paraphrase

depends on the possibility of *synonymy*: the availability of more than one expression for the same meaning. The theory of STYLE seems to demand belief in the possibility of paraphrase, and consequently in a model of language which distinguishes form and content, expression and meaning.

These assumptions have been vigorously challenged by neo-Romantic critics, taking as their battle-cry Shelley's assault on 'the vanity of translation' and drawing support from the many linguists and linguistic philosophers who have denied the existence of synonyms or asserted that a word in context has a unique and unmatchable meaning. (Chomsky's generative-transformational grammar is built on a theory which accepts synonymy, but more recent writers such as Wallace Chafe are attempting to reconstruct a theory which, while admitting ambiguity, is more traditional in rejecting synonymy.) The most vocal advocate for the inseparability of form and content is Cleanth Brooks, who attacks what he calls 'The heresy of paraphrase' (*The Well Wrought Urn*, ch. 11): 'the imagery and the rhythm are not merely the instruments by which this fancied core-of-meaning-which-can-be-expressed-in-a-paraphrase is directly rendered'. The alleged heresy is a belief that a poem reduces to an arbitrary conjunction of a 'meaning' (statement, theme, etc.) and a decorative surface. Brooks asserts, quite correctly, that the surface is not merely decorative: we apprehend meaning by way of the 'words on the page', and changing the words may change our conception of the poem. In lyric poetry (Brooks's paradigm), where the concrete properties of language are heightened, this is certainly the case—poems are *in practical terms* unparaphrasable. But it would be unwise to deny the validity of the idea of paraphrase on the basis of arguments concerning an extreme case. And we would do well to scrutinize our own critical techniques. Paraphrase is, willy-nilly, part of the critic's normal procedure. See also CONTENT, FORM, STYLE, TEXTURE.

See David Lodge, *Language of Fiction* (1966), 18–26, which rehearses some of the literary arguments on this issue.

RGF

parody

is one of the most calculated and analytic literary techniques: it searches out, by means of subversive mimicry, any weakness, pretension or lack of self-awareness in its original. This 'original' may be another work, or the collective style of a group of writers, but although parody is often talked of as a very clever and inbred literary joke, any distinctive and artful use of language—by, for example, journalists, politicians, or priests—is susceptible of parodic impersonation. Although it is often deflationary and comic, its distinguishing characteristic is not deflation, but analytic mimicry. The systematic appropriation of the form and imagery of secular love poetry by the sacred lyric is an example of parody in this basic sense. It is one of the ways for a writer to explore and identify available techniques, and may focus on their unused potentialities as well as their limitations. As an internal check that literature keeps on itself, parody may be parasitic or creative, and is often both. Perhaps because parodic works are themselves highly critical, they are more frequently annotated than analysed; sometimes the parodist is so self-conscious that he pre-empts his would-be critic, providing his own footnotes and explanatory comments (like Vladimir Nabokov in *Pale Fire*, 1962). The parodist addresses a highly 'knowing' and literate audience, for whom criticism is merely a part of literature, not a separate industry. He is often an ironist, affecting admiration of the style he borrows and distorts (Pope 'compliments' Milton in this way in *The Dunciad*, 1728); sometimes he explicitly and systematically undermines a rival mode (as Jane Austen does with the Gothic novel in *Northanger Abbey*, 1818); impersonation of the alien style is always the basic technique. In various periods, particularly in the eighteenth century, attempts were made to distinguish different kinds of parodic appropriation: 'burlesque' was said to be the kind where some new 'low' subject was treated incongruously in an old 'high' style, and 'travesty' the opposite (with Juno using the language of a fishwife). Such distinctions can seldom in practice be sustained, since one parodic work habitually exploits a whole range of incongruous juxtapositions, and the categories obscure the complex intermingling of parodic effects. Both terms, however, are useful to indicate the kind of response a work appeals to: 'travesty' (as in its popular use) implies something savagely reductive, and 'burlesque' the comic immediacy of a theatrical 'spoof'. A distinction can be made, however, between all forms of parodic imitation and 'caricature': the analogy between caricature in painting and parody in writing (established by Fielding in his parodic novel *Joseph Andrews*, 1742) is misleading. Parody attacks its butt indirectly, through style; it 'quotes' from and alludes to its original, abridging and inverting its characteristic devices. The caricaturist's 'original' is not some other already existent style or work: he holds a distorting mirror up to life, whereas parody is a mirror of a mirror, a critique of a view of life already articulated in art. Parody is so common an element in literature precisely because it adds this extra level of critical comment which is lacking from caricature. See also PASTICHE, SATIRE.

LS

pastiche,

whether applied to part of a work, or to the whole, implies that it is made up largely of phrases, motifs, images, episodes, etc. borrowed more or less unchanged from the work(s) of other author(s). The term is often used in a loosely derogatory way to describe the kind of helpless borrowing that makes an immature or unoriginal work read like a mosaic of quotations. More precisely, it has two main meanings, corresponding to two different *deliberate* uses of pastiche as a technique. There is a kind of pastiche, often serious and loving, which seeks to recreate in a more extreme and accessible form the manner of major writers. It tends to eliminate tensions, to produce a more highly-coloured and polished effect, picking out and reiterating favourite stylistic mannerisms, and welding them into a new whole which has a superficial coherence and order. Unlike plagiarism, pastiche of this kind is not intended to deceive: it is literature frankly inspired by literature (as in Akenside's poem 'The Pleasures of Imagination', 1744). The second main use of pastiche is not reverential and appreciative, but disrespectful and sometimes deflationary. Instead of ironing out ambiguities in its source(s) it highlights them. It cannot be distinguished absolutely from PARODY, but whereas the parodist need only allude to his original intermittently, the writer of pastiche industriously recreates it, often concocting a medley of borrowed styles like Flann O'Brien in *At Swim-Two-Birds* (1939). A closely synonymous term, nearly obsolete, 'cento' or 'centonism', is relevant here: in its original Latin form it meant a garment of patchwork and, applied to literature, a poem made up by joining scraps from various authors. Many of the specialized uses of pastiche are reminiscent of this literary game: it may give encyclopaedic scope to a work, including all previous styles (Joyce's *Ulysses*); it is used by writers who wish to exemplify their ironic sense that language comes to them secondhand and stylized (George Herbert's 'Jordan I'). And a general *air* of pastiche is created by many writers who, for various reasons, refuse to evolve a style of their own, and who (like John Barth) employ other men's cast-off phrases with conscious scepticism. Although it remains a specialized technique, pastiche has been underplayed by Romantic-influenced criticism with its stress on particularity and uniqueness in literature.

LS

pastoral

in classical and neo-classical definitions is a mode with conventional prescriptions about setting, characters and diction. In drama, poetry or prose it employs stylized properties and idealized Arcadian situations from rural life—'purling streams', 'embowering shades'; singing contests, mourning processions—as a deliberate disguise for the preoccupations of urban, sophisticated people. Pastoral focuses on the contrast between the lives of the people who write it and read it, and the lives of those country people it portrays (both ends of society often appear, as in Shakespearean comedy). It relies on conventions shared with the audience: traditional names (Corydon, Thyrsis, Adonais), inherited motifs (the flower catalogue), plots based on transparent disguises. It may be idyllic, but is more often (as in Spenser's 'Shepheardes Calender' or Milton's 'Lycidas') tinged with melancholy and satire; because of its dimension of reference to contemporary society, pastoral invites allegory and symbolism. The proliferation of stock features made it, in Greece, Augustan Rome and Renaissance Europe, an extremely precise medium for exploring the attitudes (rural nostalgia, narcissism, self-doubt) of consciously civilized and cultured people—poets particularly (N.B. the heightened self-consciousness of the pastoral ELEGY for a dead fellow-poet).

The artificiality of pastoral is not an evasion of realism: its rural setting is metaphorical, a means rather than an end. Like other conventions, it decays when the means cease to be viable, not because it is false (since it was never true). Many uses of the term are distorted by criteria adopted from realistic fiction. Documentary 'truth to the object' is irrelevant in pastoral, which is a mirror reflecting back its audience and writer rather than a transparent window. Pastoral is a product of pre- or anti-realistic world-views which stress imaginative projection (e.g. the PATHETIC FALLACY) rather than passive perception. Thus it lost its credibility with the rise of empiricism (and of the novel) during the eighteenth century, and has been partially reinstated in the twentieth by writers like the American poet Wallace Stevens who argue that 'Life consists/Of propositions about life.' 'Failed realism', and 'anything depicting country life' are both uses of 'pastoral' based on unexamined realist assumptions.

Exploratory modern use of the term dates from William Empson's *Some Versions of Pastoral* (1935), a model for the lively use of apparently moribund critical categories. He pointed out that essentially pastoral was not a bundle of conventional properties, but a particular structural relationship ('putting the complex into the simple') which survived and extended beyond the limits of the formal mode. Empson's best example was *Alice in Wonderland*, where the heroine, like the 'shepherd of sixteenth century pastoral, explores the anxieties and complacencies of her society'. While retaining its function as a label, 'pastoral' has acquired an extended application which relates to the search for literary MYTHS and archetypes. This use of 'pastoral' is part of a more general critical pressure towards the mapping and analysis of recurrent structures in literature, which is a convincing corrective to the New Critical and modernist erosion of generic categories. Cf. RURAL NOVEL

LS

pathetic fallacy

Ruskin introduced this notion (*Modern Painters*, vol. 3, 1856) to account for the attribution to inanimate nature of animate, even human, characteristics. He gives 'the cruel, crawling foam' as an example. Men, he claims, fall into four categories: those who see nature clearly because their emotions are too dull to interfere (non-poets), those whose emotions are too strong for their intellect (second-order poets), those who, having strong intellect and passions, achieve a balance between the two (first-order poets), and finally those who perceive realities too great for man to bear and who revert to expressions which reason no longer controls (prophets). The second and last make use of the pathetic fallacy, but only the former do so through weakness. Ruskin argues, moreover, that the poet who sees nature as having 'an animation and pathos of its own' (rather than borrowed from man) does not commit the fallacy but merely shows 'an instinctive sense . . . of the Divine presence'. What constitutes a 'pathetic fallacy' must therefore vary with the dominant idea of the time: many would now see in such an 'instinctive sense' a fallacy rather than the perception of a truth.

It is perhaps more in keeping with modern critical methods to treat the pathetic fallacy as a device with special effects on a reader's sensibility (instead of a mode of expression revealing the writer's state of mind). On this view, logical and literal criteria are as inappropriate to the evaluation of this figure as they are to the evaluation of metaphor. Literature is, after all, a means of communicating truths of experience rather than of inanimate matter. As Erwin Schroedinger argues in *Mind and Matter* (1959), even basic perceptions which few of us question (such as that of colour) are, scientifically speaking, fallacious.

AAAC

peripeteia
see NARRATIVE STRUCTURE

persona
Originally used to denote the acting masks of classic Greek theatre, the term 'persona' has developed extensive critical connotations. It is commonly used to indicate the difference between the man who sits down to write and the 'author' as we realize him in and through the words on the page. This persona, or 'second self' of the author has to be distinguished from the narrator even in first-person narration. The degree of correspondence between narrator and persona may vary greatly. In Fielding's *Tom Jones* (1749), for instance, the narrator shares many qualities with the persona—tolerance, humour, wide understanding of human behaviour, and humanistic learning. But in the case of Swift's *A Modest Proposal* (1729), to assume continuity between narrator and persona would be disastrous. The narrator deliberately heightens and distorts the view Swift seeks to expose. The distortion establishes the *tone* which makes us aware of Swift's *voice* in the prose. The persona clearly recommends the very opposite view, the amelioration of conditions and the implementation of social remedies, *not* the breeding of children for food etc.

As Wayne C. Booth points out in *The Rhetoric of Fiction* (1961), the complex problem of reliable and unreliable narrators involves the persona or, as he calls it, the implied author. Thus, 'I have called a narrator *reliable* when he speaks for or acts in accordance with the norms of the work (which is to say, the implied author's norms), *unreliable* when he does not.' Recognizing the persona is therefore central to the act of effective reading, since the persona represents the sum of all the author's conscious choices in a realized and more complete self as 'artist'.

This idea of persona as 'second self' incorporates the metaphorical roots of the 'mask' concept, implying the total being presented to the audience, outside and beyond the actor who assumes it. This, in turn, is rooted in magic ritual where 'masks' are independent beings who *possess* the man who assumes them. Metaphorically, mask belongs to the group of concepts which imply that artists discover a more fully integrated vision than exists in 'reality'. It implies, too, a way out of the closed world of the ego into an objective vision communicable to others. Late Romantics, like Yeats, turn to the 'mask' concept to express a longing for an art which permits the artist to objectify his experience and free it from mere subjectivity. See also NARRATIVE.

GG

picaresque

A kind of realistic fiction which originated in Spain with the anonymous *Lazarillo de Tormes* (1554) and the more influential novel by Mateo Alemán, *Guzmán de Alfarache* (1559 and 1604), which was widely translated. Other important novels in this genre include in German, Grimmelshausen's *Simplicissimus* (1669), and in French, Le Sage's *Gil Blas* (1715–35). The Spanish *picaro* or *picarón*, the anti-hero of such a novel, was translated into English as the *picaroon*; he was a scoundrel of low birth and evil life, at war with society. He was on his own, and the form of the novel is commonly an autobiographical account of his fortunes, misfortunes, punishments and opportunism. The tales are episodic, frequently arranged as journeys. The endings are abrupt, either as the picaroon sets off for America for a 'new life', or for the galleys. This allows a sequel to be added; but the mode is not formless. The pessimistic judgment of life does not allow a neat dénouement. Life is just more of the same. The stories inflict physical damage on their characters, and the damage is a sign of experience. Experience, however, is only more instances for the picaroon of his irrepressible independence and society's unalterable hostility. The novels allow a statement of man's freedom and independence but invoke the counter-balancing, restraining oppression of society. All picaroons have a series of tyrannical masters, and the servile relationship which demands abasement and allows cheating is a microcosm of the human state.

Picaresque is a term that must refer to the nature of the subject matter as well as to the superficial autobiographical and episodic features of the fiction. Unfortunately, in English it is the accidental arrangements that are usually indicated by *picaresque*: a low-life narrator, a rambling tale. There was plenty of rogue literature in England from Nashe's *Unfortunate Traveller* (1594) onwards. Obviously Defoe in *Moll Flanders* (1722) has some affinity with the picaresque. The novel is episodic; it has an autobiographical narrator and it is realistic. Moll, though, does not seem to be a real *picaro*. She is that peculiarly English figure, a temporary *déclassé(e)*. Smollett's *Roderick Random* (1748) is similar. Random is only temporarily of low estate; he ends by being restored to his own level. He is really a master, not a servant. The same author's *The Adventures of Ferdinand Count Fathom* (1753) is more nearly a real picaresque. Various features of the picaresque are found in different English novels: *Tom Jones* is organized along a journey; Dickens's *Nicholas Nickleby* allows realistic description of scenes of real life; Joyce Cary's *The Horse's Mouth* presents physical decay as the sign of experience, and Gully Jimson enjoys the 'free life'.

See Robert Alter, *Rogue's Progress: Studies in the Picaresque Novel* (1964); A. A. Parker, *Literature and the Delinquent: A Study of the Picaresque Novel* (1947).

AMR

plagiarism
see PASTICHE

Platonism

In his utopian *Republic* (written c. 380 B.C.) Plato banished the artists, having diagnosed the arts as indulgent imitations of a perceptible universe which was itself a misleading shadow of the eternal Ideas. He allowed only propagandist myths ('noble lies') as a concession to the irrationality of the majority, and suggested ironically that the arts were lower than practical crafts—better make a chair than a painting of one.

But Plato's own highly fictionalized method, his use of dialogue and of myth (the Cave, the Spindle of Necessity) undermined his attack on the arts. Plotinus (A.D. 204–70), founder of neo-Platonism, reinterpreted Plato in the direction of subjective mysticism (stressing the visionary elements in Book 6 of the *Republic*, and the *Symposium*)— and his version of Plato the myth-maker and *vates*, mingling with the more practical original, became the source of the most far-reaching claims *for* the arts in Western culture.

The Platonic artist, whether renaissance or romantic, is a philosopher, who aspires to change the world by changing men's attitudes and values. His 'poem' may be an institution or an epic; what makes him an artist is 'that idea or fore-conceit of the work, and not . . . the work itself' (Sidney, *Defence of Poesie*, 1595). 'Imitation' in Platonic terminology can be misleading—theoretically at least the poet will 'to imitate borrow nothing of what is, hath been or shall be' (Sidney). Platonism does not distinguish the arts by media: metaphors from statecraft are used about poetry—'Poets are the unacknowledged legislators of the world' (Shelley, *Defence of Poetry*, 1821)—and metaphors from poetics about politics or music.

It follows that Platonic criticism avoids classification of genres or of rhetorical figures; the Platonist's interest in language and form is compounded of miraculism and frustration: on the one hand the aspiration towards a fixed, innocent, 'golden' language, in which metre, image and syntax will embody that essential harmony towards which creation strives; on the other a profound scepticism which pushes language to its limits, destroys and impoverishes it as if to prove its eternal enmity to the ideal. The Platonic theorist is always likely to dismiss the product—the words, the rhythms—as 'a feeble shadow of the original conceptions of the poet' (Shelley). This pressure on the medium unites with the idealist yearning towards the One to produce hybrid forms (allegorical epics, lyrical dramas). Again, this is paradoxical: Platonism produces a subversive multiplication of forms in the strife for order.

In literary history, too, the idealist pressures have proved liberating: literature is outside space and time, eternally subversive. Shelley's reading of Milton (like Blake's) is characteristically Platonic:

He mingled . . . the elements of human nature as colours upon a single pallet, and arranged them . . . according to the laws of epic truth, that is, according to the laws of that principle by which a series of actions of the external universe and of intelligent and ethical beings is calculated to excite the sympathies of succeeding generations of mankind.

Platonic literary history is repetitious or circular (Yeats), a continual return to mythic figures and structures only incidentally clothed in the trappings of a particular culture.

Platonism is the poets' poetics; more than any other theory it has been responsible for poetic self-consciousness (Collins's 'Ode on the Poetical Character' (1746), Stevens's *Notes towards a Supreme Fiction* (1942)). This fact alone indicates its particular freedoms and limitations: it may set the poet squarely at the centre of his world (refusing to distinguish between him and the philosophers) but it undermines the world's reality and solidity for him. The result is that the processes of creativity become what the work itself is about. See also IMITATION.

See W. H. Auden, 'The Poet and the City', *The Dyer's Hand* (1962);

Christopher Butler, *Number Symbolism* (1970); R. S. Crane (ed.), *Critics and Criticism* (1957); Wallace Stevens, *The Necessary Angel* (1951); Edgar Wind, *Pagan Mysteries in the Renaissance* (1958).

LS

pleasure

Some texts stimulate rather than satisfy, and indeed Novalis cultivated the fragment as a genre with this intention. But for many Neoclassicists (e.g. Kant), art is made pleasurable by its satisfying harmony of design: once we have discovered a great work's central theme or 'core' (Spitzer), all other features (such as versification or plot) can be seen as closely related to it, creating a complex yet powerfully unified effect. Nevertheless, the problems of applying this view to the disturbing, fearful events in TRAGEDY led Kant and others to postulate a radically different pleasure, aroused by the 'sublime' rather than the 'beautiful': we thrill to see tragic heroes rise above adversity and their self-preservation instinct because we feel ourselves participating in and aspiring towards the potential indomitability of the human spirit. By accepting guilt and the destruction of his achievements, Oedipus transcends them. Note that both 'beautiful' and 'sublime' pleasure require distance: Oedipus and Lear do not enjoy their tragic experiences as their audiences may, and what distinguishes aesthetic enjoyment of form from a factory owner's admiration of a complex machine or a lecher's of a beautiful body is its disinterestedness: we seek satisfaction neither of self-interest nor of aroused desire, experiencing pleasure in our temporary freedom from such feelings.

Totally unenjoyable literature would probably cease to be published. Yet pleasure, especially if distanced or restful, is often considered suspect and self-indulgent. If we find Diderot's *The Nun* a good read, rather than feeling indignation at the heroine's suffering, we perversely refuse to be disturbed by how human beings can treat one another in society. And is it irresponsible, in our world which perpetually generates new problems and challenges, to enjoy Mörike's Orplid poems, which create a harmonious, limited, self-contained alternative world?

Roland Barthes detects insufficiently challenging pleasure in almost all pre-Modernist literature. He too postulates two radically different kinds of pleasure. He argues that we interpret what we read (as also our other experience) by applying already familiar conventions: our previous novel-reading and acquaintance with social assumptions create a large yet finite set of expectations, activated when we tackle another novel. A text might work totally within these limits, avoiding surprise and confirming our cultural expectations: Balzac, despite his complexity, can be seen as very readable (*lisible*), offering pleasure in reassuring recognition of the familiar. But the ideal text is for Barthes totally plural, in the sense that it refuses to imprison its readers within conventions or compel any particular interpretation: such a text he calls *scriptible*. For example, as we read Joyce's *Finnegans Wake* (1939) or Philippe Sollers's *Paradis* (1981), small segments of text, at first apparently disconnected, can be related in innumerable different ways. This experience, in which each reader 'writes' or constructs his own text, Barthes sees as liberating.

Although such works may indeed be used by the patient and inventive for individualistic self-expression, Barthes implies a heedlessly optimistic view of the reader. Faced with segments which can mean almost anything and an absence of authorial direction, readers will imagine and impose interpretations deriving from their previous habits of sense-making and thus from their acquired conventions: supposedly liberated reading becomes indistinguishable from uninventive, self-indulgent mental drift. A more useful approach to pleasure's origins is to analyse the experience of having expectations sometimes confirmed, sometimes surprised by a text (impossible if it is *totally* plural). At a first reading, there is delight in a release from and expansion of our limited consciousness as we compare our responses with the text's; at a later reading, the no less pleasurable realization that our perceptions of it have altered and that therefore our relation with it remains fruitful. This indicates why, without being restful, books are often valued much as are developing relationships with friends. See also AESTHETICS, READER.

See Roland Barthes, *The Pleasure of the Text* (trans. 1976), *S/Z* (trans. 1975); Donald W. Crawford, *Kant's Aesthetic Theory* (1974); William Wordsworth, 'Preface' (1802 version) to *Lyrical Ballads*.

MHP

plot

in criticism is a term of highly varied status. It can mean just the paraphrasable story of a work—the simple narrative line which we can then flesh out by considering character and description, tone and texture, pattern and myth; Forster's 'low', 'atavistic' story-telling. So writing-schools offer compendia of plots; so many works (lyric poems, modernist novels) can be 'without' it. The usage is partly a bastardization of Aristotle's word *mythos* in the *Poetics*, commonly translated as 'plot'; and for a richer sense of the term it is worth recalling what he said. Aristotle's plot was the mimesis (i.e. the analogous *making*) of an action. He distinguished six parts in his exemplary species, tragedy, but did not reduce them to equivalence: plot constitutes the dynamic whole to which the other parts relate, the necessary order as opposed to the enabling features of development. It is the distilling centre of the choices available to the author; having determined his medium (stage, book) and his mode (lyric, dramatic), he must also choose other essential principles of coherence. His plot must have a shape (e.g. a rise in the hero's fortune followed by a descent); it must have a sequence or order determining the kind and degree of effort at particular points (beginning, middle, end); it must have a size (magnitude, duration) which will help determine that shape and sequence. It must have agents and a society: for these there must be a language, appropriate not only to them but to the other elements of the structure. It must have a developing psychology culminating internally in good tragedy in the protagonist and externally in an effect on the audience (CATHARSIS); and it must accord with and seek out general human experience (universality). Aristotle's *mythos* is close to Henry James's assumptions in his preface to *The Portrait of a Lady*, when he distinguishes a *donnée* and then sees certain elements as being of the essence and others of the provision. This adds what is perhaps implicit in Aristotle; that there is play in writing for *continuous* choice; plot is *emergent* from the selective logic of the writerly act.

Few modern critics have taken up this complex usage, viewing plot as a necessary order of a fiction. An exception are the Chicago Aristotelians (see CHICAGO CRITICS), who have spoken persuasively of its value as a means of distinguishing the determining order of a work. (The Russian FORMALIST critics have also usefully explored the concept.) What (here to adapt Aristotle considerably) seems apparent is that the 'deep' definition of plot approximates to the difficulties of the writing process before and during composition: it involves recognizing an essential relationship, familiar to writers if not always to critics, between 'plot' in its simple story sense and other elements much more complicated than is usually understood—characters, local linguistic devices ('speeches', 'descriptions'), general linguistic devices (rhetorical strategies, pervasive symbols), generative sequence in actions at narrative and tonal levels, starts and finishes. The tendency in modern criticism to isolate 'human plot' from 'verbal plot' (preferring often the latter) or to regard story as a low, summary thread on which to string higher things can be a dangerous, diminishing scheme; this is not Aristotle's predicate, since he would assume that plots can be of all kinds (e.g. a lyric poem must have one). Plot is a compositional whole. Even then, it *can* seem a deterministic grid, making the writer of a fiction a God-figure whose command over his characters is absolute. (This analogue—character as liberal, plot as determinist—has often been a theme in fictions: Muriel Spark's *The Driver's Seat*, 1970 is a recent example.) This is a possible derivative of the concept of plot, and suggests its coherent wholeness. But should we separate out character? Do we not, generally, need an organizational concept less rigid than this: one that presumes the multiplicity of necessary orders in fictions, recognizes that these are not all pre-formed but are emergent factors of literary creation, yet still assumes that the writer characteristically pursues an organizational coherence we can term a 'plot'? See also CHARACTER, NARRATIVE STRUCTURE, STRUCTURALISM, STRUCTURE.

See Aristotle, trans. I. Bywater, *Poetics* (1909); R. S. Crane, 'The concept of plot and the plot of *Tom Jones*' in Crane (ed.), *Critics and Criticism* (1957); E. M. Forster, *Aspects of the Novel* (1927); Henry James, 'The art of fiction' (1888), reprinted in Morris Roberts (ed.), *The Art of Fiction and Other Essays by Henry James* (1948); Tony Tanner, *City of Words* (1971). For the Formalist/Structuralist tradition, see Lee T. Lemon and Marion J. Reis (trans.), *Russian Formalist Criticism: Four Essays* (1965); *Russian Poetics in Translation*, Vol. 4, *Formalist Theory* (1977); Tzvetan Todorov, *The Poetics of Prose* (trans. 1977); Seymour Chatman, *Story and Discourse* (1978).

MSB

pluralism
see CHICAGO CRITICS

poetic diction
see DICTION, POETRY

poetic licence
It has sometimes been argued that, because of the difficulty of satisfying the additional voluntary restrictions of poetic form, the poet has a 'licence' to relax some of the normal restrictions of his language-system. But if poetic licence is to be anything more than an excuse for technical incompetence, a deeper justification must be sought for the tendency of poetic language to deviate from the grammatical, and lexical, norms. The most thorough attempt to find such a justification was made by the Russian Formalist and Prague Structuralist critical schools. According to Shklovsky, people living by the sea grow impervious to the sound of the waves. 'By the same token, we scarcely ever hear the words which we utter. . . . We look at each other, but we do not see each other any more. Our perception of the world has withered away, what has remained is mere recognition.' By disturbing language, and therefore the view of reality which we receive through language, the poet refreshes perception and replaces recognition by an impression of novelty. Or, as Roman Jakobson has put it, 'The function of poetry is to point out that the sign is not identical with its referent.' On this view, the kind of 'licence' we ought to grant should cover neither technical incompetence nor novelty for its own sake, but only deviations which bring about a keener sense of inner and outer realities. Many writers, even prose-writers, would agree. Conrad, for example, wrote that 'the

development of . . . phrases from their (so-called) natural order is luminous for the mind'. See also FOREGROUNDING, FORMALISM, ORIGINALITY.

See Victor Erlich, *Russian Formalism* (1965) for a general discussion of the topic and for the quotations from Shklovsky and Jakobson above.

AAAC

poetics

In modern usage, not the study of, or the techniques of, poetry (verse), but the general theory of literature. From the Russian FORMALISTS, Prague School and French STRUCTURALISTS to current structuralist and POST-STRUCTURALIST writers there has been an appeal for a science of literature which should be devoted not to the piecemeal criticism or interpretation of specific literary texts, but to identifying the general properties which make literature possible: one should study 'literariness' rather than existing works of 'literature'. The search was, then, for general laws underlying particular texts: for an 'essence' to literature. For a clear programmatic statement, see T. Todorov, 'Poétique' in O. Ducrot *et al.*, *Qu'est-ce que le structuralisme?* (1968).

Universals of literature might seem an over-abstract and over-ambitious goal, given the great formal diversity of poems, plays, novels, oral stories, etc., and most work in poetics has consisted of descriptive studies of specific kinds or genres of texts. Narrative genres from the oral anecdote and fairy tale to the epic and novel have been analysed in terms of claimed universal elements such as 'functions' of characters and the relations between them in fable, plot or narrative structure, or the relations between these internal elements and relationships and the position of the narrator or reader (see Shlomith Rimmon-Kenan, *Narrative Fiction: Contemporary Poetics*, 1983). Dramatic genres involve the same elements and relationships with the additional modalities of character/actor and stage/audience relations (see Keir Elam, *The Semiotics of Theatre and Drama*, 1980). Poetic genres have been studied in terms of the formal patterning of sounds (assonance, alliteration, rhymes); rhythms (metre, phrase- and sentence-rhythm), relations of lines, stanzas, sections, syntax, point of view, etc. (the verse analyses of Roman Jakobson have been an important model and focus for controversy). Poetics does not aim, however, to study these 'devices' piecemeal, but seeks the determining patterns of literary structure such as the relationship between automatism and FOREGROUNDING and the master device of the 'dominant' (Jakobson), that component of a work which sets in motion and determines the relations between all other components.

Theory and description in contemporary poetics has been much influenced by the analogies provided by the 'generative' linguistics of

Noam Chomsky (cf. LANGUAGE): hence *generative poetics*. Chomsky proposed that mature native speakers possess 'linguistic competence', based on universal properties of language, which allows them to produce and comprehend an unlimited number of new sentences; a grammar of a language captures this linguistic competence and assigns structural descriptions to sentences of the language. Such a grammar is said to 'generate all and only the grammatical sentences of the language'. Analogously, argued the poeticians, experienced readers of literature possess 'literary competence', a knowledge of the essential universal properties of literature which gives them access to the significance of specific literary texts: just as we know the grammar of our own language, we may in some sense know the 'grammar' of (e.g.) story construction, and even a naïve reader or listener senses when a story is deviant, if it is incomplete, if events seem to be in the wrong order, or if causal and sequential connections between elements are inconsistent or suppressed.

Although, as suggested above, universal literary competence is implausible, competence in particular genres with which the reader is familiar is reasonable, and grammars of genres of the kind suggested by Todorov could be regarded as accounting for such competence. At this point the linguistic analogy can be brought closer: the particular technical concepts which linguists use for describing sentences (e.g. deep structure, transformation, embedding, semantic feature, lexical item, etc.) can be applied to the larger unit, text, on the SEMIOTIC assumption that texts are structured analogously to sentences. A strictly generative poetics involves the analogic use of linguistic concepts in accounting for a text as derived from underlying abstract units of significance. We may distinguish between *syntactic* and *semantic* approaches to the generation of literary texts. Working with syntactic analogies, Todorov and Kristeva in France applied traditional grammatical terms to the analysis of narrative structures: 'proper name' represents character; 'adjective' represents properties of or states experienced by the characters; 'verb' represents actions by the characters that modify situations or affect the characters. See T. Todorov, 'The grammar of narrative' and 'Narrative transformations' in *The Poetics of Prose* (trans. 1977); J. Kristeva, *Le texte du roman* (1970). In America, the syntactic transformations of Chomsky's grammar have been applied to the ordering of narrative functions analysed by Propp in his *Morphology of the Folk-Tale* (1928, trans. rev. ed., 1968): a story consists of 'moves' or sequences of actions, and it is these, not individual verbs, which may be reordered, inverted or embedded (three typical transformations). Moreover, there is a semantic congruence between key sequences, such as the hero's struggle to solve a riddle set by the donor of a magic aid and his struggle to overcome the villain and thus achieve victory and rewards. A similar exploration of narrative transformations which underlie the shifting roles of characters was attempted by Todorov in his analysis of the novel *Les liaisons dangereuses* (see *Littérature et signification*, 1967).

Two Russian poeticians, Zholkovsky and Scheglov, take a more radically semantic line: literary *texts* are generated from *themes* (the object of search in traditional literary analysis and interpretation). The entire literary work is an expansion of a basic theme, and our ability to move to and fro between text and theme must depend on some rather consistent psychological mechanisms ('expressiveness devices') whereby simple meanings are 'processed' into more complex meanings. The number of such mechanisms is probably quite small, but it must include 'concretization', 'multiple realization', 'augmentation', 'contrast', 'antecedence', 'reversal' and 'ellipsis'. These may operate at any level of structure and at any phase in the generation of the text, so that their operation is not confined to specific sentence-like structures and sequences, as with the syntactic generative models. This model provides a set of procedures whereby we can trace the derivation of a literary text from its deep theme while making explicit at every stage our interpretative and analytical processes. See Yu. K. Scheglov and A. K. Zholkovsky, 'Towards a "theme-(expression devices)-text" model of literary structure' in *Generating the Literary Text, Russian Poetics in Translation*, I (1975); L. M. O'Toole, 'Analytic and synthetic approaches to narrative structure: Sherlock Holmes and "The Sussex Vampire" ', in R. Fowler (ed.), *Style and Structure in Literature* (1975).

Although founded on the generative model of linguistic competence, this generative poetics does not confine itself to studying the sequential arrangement of quasi-grammatical elements, but focuses on the specific mechanisms of literary competence. For other questions which are traditional concerns of poetics, see LITERATURE.

See also J. Culler, *Structuralist Poetics* (1975); V. Erlich, *Russian Formalism: History, Doctrine* (1965); R. Fowler, *Literature as Social Discourse* (1981), Chs 9 and 10; R. Jakobson, 'Linguistics and poetics' in T. A. Sebeok (ed.), *Style in Language* (1960). Relevant journals include *Communications, Journal of Literary Semantics, Poetics, Poetics Today* (formerly *Poetics and the Theory of Literature), Poétique, Russian Poetics in Translation*.

MO'T

poetry

The cluster of terms 'poem', 'poetry', 'poetic' and 'poetics' seem to be necessarily frequent in critical writing, various in their senses, and consequently dangerous. The commonest use of 'poem' is 'any composition in verse': VERSE referring to a set of technical conventions for regulating a composition by line-length, for making the *line* part of the expressive form, and 'poem' claiming to be a genre-term subsuming any production which utilizes that convention. There is some redundancy here, if poetry is equated with verse, but perhaps we need the term, for we have no other word, parallel to, say, NOVEL in prose, for a complete set of verses. However, poetry is also commonly *contrasted* with verse, both in a quantitative way, as using more tropes, more linguistic reverberations, and in a qualitative way, as using them better. So there is an implicit value-judgment, 'verse' being a metred production merely mechanically achieved, 'poetry' being an excellent set of verses. Verse may also be considered 'prosy', that is, mechanically correct but uninspired: this characterization merges with the idea of poetry as a metaphysical quality, an intangible, romantic, virtue. So the technical, descriptive, distinction between prose and verse is blurred: verse may be poetic or prosaic, prose may be poetic (ambiguously a good or bad quality) or not. The overtly evaluative 'poetic' hazardously transcends formal categories, except in such usages as 'poetic diction' by which is meant the artificial vocabulary conventions obeyed in, say, Anglo-Saxon or Augustan verse: *purling streams, finny tribes* and the like.

The technical imprecision of 'poem' and its derivatives is allowed by its etymology: Greek *poesis*, meaning a 'making', in verse or not. The contrast invoked is between that which is *constructed* and that which is natural. Traditionally 'poetry' has narrowed to the sense of a *verbal* making (as opposed to *poesis* in the other art media), but is still more general than 'verse', so again obscuring the distinction between metred and unmetred language which common usage supports. So 'poetics' comes to mean the general aesthetics of literature-as-opposed-to-other-arts and, more particularly, literature-seen-as-verbal-construct. The latter, more restricted, usage derives from the current extension of NEW CRITICAL doctrine, which stipulates that the method of analysis must be basically verbal (see David Lodge, *Language of Fiction* 1966, and articles by several hands in early issues of the new periodical *Novel*); critics can move easily to such apparently self-contradictory phrases as 'the poetics of fiction', considering the novel as a fundamentally verbal construct and its peculiar inner 'world' as ultimately linguistically created. So a novel can be a 'poem', and again the verse criterion for poetry disappears. So the unfortunate situation has arisen whereby any literary production may be called a poem: the word is short, etymologically unimpeachable, so various in its presuppositions as to appear to be minimally objectionable in any usage. As we have said, the term seems unavoidable. But the generalized senses, even if apparently etymologically justified, are surely misleading. It would be better if 'poem' were restricted to 'a complete set of verses'. If critics persist in exploiting the semantic variousness of the term, they must not let it betray them into a lazy romanticism; readers of criticism should look on it with scepticism (being careful to diagnose presuppositions) and students should use it with the utmost caution. Where a technical characterization is called for, other labels may be less misleading (e.g. 'verse', 'literary artefact'); where evaluation is implied, the criteria for judgment are more honestly faced and more securely applied if we avoid 'poetic' altogether.

RGF and AER

point of view

is a term used in the theory and criticism of FICTION to designate the position from which a story is told. Although a large number of these have been distinguished by some critics, there are basically only two: first-person and third-person narration. (Michel Butor's virtuoso use of the formal second-person '*vous*' in his novel *Second Thoughts*, 1957, is an idiosyncratic and isolated exception.) Narration from the first-person point of view has some obvious advantages in that it enables the author, without artificiality, to enter the intimacy of his protagonist's mind and betray its most secret thoughts and feelings to us, in a STREAM OF CONSCIOUSNESS manner or otherwise. But there are also serious drawbacks to this form of narration: if access to the hero is privileged and extensive, by the same token, since we are not able to read the minds of other people, the thoughts and feelings of the other characters must remain a matter of conjecture to hero, author and reader alike. Needless to say, some novelists turn this opaqueness to good ironic account (cf. *The Outsider* by Albert Camus (1942) which relies heavily on the inscrutability of others). The third person is, however, the more natural and widespread mode of narration, and most novelists have assumed it grants them licence to virtual omniscience. In a famous essay Jean-Paul Sartre pilloried François Mauriac for usurping wisdom reserved only to God, who—Sartre concluded with cutting emphasis—is no artist, 'any more than Mr Mauriac is.' As if to forestall this sort of broadside, some novelists have followed the example of Flaubert in *Madame Bovary* (1857) and used omniscience with such discretion that it passes virtually unnoticed. Others, again, have adopted Dickens's practice in *Bleak House* (1852–3) (intercalating Esther's narrative with omniscient narrative, and allowing Esther occasionally to narrate things not observed by her but reported to her by others), or have imitated the skilful manner in which Conrad, in *Under Western Eyes* (1911), employs an intelligent first-person narrator having privileged access to the mind of another through the perusal of a private diary or correspondence. And some contemporary experimental novelists like Alain Robbe-Grillet transcend the issue altogether by abrupt and unsignposted shifts from one point of view to another, in line with a systematic undermining of the entire traditional notion of consistency, and produce works which read as William Faulkner's *The Sound and the Fury* (1929) would, if all its paragraphs were placed in a hat and pulled out in random order. See also NARRATIVE.

See Norman Friedman, 'Point of view in fiction', *PMLA*, 70 (1955), 1160–84, updated by Wayne C. Booth, *The Rhetoric of Fiction* (1961); G. Genette, *Narrative Discourse* (1980); S. S. Lanser, *The Narrative Act: Point of View in Prose Fiction* (1981); F.Stanzel, *Narrative Situations in the Novel* (1969); B. Uspensky, *A Poetics of Composition* (trans. 1973).

JWJF

polyphony
see DIALOGIC STRUCTURE

polysemy
see AMBIGUITY

pornography,
classified by the Library of Congress as 'Literature, immoral', has evaded definitions by critics and courts alike precisely because of the difficulty of establishing the exact relationship between literature and morality. Lawyers have tended to describe it in terms of its effects—the pornographic is that which tends to deprave or corrupt—while recognizing that the pursuit of literary or scientific objectives may be held to justify even the potentially corrupting.

Pornography cannot simply be equated with eroticism, although the word originally signified accounts concerned with prostitutes. Lawrence, for example, saw eroticism as an essential element in human relations and as a reassuring contrast to the sterility of the modern environment; the SURREALISTS discovered in the erotic evidence of the central role of intuition and evidence of that reconciliation of opposites which was their chief aim. In other words eroticism could be seen as an essential aspect of the battle between humanity and its social determinants, as a key to mystical experience, and a salutary reminder of a non-rational dimension to existence. Pornography, on the other hand, has no aim beyond sexual stimulation. As Lawrence suggested, pornography is a result of the separation of sexuality from a notion of the whole man; it stems, at least in part, from a refusal, for religious, moral or aesthetic reasons, to admit in a public way to the centrality or the detailed reality of the sexual impulse. By this argument pornography is the inevitable by-product of prudery, and it is scarcely surprising, therefore, to discover the extent of pornography during the Victorian years: see Stephen Marcus, *The Other Victorians* (1966).

Pornography may constitute a conscious defiance of conventional standards of taste and propriety; it is thus potentially a subversive, even a revolutionary, force. It appears to push sensibility to its limit and to stand as an implicit criticism of a society intent on denying freedom of thought and expression. It is perhaps significant that pornography was permitted for a brief period during the French Revolution. Yet, if it is subversive in its appeal to anarchic impulses it is cathartic in its purgation of such impulses. Finally, therefore, pornography is perhaps little more than the perfect consumer product, simultaneously creating and doing its best to satisfy a specific need.

See Anon, *The Obscenity Laws* (1969); John Chandos, *To Deprave and Corrupt* (1962); Ludwig Marcuse, trans. K. Gershon, *Obscene: The History of an Indignation* (1965); Norman St John Stevas, *Obscenity and the Law* (1956).

CWEB

poststructuralism,

as a general term for recent developments in literary theory and criticism, became common in the 1970s. Like all such compounds, it is ambiguous. Is the relation to STRUCTURALISM one of succession or supercession?—that is, do we see poststructuralism as simply later than its predecessor, or is it in some sense an advance? Both usages can be found; and poststructuralism covers so many practices that it is impossible to define. But it can be approached as a working through, in various fields of inquiry, of some implications of DECONSTRUCTION. Derrida's influential lecture on 'Structure, sign and play in the discourse of the human sciences' (*Writing and Difference*, 1967, trans. 1978) proposed a disruption in the very concept of structure as a stable system, mischievously quoting Lévi-Strauss against himself. The effects of deconstruction, though, were not confined to a critique of structuralism. They rather emphasized a methodological shift, a move away from explanation by origin, order by opposition, fixed or closed signification, and the person as a unified subject. Recent PSYCHOANALYSIS, notably that of Jacques Lacan, encouraged the latter move, and psychoanalytic criticism is one variety of poststructuralism. It can also be traced in cultural and ideological analysis like that of Michel Foucault or Gilles Deleuze, and in the feminism of Hélène Cixous or Luce Irigaray. Divergent accounts of the READER, like Bloom's 'misreading', can be cited; so, of course, can the literary studies listed under DECONSTRUCTION. Roland Barthes's career shows the poststructural shift with particular emphasis, as in the sardonic opening of *S/Z* (1970, trans. 1974): 'There are said to be certain Buddhists whose ascetic practices enable them to see a whole landscape in a bean.' Such tidy encapsulation had been Barthes's own ambition in the mid-1960s, and it is precisely what poststructuralism rejects.

There are two useful anthologies: *Textual Strategies: Perspectives in Post-Structuralist Criticism*, edited by Josué V. Harari (1979); and *Untying the Text: a Post-Structuralist Reader*, edited by Robert Young (1981). The *Oxford Literary Review* and *Diacritics* publish relevant articles.

EC

practical criticism
see ANALYSIS, CRITICISM, NEW CRITICISM, READER.

prose
Though apparently the natural antithesis or sibling of verse, prose suffers from a lack of the precise definition which readily delimits its formal counterpart. From its 'different' look on the page, verse at first glance announces itself as something formed, pretentious, arresting; the claim to coherence, the inescapable frequency of line-endings, the alternate acceptance of and resistance to the potentially monolithic control of metre, gives verse a tenseness which may render it inadequate to explore modes of experience which are untense, only partially coherent, not attainable except by free-and-easy groping such as that of Montaigne. But theories of prose are heavily outnumbered by those of poetry, many of which, willingly blinded by the partially incidental etymological relationship between 'prose' and 'prosaic', are liable to stigmatize prose as irredeemably more ordinary, diffuse, unrefined, straightforward, and thereby to assume an often unexplained superiority for extraordinariness, compression, and refined obscurity.

Prose, like the Homeric epic, becomes formulaic if it aims at fixity and crystallization. Flaubert, for example, in attempting to refine it, eventually subjects it to a near-monolithic discipline, an impoverishment of language to a finite, recurring range of devices, not unrelated perhaps to the formulaic meagreness of memoranda and scientific discourses. His prose can often be read only one way: many of his ternary sentences are so clear in structure and cadence, so controlled in meaning, that the alert reader's initial experience of them can scarcely avoid being total; this excludes any search for alternative groupings of word or idea, and presents us with a bareness where language, thought and character lie unrelievedly open to our merciless gaze. Indeed, one resource of prose, which makes it an eminently suitable vehicle for realism, is the relative looseness of its context, its refusal to presuppose the inevitability of complex pattern, its ability to acknowledge the right of something to exist as itself and not some other thing, as a self-sufficient detail which may be absorbed only slowly into an organized perception.

Stanzas, by their visual shape, announce their separateness and monumentality; the appearance of the most frequent prose forms (essay, novel, short story) asserts an often reassuring substantiality and continuity. A danger, yet also a resource of longer forms, is repetition: the early pages of Dostoevsky's *Crime and Punishment* (1866), for instance, make much use of adjectives such as 'petty', 'disgusting', 'filthy', 'loathsome', 'ill-tempered', 'weary', which come increasingly to share each other's overtones, so that the qualitative unvariedness of Raskolnikov's perceptions is rendered, as well as the ebb and flow of their intensity. Frequently a variety of strands are sustained and repeated during a prose work: throughout *Mutmassungen über Jakob* (1959), Uwe Johnson sustains various possible interpretations of the central character's death; none is a full interpretation, but no satisfactory unified view emerges either, the various strands attempting to fuse but partly failing to do so: the book's continuing hesitation between them generates a highly complex view of an insoluble riddle, while also conveying a view of East German life as paralysingly slow. Slowness, as prose has perhaps realized better than the verse paragraph, is no barrier to complexity; the groping centrifugal incompleteness of a vision (e.g. in Proust) is no barrier to intensity.

The reassuring substantiality of prose, its ability to exist at low tension (enhanced in some authors by a casual colloquial tone approaching everyday speech, or other temporary or permanent withdrawals from a consciously literary mode of narration) makes it easier for prose to establish clear hierarchies of significance than verse: some parts of an essay or novel may be less important without being unimportant. Prose can without mockery admit and accept that something plays a minor role; it can if it wishes avoid being cleverer than life, whereas verse, with its evidently deliberate patterns, imposes an air of absoluteness on its material. See also VERSE.

See Robert Adolphe, *The Rise of Modern Prose Style* (1968); Ian A. Gordon, *The Movement of English Prose* (1966); George Levine and William Madden (eds), *The Art of Victorian Prose* (1968); Tzvetan Todorov, *The Poetics of Prose* (1971, trans. 1977).

MPH

protagonist
see CHARACTER, HERO, PLOT

psychogogia
see CATHARSIS

psychology and psychoanalysis
The connection between literature and psychology is an ancient one. The classic locus is Aristotle's series of attempts to account for the effects of tragedy and his deployment of the term CATHARSIS. Such a

play as *Hamlet* has traditionally been seen as offering us an inward account of the psychological consequences of chronic circumstantial dilemma. With the rise of the novel, a new dimension of psychological intensity comes on to the literary agenda; Pamela, in the eponymous Richardson novel, supplies us with a set of insights into a mind; but a mind which demands to be read simultaneously as typical of a particular historical moment, the rise of individualism as an accompaniment of the social transition to capitalism. In the eighteenth century in the West, the whole structure of the mind's relation to society and nature becomes the problematic site on which the literary is constructed.

It is partly because of this that, with the arrival in England of ROMANTICISM, we see a shift of attention onto the creative activity itself. Following on from Kant's classifications of mental activity, and from Schelling's delineation of an aesthetic philosophy, Coleridge provides another crucial locus in *Biographia Literaria*. His principal contributions are in giving an account of the kind of activity in which the poet engages, and in fitting this into a hierarchy of mental activities. The central term is IMAGINATION; Coleridge conceives of this semi-theologically, comparing the task of the poet with the divine creative task, but his attempts to differentiate between imagination, reason and understanding nevertheless constitute an early psychology of creativity. It was also Coleridge who provided the first useful coinings of the word 'unconscious', parallelling Hegel's efforts to detect the mind's mode of recapitulating past history. This interest in the creative urge continues through Shelley, and is later given an added twist by Darwin's problematic assertion of human kinship with the animals: problematic because it implies the possible operation within the mind of forces beyond individual or species control.

Psychological speculation in English criticism continues through the 'appreciative' but subtle essays of Swinburne and Pater, and into T. S. Eliot's major work on the relations between the writing of poetry and the presence of the TRADITION. But all of this was largely overtaken by the work of Freud, whose evolution of psychoanalysis as a technique which eventually generated a 'metapsychology' fundamentally altered the field of speculation. The most basic of Freud's discoveries was that there does exist a large part of the psyche which is not under the direct control of the individual. In referring to this as the unconscious, Freud generated a paradox: how can we know of the existence of the unknowable?

We know of it, Freud contends, in three ways: through dream; through parapraxes, principally slips of the tongue; and through the technique of analysis and its main tool, free association. These phenomena demonstrate that memory is merely a filtering mechanism, and that a large part of what we apparently forget is in fact stored. A major image for this occurs in his late work *Civilisation and its Discontents* (1930), where he compares the unconscious to an ancient city, but one where all the preceding versions of that city continue to exist, superimposed one upon another: from the unconscious nothing ever goes away. The forms in which we become aware of these suppressed areas of the psyche are linguistic. For language, according to Freud, is a double structure: while we think we speak what we mean, something else is always speaking through us. See, e.g., *Jokes and Their Relation to the Unconscious* (1905). Literature is deeply implicated in this double structuring: Freud says that much of what he has discovered was already known to us in the works of Goethe and the great German writers, because the great artist has privileged access to unknown realms.

The techniques of psychoanalysis are essentially the techniques of close reading, and the posture of the analyst is that of the disinterested but observant interpreter of a text, seeking to unearth the unconscious level which can be discerned beneath, or within, the everyday chains of discourse. But that relationship is always complicated: in dreamwork— our attempted recollections of dream—we are always performing an activity of naturalization, trying to represent our inadmissible wishes in forms which will not severely dislocate cultural norms. This activity relies on certain crucial devices, principally condensation and displacement, which have since been assimilated to the structuralist categories of metaphor and metonymy. Other Freudian insights include the supposition that the interplay of characters in a literary work can be read as an interplay between elements in the psyche; and in his later work, Freud begins to suggest that psychoanalytic diagnosis can be applied to whole cultural formations as well as to individual pieces of discourse.

Freud's dissident disciple Jung concentrated on the transindividual, collective unconscious; and his involvement with the arts has generated a set of readings in which the main focus is on the discernment of specific 'universal' symbols. Jung moves further back into the realm of biologism, asserting that the central shapes of the organism are responsible for the structuring of works of art. This approach has proved more fruitful in the visual arts; where writing has been concerned, some post-Freudian developments have been more concerned with the relation between the instincts and socio-historical change. Herbert Marcuse, for instance, working both with psychoanalysis and with a version of Marxism mediated through the Frankfurt School, suggests that different 'instinctive' shapes emerge in response to different social conditions (e.g., the 'performance' principle within capitalism; the necessity of an element of 'surplus repression' to the smooth running of the State). His claims for literature, and particularly for the more surrealist kinds of lyric poetry, are high; he regards them as ways of uttering the otherwise unutterable, as modes of escape from the bondage of ideology. See Marcuse, *One Dimensional Man* (1964) and *Eros and Civilisation* (1966).

This 'cultural transcendentalism' may be seen as a phenomenon of the 1960s; more recent post-Freudian developments have moved into a different area, taking on board the concepts of STRUCTURALISM, and offering new ways of describing the displacement of the subject. The most visible thinker has been Jacques Lacan, who has fashioned a remarkable discourse from Lévi-Straussian anthropology, linguistics, recent French philosophy and his own clinical experience. His central ideas can be found in *Écrits* (1977) and *The Four Fundamental Concepts of Psycho-analysis* (1977). Language, he claims, is the major force through which the human individual is constituted as a structured, gendered subject; the entry upon language is a simultaneous submission to social authority, in which the individual passes under the 'name of the Father' and is coloured with patriarchy at the very moment of emergence from undifferentiation. Lacan's discovery of the 'mirror-phase' and his less well-known work on psychopathology offer versions of the construction of the subject which have proved congenial to literary and other critics searching for explanations of the constitutive power of language and image. See, e.g., *Yale French Studies* (1977): *Literature and Psychoanalysis*; Tony Tanner, *Adultery in the Novel* (1979); Christian Metz, *Psychoanalysis and Cinema: The Imaginary Signifier* (1982).

This work has been followed to cultural conclusions by Gilles Deleuze and Félix Guattari (*Anti-Oedipus: Capitalism and Schizophrenia* (1977)); but more particularly, it has been taken up in FEMINIST CRITICISM. The writings of Juliet Mitchell, Jacqueline Rose and others offer a deconstructive approach to Freud's inadequate accounts of female sexuality; mediated through Lacan, they seek to establish a specifically female location in relation to language, and to prescribe a practice of writing. Some feminist approaches define grammar itself as a form of patriarchal power, while seeking to avoid a logocentric prescription of a utopian alternative. In the work of Hélène Cixous we see the opposition male/female modulated into other categories: single/collective; quasi-permanent/recognizedly transitory. Recent work in feminist psychoanalysis, notably by Nancy Chodhorow, suggests a whole new pattern in which female skills in nurturing are seen as having been systematically downgraded in the interchange between the generations in favour of the phallocentric, and feminist critics have discerned this power-structure in particular literary works. See Mitchell, *Psychoanalysis and Feminism* (1974); Marks and de Courtivron (eds), *New French Feminisms*

(1980); Jane Gallop, *The Daughter's Seduction* (1982).

There are several further contemporary developments worth pointing to. The work of Melanie Klein on young infants, and her descriptions of familially-induced psychosis, are now being seen as capable of generating accounts of the origins of creativity and symbolism in early infancy; Klein also presents a version of what it is like to be human which has a revisionary relationship to the now conventional theorizing of sexual difference. Her work is sometimes referred to as 'object-relations psychology'; referred to under the same heading, although it has significant differences, is the work of such analysts as D. W. Winnicott. From Freud and Klein have come the attempts to read a whole culture and its myths suggested by the group relations practice of Wilfred Bion and pioneered by the Tavistock Institute, a project of cultural analysis which is convergent with Foucault's institutional histories. Finally, it should be noted that one of the great charges levelled against Freud was that he had prevented the world from ever again indulging in the primal innocence implied in fantasies of the free individual: certainly this development now finds an echo in the work of a large number of creative writers—Thomas Pynchon, J. G. Ballard, John Barth, Angela Carter—where the complexity of subject construction which Freud originally proposed is increasingly being taken as an alternative to traditional notions of character autonomy, a development which itself follows from earlier twentieth-century writers of the bureaucratic State—Chekhov, Kafka, Lu Xun—and their perceptions of the intense relationship between the psyche and the external forces which condition its development and shape.

See also Freud, *The Interpretation of Dreams* (1900) and *Introductory Lectures on Psycho-Analysis* (1916–17). A useful anthology of Jung is Anthony Storr (ed.), *Selected Writings* (1983). On object-relations psychology, see Michael Rustin, 'A Socialist Consideration of Kleinian Psychoanalysis', *New Left Review* (1982). The best general account is Elizabeth Wright, *Psychoanalytic Criticism* (1984). See also Joseph H. Smith (ed.), *The Literary Freud* (1980); Alan Roland (ed.), *Psychoanalysis, Creativity and Literature* (1978); Peter Fuller, *Art and Psychoanalysis* (1980); Samuel Weber, *The Legend of Freud* (1982); D. W. Winnicott, *Playing and Reality* (1974); Julia Kristeva, *Desire in Language* (1980).

DGP

R

reader

Is 'reader' a critical term that warrants attention? Or are readers unproblematically obvious in any consideration of literature? For a long time, the second view prevailed. Classical theory, seeing literature as an affective medium, necessarily assumed a reader to be affected, but did not emphasize the reader as such. Horace, in his *Art of Poetry*, says that the poet's aim is either to profit or to please—but readers are dismissed with the casual comment that elders prefer profit and youngsters pleasure. To cite 'the poet's aim' as Horace does is to shift from affect to intention, a typical move in author-centred criticism. Neoclassical discussions of taste suggest attention to what would now be called the reader's competence. Eighteenth-century fictional practice goes further, enacting the dynamics of reading: an inscribed reader for Fielding or Sterne is functionally engaged in a temporal process of challenge and response. Nineteenth-century novelists often imply a social dimension for readers, including them by address in some actual or imagined community; but contemporary didactic criticism usually glossed this by a return to authorial intention. As usual, it is Henry James who offers crucial insights into the question of author vs. reader. An early formulation suggests that the balance of power is on the author's side: 'the writer makes the reader, very much as he makes his characters.' But James described his own reading practice in terms of 'reconstruction', and his emphasis is increasingly on the reader as an active figure rather than a mere affective target for experience or instruction.

One twentieth-century study of reading is the 'practical criticism' of I. A. Richards, which uses empirical accounts by actual readers. It is not, however, pure empiricism, since it is informed by a motive: the production of a totally unified reading, in which all inconsistencies are resolved. And this totalization in turn produces a claimed psychological result of synthesis and harmony. Reading is thus seen as therapeutic, in a tradition that goes back to Aristotle. Unified readings are also the concern of Anglo-American New Criticism; here, in the famous article on 'The Affective Fallacy' by Wimsatt and Beardsley (*The Verbal Icon*, 1954), affect is ruled out as a confusion between the poem and its results. To see the work as autonomous is to forbid specific attention to readers.

More recently, reaction against NEW CRITICAL autonomy has prompt-ed studies of readers and their responses which tend to use a dynamic rather than an affective orientation. It is important to note that reader study is *only* an orientation, not a method. It is indeed possible to convert any formal description into a 'readerly' account simply by changing terms, so that a reader instead of a critic discovers formal distinctions. Theories that try to go further than this can be categorized in terms of the methods that they seek to appropriate. Similar appropriations do not necessarily produce similar results. Thus, Norman Holland and Harold Bloom both study reading through psychology or psychoanalysis; but while Holland uses the reader's 'identity theme' to produce unified, convergent readings, Bloom stages an Oedipal conflict which prompts *mis*readings that diverge from the authority of their predecessors. This split between convergence and divergence, or be-tween total and plural readings, can also be found in appropriations of SEMIOTICS. It can be seen from my discussion under that heading that Riffaterre's reader, transforming the essential 'matrix' of a text, is a supreme exemplar of convergent activity; while Umberto Eco's work seems to offer both convergent and divergent emphases. In so far as he attempts a systematic account of how readers extend their codes, he seems to offer a positive, total study. But in so far as he follows Peirce on the unlimited nature of semiotic process, any such account must be provisional, one of many plural readings. Plurality or divergence are emphasized in borrowings from SEMIOTICS that have felt the impact of DECONSTRUCTION; the later work of Roland Barthes is a case in point. *S/Z* (1970, trans. 1974) studies reading through the interplay of semiotic codes yet refuses to codify that interplay. Where Eco offers diagrams, Barthes prefers the undecidable model of an interwoven textile. Barthes's presuppositions are also evident in his hedonism. *The Pleasure of the Text* (1975) may recall Horace by its title, but the Barthesian reader thrills to the decidedly unHoratian qualities of transgression, discord and excess.

Reader studies from the University of Constance offer a more sober set of appropriations. H. R. Jauss's approach derives from sociology and HERMENEUTICS. His 'reception aesthetics' moves away from intrin-sic accounts of an individual reader's response to consider the commu-nal 'horizon of expectations' against which any work is received. These horizons are historically generalized as 'paradigms', following Thomas Kuhn's work in the history of science. In his earlier writing, Jauss betrayed a modernist bias in his emphasis on innovation, evaluating works by their degree of distance from the horizon against which they appeared. And though he now repudiates it, Jauss was by no means alone in this approach. Theorists as different as Barthes, Iser and Fish also concentrate on the change or frustration of a reader's expectations;

change is always seen as somehow salutary, a variety of Horatian 'profit'. Jauss's colleague Wolfgang Iser builds on the phenomenology of Roman Ingarden. They consider the reader's activity in 'actualizing' what is only potential in any text. Iser attempts a compromise in the balance of power between text and reader. The text offers a 'structure of appeal' which calls for its 'implied' reader; their interaction creates the aesthetic object, as the reader works through gaps and indeterminacies in the text, through shifts of vantage point, through distinctions of theme and horizon. This process, though idealized, is one of the most intimate accounts of reading yet produced; but it has been fundamentally challenged by Stanley Fish. Fish's approach derives in part from linguistics and stylistics, but he is both eclectic and variable; what I describe here are his recent claims, in which the balance of power tilts toward the reader. Instead of implying a reader, the text now becomes itself a product of the reader, in that its significant structures are not given but ascertained by prior interpretive procedures that are always already in place. 'Strictly speaking,' says Fish, 'getting "back-to-the-text" is not a move one can perform.' To get rid of the text as an autonomous authority might seem to open the way for the most widely divergent readings, but Fish differs from Barthes or Bloom in preserving a convergent factor. Reading is not a radically private affair. It always takes place within an 'interpretive community', social or institutional or both. Though communities and their memberships change, there is always a set of normative procedures available—if only for challenge—at any given time.

Though Fish himself does not pursue the point, to speak of communal constraints is to suggest a politics of reading. Barthes's apparent perversity, for example, is politicized by his claim that power is inscribed in the language itself. He thus produces a rhetoric of contestation which, in different forms, is echoed by a range of oppositional reading practices that seek not simply to actualize the meaning of a text but to call it into question. This activity is especially strong in FEMINIST CRITICISM, and it is neatly characterized in the title of a book by Judith Fetterley: *The Resisting Reader* (1979).

Two useful anthologies are edited by Jane P. Tompkins, *Reader-Response Criticism: from Formalism to Post-Structuralism* (1980); and by Susan R. Suleiman and Inge Crosman, *The Reader in the Text: Essays in Audience and Interpretation* (1980). The Constance School is described in Robert C. Holub, *Reception Theory: A Critical Introduction* (1984). William Ray, *Literary Meaning: from Phenomenology to Deconstruction* (1984) covers the major theorists.

EC

realism,

in literary history, is usually associated with the effort of the novel in the nineteenth century, particularly in France, to establish itself as a major literary genre. The realism of Balzac and the Goncourt brothers was essentially an assertion that, far from being escapist and unreal, the novel was uniquely capable of revealing the truth of contemporary life in society. Balzac, in *La Comédie Humaine*, saw himself as a scientific historian, recording and classifying the social life of France in all its aspects. The adoption of this role led to detailed reportage of the physical minutiae of everyday life—clothes, furniture, food etc.—the cataloguing of men into social types or species, and radical analyses of the economic basis of society. The virtues pursued were accuracy and completeness of description. However, such an effort necessarily begs the question: accuracy to what? completeness in what terms? At its extreme the realistic programme runs into two difficulties. Technically it becomes obsessed with physical detail and topographical accuracy for its own, or history's sake, and so novels may amount to little more than guide books or social documents. Secondly, it becomes confused about the distinction between art and history or sociology: the novelist is only metaphorically and incidentally a historian; whatever the relations of his art with the 'realities' of society, he is finally involved in the making of fictions, and has responsibilities to FORM that the historian or sociologist does not.

The failure to acknowledge this crucial distinction is evident in the development of realistic theory into *Naturalism*, whose claim for an even greater accuracy and inclusiveness rested on an analogy with scientific method. Naturalism, notably in the theories of Emile Zola, borrowed its terms from post-Darwinian biology and asserted the wholly *determined* character of man and society. Since man was simply a higher animal, his nature was controlled by the regular forces of heredity and environment. So the novelist as social historian now appeared as the taxonomic biologist, displaying his scientific objectivity in elaborate documentation and unwonted frankness in regard to bodily functions. Fortunately many of Zola's novels, at least, managed to survive their methodology.

The theory of realism in England was much less coherent and scientific. Until the 1880s, when the debate on realism and naturalism was imported from France, critics and novelists tended to talk rather of the novel's duty to be true to 'life'. The central concern in this injunction was not the representation of material reality—cataloguing the environment—but the investigation of the moral behaviour of man in society. The mechanistic and deterministic elements of realism were alien to the temper of Victorian novelists and their critics. But the concern for truth, for morality, and for an accurate and unromanticized description of contemporary society, defined an unmistakably realistic concept of the novel. Of course such demands implied a general agreement about the nature of reality, about certain self-evident truths concerning man and society, for without these there could be no way of identifying the abnormal, the deviant, the novels that were untrue to life. At the worst this critical demand could narrow to a prescription for a conformist fiction of the commonplace, novels for Mrs Grundy. Dickens, George Eliot and James, all major realists in different ways, found it necessary to assert a larger idea of realism that might answer to more complex views of the possibilities of life.

All theories of realism, however sophisticated, rest on the assumption that the novel imitates reality, and that that reality is more or less stable and commonly accessible. But it is possible to conceive of the relationship between art and reality in terms of imaginative creation rather than imitation. The artist may be said to imagine, to invent a fictional world which is more than a copy of the real one. Such a shift in conceptual metaphors produces attitudes to the novel, and perhaps even novels, with quite different priorities from those of the realist tradition. The emphasis moves from accuracy of representation to aspects of form—narrative structuring, symbolic patterning, linguistic complexity and so on. Much of the major fiction of this century—the later James, Conrad, Joyce, Woolf—and many contemporary novels, seems to exist in terms of this alternative poetic; they advertise their fictionality. Of course all novels relate in some way to the general complex of realism, but relatively few can be fully understood in the terms of the specific theory of realism.

This is why attempts to use 'realism' as a critical term to define the essential nature of the novel, rather than as a label for a diverse but identifiable tradition, prove unsatisfactory, if initially attractive. Ian Watt, in *The Rise of the Novel*, points out that we find in nearly all novels, in comparison to other genres, an accentuation of the temporal and spatial dimensions. Novels give us a sense of man existing in continuous time, and locate him in his physical world more specifically than any other kind of literature. In *this* sense *Ulysses* is the supreme realist novel. The difficulty arises when Watt goes on to specify, as a defining element of realism, 'the adaptation of prose style to give an air of complete authenticity', and takes, as models of authentic report, the novels of Defoe and Richardson. The implication is that the novelist attempts to divert attention from the fictionality of his work by avoiding all eloquent and figurative language. He writes the neutral prose of the dispassionate reporter so that reality, or his image of reality, may seem more purely itself. On this view of realism the ideal novel would be a flawless mirror to the world; but since language is never neutral, such a novel is impossible. More importantly, it is doubtful whether many novels, even within the realist tradition, have any such ambitions for linguistic transparency. Perhaps Arnold Bennett, Sinclair Lewis, or Theodore Dreiser longed for the anonymity of reportage, but there is nothing self-effacing about the language of Flaubert, Dickens, or James.

So as a critical term 'realism' identifies some important character-istics of the novel form, but fails to define it. Most novels are too complex to be accounted for in terms of their representational authen-ticity, and the languages of the novel are too various to be subsumed under the model of direct report. The art of the novel is rhetorical as well as representational; 'realism' gives us an account of only one of its dimensions. See also FICTION, IMITATION, NOVEL.

See Harry Levin, *The Gates of Horn: A Study of Five French Realists* (1963); R. Stang, *The Theory of the Novel in England, 1850–1870* (1961); Ian Watt, *The Rise of the Novel* (1957); René Wellek, 'The concept of realism in literary scholarship', *Neophilologus* 44 (1960), 1–20; reprinted in *Concepts of Criticism* (1963); D. Grant, *Realism* (1970); G. Lukács, *Studies in European Realism* (1950); J. P. Stern, *On Realism* (1973); *Representation in Modern Fiction,* special issue of *Poetics Today*, 5 (1984).

PM

reason
see FEELING, IMAGINATION, SENSIBILITY

reception
see READER

refrain
A refrain is a line, or a group of lines, of verse, repeated in its totality so regularly or in such a specific pattern as to become a controlling (ballad) or defining (fixed forms) structural factor.

In the BALLAD, much of the effect of a refrain depends on the narrative not at first comprehending it: each goes its own way. But as the poem proceeds, the narrative increasingly invests the refrain with circum-stance and an awful aptness, while the refrain makes of the narrative something pre-ordained and lyrically self-engrossed. Ultimately, the poet may anticipate the refrain and explore the various opportunities it offers for indulging his self-assurance, frustration, morbidity etc. (e.g. Poe's *The Raven*). For an exceptional reversal of refrain's irreversibil-ity, see Pound's *Threnos*, in which the refrain—'Lo the fair dead!'—is finally ingested into the body of the verse, parenthesized by brackets and surmounted by the word 'Tintagoel', which *resurrects* the lovers, Tristram and Iseult, even as it identifies them.

In ballads in lighter or coarser vein, the refrain may act as a verbal substitute for knowing laughter, in patriotic ballads (e.g. *The 'George Aloe'*), as a mark of steadfastness in vicissitude and insolent complacency in victory. The nonsense refrain—'Heigh ho! says Rowley', 'Ay lally, o lilly lally'—seems to be a way of expressing a complete acquiescence in the mood of the poem without interfering with its meaning, a way even of momentarily backing away from the meaning of a song in order to capture its feeling nearer to its pre-verbal inarticulacy.

In many ballads and rhymes, the refrain enjoys a typographical separation which points to its origin in a dialogue, between the poet and chorus. But in many of the fixed forms (rondel, triolet, rondeau) the refrain has been absorbed into the poem and thus emerges only gradually from it; indeed, it may appear to betray the poem by becoming at once the poem's subject and limitation, formally beautifying but intellectually stultifying. The alternating refrains of the villanelle in particular suggest a choking process; the peculiar anguish of those villanelles devoted to the theme of time (e.g. Dobson's *'Tu ne quaesieris'*, Henley's *Where's the use of sighing*, Auden's *If I could tell you*), derives from the continual notation of passing time within a structure that wastes time and condemns the poet to contemplative immobility. But the fixed form may equally struggle against its refrain, not allow it to settle into a repressive role; it may outwit it with an indefatigable novelty or humanity, it may make it an instrument of novelty itself, or it may re-integrate the refrain by making its lyric intentions unknown to itself, dependent on the fancy of the 'common' lines.

cs

refunctioning

is a translation of the German term *Umfunktionierung*, which was used by certain left-wing German writers and critics of the 1930s (Bertolt Brecht and Walter Benjamin in particular) to suggest the way in which works of art and literature could be constantly put to diverse uses. Such writers rejected the view that literary works were 'timeless', stressing the historical conditions of their production and reception; but they also dismissed the notion that literary works belonged only to their historical moment, and that their meaning was 'exhausted' by what they meant to their contemporaries. On the contrary, works of literature could be given new meanings by successive generations, turned to social uses unthinkable for their authors, and so ceaselessly reinterpreted and 'rewritten'. For such a theory, the 'meaning' of a literary text does not reside within it like the core within a fruit; it is the sum-total of the history of uses to which the text is put. Such uses will naturally be constrained by the nature of the literary work itself: it is not possible to put any work to any kind of use. But it is equally impossible to read off from a literary work the various interpretations which it may validly receive in different historical contexts.

For writers like Brecht and Benjamin, the most significant meanings of a literary work are always determined by one's present situation. Though it is often enough possible to establish what a work 'originally' meant, we can of course only establish this within the limits of our own discourses, which may be quite alien to the discourse of the work itself. The German critical traditions of HERMENEUTICS and reception theory (cf. READER) ponder the interpretative problems involved in this encounter between our own social world of meaning, and that of a literary work produced in different conditions. But whereas HERMENEUTICS is on the whole concerned with the problem of how we can recapture as faithful as possible a sense of what the work originally meant, the exponents of 'refunctioning' were more concerned with lending the work a new, contemporary set of meanings, if necessary by deliberately 'misreading' it. (For certain modern critics, in particular the American Harold Bloom, all readings of literary texts are 'misreadings'; other, DECONSTRUCTIVE, critics, having rejected all notions of a 'correct' reading of a work, are consequently led to deny the very distinction between 'true' and 'false' readings.)

Refunctioning, then, is a deliberate using or appropriation of an artefact. But it would insist, against those who would regard this as scandalous or unethical, that all criticism is, inescapably, a form of use of the text: there is in this sense no disinterested criticism. The difference is between those schools of criticism which frankly admit that they are using the work—often for political ends—and those which do not. The criticism of Coleridge or T. S. Eliot would in this view be quite as 'ideological'—and ultimately political—as that of a Marxist writer; it is just that the latter makes his or her position plain.

An example of refunctioning would be Brecht's attempt to produce Shakespeare's politically conservative *Coriolanus* for socialist audiences and socialist political ends. Such an attempt, of course, may fail: it may be that changed historical conditions result in people's ceasing to extract any significant meaning from a work of the past, even a highly valued one. (It may also be that if we discovered more about the original meanings of certain past works—say, Greek tragedy—we might cease to value them as highly as we do.) If, on account of a deep historical transformation, people ceased to find relevance in the works of Shakespeare, it would be interesting to ask in what sense, if any, those works were still 'valuable'.

See T. Eagleton, *Walter Benjamin, or Towards a Revolutionary Criticism* (1981); P. Widdowson (ed.), *Re-Reading English* (1982); J. Willett (ed.), *Brecht on Theatre* (1964), *The New*

Sobriety: Art and Politics in the Weimar Republic (1978).

TE

representation
see DECONSTRUCTION, DRAMA, IMITATION, REALISM, TYPICALITY

response
see EFFECT, READER

rhetoric
Traditionally, the art of putting a thought over in a particular manner; command of a number of artfully different manners of expression or persuasion. As a result of the diversity of its products, there is and has been no certain orthodoxy in its doctrines, although spokesmen from each of its jarring sects will assure you of the others' heresies. On the other hand, in spite of the discord which has characterized it both as a subject and as a discipline, rhetoric probably does have a boundary or two and, within each of its schisms, a surprising amount of homogeneity and tradition. There is not all that much difference, for example, between two modern textbooks of English composition, say A. M. Tibbett's *The Strategies of Rhetoric* (1969) and Kane and Peter's *A Practical Rhetoric of Expository Prose* (1966). Nor are these two texts entirely unrelated to Irving Rein's *The Relevant Rhetoric* (1969), although the latter work is concerned with teaching speakers rather than writers. And in a broader sense, all three of these books are recognizable descendants of such Sophistic handbooks as the *Rhetorica, ad Alexandrum* and the *Rhetorica ad Herennium*. They share a considerable amount of subject-matter and a few attributes with even such famous philosophic rhetorics as Aristotle's or Campbell's or a respectable modern writer's in this vein, Perelman's *The New Rhetoric, a Treatise on Argumentation* (1969): a concern for grammar, figures, argumentative devices and forms, how an author credentials himself, relates to his audience, attempts to persuade—even a few pieties about ethical and intellectual truth. At the same time, no student who pays a moment's attention to epistemology, ontology, or intellectual history is likely to confuse Rein with Aristotle, a composition handbook with a formal theory of discourse, or, for that matter, fail to discover that Campbell's beliefs very often contradict Aristotle's, that neither man's first principles would be at ease with the reformed positivism of Perelman.

This inordinately broad range of opinion as to what constitutes rhetoric, from a concern with the grammatical or inflectional efforts of freshmen to the search for the mainsprings of rational discourse, is further complicated by the fact that from classical times onwards the majority of writers on the subject, despite their own particular allegiances, have dealt with rhetoric as something akin to mathematics, a more or less universally applicable tool. That it may profitably be viewed as such is perhaps so, but this bias has more often led generations of rhetoricians into a marked fondness for eccentric eclecticism, vague key terms, untenable and extreme generalizations, and a naïve enthusiasm for instant social and language reform.

The temptation to consider rhetoric as an all-embracing compositional and critical discipline, panacea, and touchstone for human motivation has also occasionally led scholars to conclude that all writers in all times have succumbed to it, that its universality is chronological as well as conceptual. Charles O. McDonald, to cite a recent case, argues in his *Rhetoric of Tragedy: Form in Stuart Drama* (1966) that English dramatists from Shakespeare to John Ford were thoroughly infected by an 'antilogistic' 'Sophistic' 'habit of mind', caught, allegedly, from a somewhat too free association with the two thousand years of rhetorical tradition which he outlines in a hundred pages of prefatory material. We are left with the provocative if eristic implication that Gorgias of Leontini made a demonstrable and significant contribution to *Hamlet*.

All of this is not to say that the 'garden of eloquence' is naught but a jungle of verbiage, nor to disparage the occasional fine flowerings in the pioneer work of such moderns as Father Ong, Wayne C. Booth, Richard McKeon, and Kenneth Burke. A fair case could even be made out to show that the infinite variety and lack of cohesion in rhetoric and rhetorical studies is favourable to independent thought, original research and heuristic scholarship. And certainly the long and complex history of the influence of rhetoric on Western thought is too important a subject to be ignored by serious investigators into language and literature. Yet the fact remains that the resurgence in the past half century of scholarly interest in rhetoric, and the noticeable acceleration of that interest recently, have not produced a substantial body of important thought or impressive research. There is not a single well-regarded general history of the subject, there are surprisingly few careful studies of the theories held in various periods, and there is a marked paucity of modern theoretical treatises which will withstand more than a few minutes' critical scrutiny. And beyond that, the relationships of rhetoric to history, literature, linguistics, homiletics, law, and philosophy have seldom been investigated in any detail, let alone understood on more than a superficial level.

Looked at from a constructive point of view these all too obvious gaps and shortcomings in contemporary rhetorical studies constitute the one major advantage which rhetoric has over many of its academic neighbours: it has yet to be exploited to the point where its body of knowledge is inevitably repetitious, replete with miniscule observations, and haunted by portents of collision with dead ends.

Cf. STYLE, a term with a similar basic meaning and a similar wide range of connotations and thus power to evoke contention. Both 'style' and 'rhetoric' signify systems of conventional (hence variously prescriptively teachable) verbal devices for the 'ornamentation' of a discourse. If style often suggests artificiality, self-indulgence or preciousness, rhetoric, because it is initially a verbal art for *persuasion* often connotes design, insincerity, even lies. Alternatively, the availability of hundreds of rhetorical handbooks—lists and examples of figures and schemes—produced over the last two thousand years may suggest a mechanical shallowness of linguistic technique. Modern attempts to make the term exploratory and critical rather than normative and technical (e.g. I. A. Richards, *Philosophy of Rhetoric*, 1936, Wayne C. Booth, *The Rhetoric of Fiction,* 1961) play down the evaluative dimension and the sinister side of 'persuasion'. Booth's book also shows that it is, unfortunately, all too easy to neglect the linguistic aspects of persuasion; here 'rhetoric' is being used in an essentially untraditional sense.

Wimsatt and Beardsley's *Literary Criticism, A Short History* (1957) provides an elementary account of the classical and medieval tradition. For more detailed information, see the many books by J. W. H. Atkins, such as *Literary Criticism in Antiquity* (1934), *English Literary Criticism: The Medieval Phase* (1943) or C. S. Baldwin, *Ancient Rhetoric and Poetic* (1924), *Medieval Rhetoric and Poetic* (1928).

TGW

rhyme

is a word in a line and a word in a scheme of things that transcends the line; and it is by virtue of this duality that it can at once act as the line's ticket to membership of a larger poetic community and counterpoint the line by suggesting with its rhyme-partner meanings extremer than or contradictory to the line's meaning. Rhyme is also the music that thought and feeling are capable of: thought when it is so just as to delight the ear as well as the mind, feeling when the consonance it achieves testifies to its participation in a principle greater than itself. In the service of rhetoric, rhyme is an insidious substitute for causality. In a rhyme like *gay*: *stray*, to take a simple example, the poet can play on the knowledge that the reader, attempting to rationalize the phenomenon of near-homonymity, will see lightheartedness as the necessary source and necessary oucome of vagabondage; as Daniel so succinctly puts it: 'Whilest seeking to please our ear, we enthrall our judgment' (*A Defence of Rhyme*). There is little difference between the poet's wanting to convince a reader and wanting to convince himself; for the poet whose song is a way of 'en-chanting' his anguish, rhyme is a powerful instrument of wish-fulfilment (*woes: repose, grief: relief*).

Rhymes in dramatic, and particularly tragic, verse, encode patterns of predestination; they are recurrent moments of irrevocability; the rhyme-words fit much too snugly for characters to be able to go back on them (*name: shame, cast: waste, success: distress*). It is also probable that in the course of a play, the audience will become familiar with rhyme-groups in their entirety; in other words rhymes act as gravitational centres for dramatic syndromes and create, ironically, a sense of freedom which however is at best limited and in the very act of rhyming shown to be illusory. The group *'cacher: chercher: attacher: approcher: reprocher: toucher'*, for example, which we find in Racinian drama, covers a whole behaviour pattern, and of the possible combinations most involve contradiction or duplicity.

It is rhyme that has allowed, encouraged the diversification of strophic forms, the rhythmic organization of lines. Rhyme-schemes, even in the abstract, execute meaningful gestures. Abab describes the thrust and parry, give-and-take of leisurely discursive development; abba describes, apart from its self-stabilizing chiastic structure, an aggressive movement in which the aa pair outflanks and envelops the bb couplet, so that the bb couplet is ever in danger of becoming a mere parenthetic insertion.

See H. Lanz, *The Physical Basis of Rime* (1931); C. F. Richardson, *A Study in English Rhyme* (1909); F. Ryder, 'How rhymed is a poem', *Word*, 19 (1963); W. K. Wimsatt, Jr, 'One relation of rhyme to reason: Alexander Pope', in *The Verbal Icon* (1954).

CS

rhythm
see METRE

ritual
see MYTH

romance
A term which can encompass the medieval narrative poem, Spenser's *Faerie Queene*, gothic horrors, and sentimental pap for the mass market is bound to be difficult to define. The linguistic history of the word (the romance, a romance, romance) reflects a movement from the definite to the indefinite which illustrates the necessary diffusion which must accompany such linguistic longevity and plasticity. As Gillian Beer points out (*The Romance*, 1970), the 'term "romance" in the early Middle Ages meant the new vernacular languages derived from Latin, in contradistinction to the learned language, Latin itself'. *Enromancier, romancar, romanz* meant to translate or compose books in the vernacular. The book itself was then called *Romanz, roman, romanzo*. The word became associated with the content of these diverse works—

usually non-didactic narratives of ideal love and chivalric adventures such as *Sir Gawain and the Green Knight* or Chrétien de Troyes's *Le Chevalier de la Charete*. Then these medieval romances, which took both poetic and prose form and which continued to influence the Elizabethan romance, tended to be regarded with some suspicion and even contempt by the classically-oriented writers of the seventeenth and eighteenth centuries (see Arthur Johnston, *Enchanted Ground: The Study of Medieval Romance in the Eighteenth Century*, 1964).

The romance is usually concerned with an avowedly fictive world, though the medieval romance was more directly rooted in contemporary fact than might seem apparent from the perspective of the twentieth century. At the same time it could be viewed increasingly as an imaginative and psychological projection of the 'real' world. In the nineteenth century, renewed interest in things medieval (cf. GOTHIC), together with a growing respect for the power of the imagination and the intangible truth of the inner world, gave new life to a form which tended now to be counterposed to the apparent facticity of the novel (cf. NOVEL, REALISM). Hawthorne saw the essential difference between the two as lying in the imaginative freedom granted to the writer of a romance which enabled him to pursue psychological and mythical truth more single-mindedly.

The main criticism of the romance, from Cervantes to Dr Johnson and Jane Austen, has been a moral one. The reader, it is argued, is seduced into applying its values, appropriate enough to the artificial world treated by the writer, to a real world in which pain has a genuine sharpness and the romantic pose is little more than a pallid gesture. This sense is retained in modern practice: sentimental ideals are presented in the knowledge that their power lies simultaneously in their apparent reality and actual ideality.

See J. M. Nosworthy, Introduction to *Cymbeline* (1955); E. H. Pettet, *Shakespeare and the Romance Tradition* (1949).

CWEB

Romanticism

The confusion surrounding the term 'Romanticism' seems only to be deepened by further attempts at definition. A. O. Lovejoy's famous essay 'On the Discrimination of Romanticisms' insists on the need for discrimination between the meanings of the term at various times and in various countries. The danger perceived by Lovejoy is that the word will lose *all* meaning unless we insist on defining our references. Other critics, René Wellek and Northrop Frye, have argued that Romanticism is not essentially an idea but 'an historic centre of gravity, which falls somewhere around the 1790–1830 period' (Frye). They accuse Lovejoy of attempting to break this historic characteristic into its component parts and of trying to insist on a romantic period or character wherever any of these components appear. This 'fallacy of timeless characterization' of Romanticism they see as destructive of the real identity of the historic romantic period. They attempt to define the romantic event from a more isolatedly critical context. Whereas Love-joy sees Romanticism as the general term for a range of related ideas, poetic, philosophic and social, his refuters would more lay more stress on the characteristic images which haunt the romantic imagination. The central distinctive feature of the romantic mode is the search for a reconciliation between the inner vision and the outer experience expressed through 'a creative power greater than his own because it includes his own' (Frye); or the synthetic IMAGINATION which performs this reconciliation and the vision it produces of a life drawing upon 'a sense of the continuity between man and nature and the presence of God' (Wellek).

The central feature of these attempts to define a Romantic entity is the development of romantic theories of the imagination. M. H. Abrams has provided an indispensable account of the origin and development of romantic theories of perception and imagination in *The Mirror and the Lamp* (1953). Underlying these theories, from the end of the eighteenth century and for the next hundred years or more, is the sense that man has become separated from nature. For a variety of reasons the romantic writer feels cut off from the world about him. The failure to understand the true *nature* of man and of his creative power has led to a false characterization of external nature as 'fixed and dead'. The romantic poet seeks a way to reactivate the world by discovering in himself the creative perceptiveness which will allow him to draw aside the veils which men have laid across their senses. He seeks a perception where the false separation of Nature (fixed, external objects) and nature (the living being of the perceiving man) can be reconciled: a new synthesizing vision. The romantic thinker often feels that such a faculty is not an invention, but a re-discovery of the truth about the way we perceive and create which has been lost in the development of more complicated social forms and the growth of rational and self-conscious theories of human thought. This belief leads to a marked historicism, to an increased interest in primitivist theories of culture; to a persistent strain of historical reconstruction in romantic writing, a medieval element in poetry and the novel, and an idealized resurrection of ballad and folk-song.

This attempt to revitalize the perceptive process is also bound up with the desire to re-discover a 'living language'. The search in ballads and in the language of the generality of men (Wordsworth) is only a side-issue. At root the romantic is trying to find a way back—or forward—to the Word, the Logos which is the act it describes. The romantic thinkers are finally baffled by their loyalty to the traditional concept of art as an embodiment or vitalized representation of a separate perceptive act in the 'real' world. But their struggles with this problem prepare the way for the more total concepts of the post-romantic artists, the SYMBOLISTS and IMAGISTS who force romantic aesthetics to its logical conclusion by identifying a desire for complete reconciliation between perception and art: 'How can we know the dancer from the dance?' (Yeats). The romantic artist suffers an agonizing struggle to grasp and express what he perceives; he is continually aware that he cannot objectively 'trust' what he sees since he is involved in *creating* what he sees. He is barred from the convenient symbolic systems available in existing mythic patterns because such public symbols falsify the truth of personal feeling. On the one hand lies the quagmire of personal mythology with its resulting lack of communicative power (Blake), on the other the terrible isolation of the specific and actual: 'the weary weight of all this unintelligible world' (Wordsworth).

The artist feels isolated, unable to discover what must exist, some objective form or Form to embody his sense of the continuity of his own imagination and the visible world. He is drawn towards those experiences which offer a blurred version of the separation of ego and event, drug hallucination or the radical innocence of childhood perceptions. But such experiences are special and not typical, and they are also transient. Thus Wordsworth, looking back at the apparent directness of childhood, sees it slipping away as 'shades of the prison house' close round him.

Coleridge saw that 'we receive but what we give' ('Dejection Ode'), but his poem celebrates this realization in the context of the inevitable pressures of time and decay. At the heart of the romantic dilemma is the agony of the disappearing dream. Life in nature is life in *our* nature, and that is subject to decay. With the romantic thinkers and poets, with Wordsworth's lost 'splendour in the grass', Keats's and Coleridge's 'fragments' ('The Fall of Hyperion', 'Kubla Khan') we have begun the artistic dilemma which leads to Yeats's desire for the immutable permanence of the golden bird of Byzantium and the modern, post-Symbolist search for unchanging form in the heart of chaos itself.

See M. H. Abrams (ed.), *English Romantic Poetry* (1960) (includes Lovejoy's essay cited above); M. H. Abrams, *The Mirror and the Lamp* (1953); D. Aers, J. Cook and D. Punter, *Romanticism and Ideology* (1981); D. Bush, *Mythology and the Romantic Tradition in English Poetry* (1937); M. Butler, *Romantics, Rebels and Reactionaries* (1981); P. De Man, *The Rhetoric of Romanticism* (1984); N. Frye (ed.), *Romanticism Reconsidered* (1963); J. B. Halstead, *Romanticism* (1969); F. Kermode, *Romantic Image* (1957); S. Kumar (ed.), *British Romantic Poets: Recent Revaluations* (1966); J. J. McGann, *The*

Romantic Ideology (1983); D. Morse, *Romanticism: A Structural Analysis*; I. A. Richards, *Coleridge on Imagination* (rev. ed., 1950); R. Wellek, 'The concept of romanticism in literary history', *Comparative Literature* 1 (1949), reprinted in his *Concepts of Criticism* (1963).

GG

rural novel

Works which restrict themselves to portraying rural characters in a rural environment are rare before Gotthelf's *Der Bauernspiegel* (1838). The genre enjoyed a wave of popularity in German literature of the middle and late nineteenth century (e.g. Ludwig Anzengruber, Wilhelm von Polenz) and in France more sporadically (e.g. George Sand, *Les Maîtres Sonneurs*, 1853; Maurice Genevoix, *Raboliot*, 1925). English writers often concentrate lop-sidedly on the creation of a mystical, impalpable atmosphere: many readers find their ability to suspend disbelief cannot cope with the farmers of Sheila Kaye-Smith and Mary Webb.

Habits of mind attributed to peasant communities often assort ill with the modern novel, which tends towards irony rather than unequivocal approval or disapproval, which uses plot as an important element and sets up tensions between and within characters, and which has developed a high degree of emotional and intellectual sophistication, sensitivity and alertness. Among the features presenting problems to the rural novelist are: the usually even pace of country life; the central fact of unremitting toil, which may be therapeutic where introspection and leisure would exacerbate anxieties; the self-sufficiency, resilience and limited ambition of many peasants; their frequent inarticulateness and guarded taciturnity, which may prevent them from putting their feelings into words and thus becoming aware of them, yet which may also make them seem possessors of valuable and elemental but incommunicable insights and knowledge; their resolute practicality and acceptance of things, often without any strong emotional reaction to them; and the narrowness of their childhood and adult experience, which reduces the possibilities of conflict within the personality between different hopes, expectations and desires.

Almost invariably, rural novels are read by a non-peasant public; the notions of 'distance' and POINT OF VIEW are therefore important. Some novelists avoid ironic tension by presenting peasants as less than human, with many potentialities undeveloped and others debased (e.g. Zola, *Earth*, 1887); similarly others, by making them seem more than human in their capacity for contentment and stability of personality (e.g. Berthold Auerbach, *Schwarzwälder Dorfgeschichten,* 1843–54), evoke a nostalgia for a mode of feeling the reader himself can never enjoy. More subtly conceived novels (e.g. many of Gotthelf's works;

Hardy, *Tess of the D'Urbervilles*, 1891; Alphonse de Châteaubriant, *La Brière,* 1923) exploit both these reactions and set them in tension with each other. A frequent structurally organizing device in rural novels is an intrusion from outside the closed community, the provoking of a sudden crisis (e.g. by Tess's loss of virginity, or by the rock fall in C. F. Ramuz's *Derborence*. 1936); faced with the unusual or unprecedented, characters reveal adequacies and inadequacies different from those of urbanized man, exploring areas of endurance and weakness new both to themselves and to the cultured reader.

See Glen Cavaliero, *The Rural Tradition in the English Novel 1900–1939* (1977); Stella Gibbons, *Cold Comfort Farm* (1932); M. H. Parkinson, *The Rural Novel* (1984); Raymond Williams, *The Country and the City* (1973); Peter Zimmermann, *Der Bauernroman* (1975).

MHP

S

satire

is a genre defined primarily, but not exclusively, in terms of its inner form (see GENRE). In it the author attacks some object, using as his means wit or humour that is either fantastic or absurd. Denunciation itself is not satire nor, of course, is grotesque humour, but the genre allows for a considerable preponderance of either one or the other. What distinguishes satire from comedy is its lack of tolerance for folly or human imperfection. Its attempt to juxtapose the actual with the ideal lifts it above mere invective.

From this need to project a double vision of the world satire derives most of its formal characteristics. IRONY, which exploits the relationship between appearance and reality, is its chief device, but as Northrop Frye points out in his essay on satire and irony (*Anatomy of Criticism*, pp. 223–39) it is irony of a militant kind. 'Irony is consistent both with complete realism of content and with the suppression of attitude on the part of the author. Satire demands at least a token fantasy, a content which the reader recognizes as grotesque, and at least an implicit moral standard'.

The moral standard referred to here is often only discernible in the satirist's tone of indignation, and in forms which effectively deny the author any tone of voice, satire is achieved differently. For example, much critical discussion of Restoration Comedy has fruitlessly pursued the question of the dramatists' attitudes towards their subjects. Where an author is forced to efface himself from his creation, or chooses to mask his own attitude, as Swift does in *A Modest Proposal* (1729), he must rely on the reader to make the necessary comparison between the grotesque fantasy he creates and the moral norms or ideals by which it is to be judged. The best clue to the intentions and the achievements of the Restoration dramatists lies in the techniques of distortion they employ—or fail to employ—in the creation of a fantasy world.

In some satires distortion takes the simple form of displacement: the substitution of an animal world for the human in Swift's *Gulliver's Travels* (1726) or Orwell's *Animal Farm* (1945). In others, inverted values serve to distort reality. This technique makes possible the sub-genre of MOCK-EPIC. Yet again, writers may use a variety of devices—caricature, exaggerations, parallelism, or parody—to achieve similar ends.

See R. C. Elliott, *The Power of Satire; Magic, Ritual, Art* (1960); John Heath-Stubbs, *The Verse Satire* (1969); Ronald Paulson, *Satire and the Novel in Eighteenth Century England* (1967); James Sutherland, *English Satire* (1958); David Worcester, *The Art of Satire* (1940).

BCL

scansion
see METRE

scheme
Redefined by classical rhetoricians and grammarians until its meaning became indeterminate, 'scheme' in the sixteenth and seventeenth centuries was enormously popular in the vocabulary of literary and rhetorical theorists who, exploiting their new methods, managed to repeat the process. Any reasonably accurate reading of the versatile definitions and usages of the term in such works as Richard Sherry's *Treatise of Schemes and Tropes* (1550), Henry Peacham's *Garden of Eloquence* (1577), or John Prideaux's *Sacred Eloquence* (1659) will arm the modern critic with sufficient authority to explain and defend as 'schemes' all known figures and tropes in English and Mandarin Chinese, the 'conceits' of seventeenth-century poetry, the rhetorical strategies of Robespierre, the designs, foils, plots, and prosody of Vladimir Nabokov, and Owen Barfield's theory of metaphor. Or, conversely— and this has been the actual trend among the twentieth-century scholars from Morris Croll to J. W. H. Atkins to Lee Sonnino in her recent *Handbook to Sixteenth Century Rhetoric* (1968)— 'scheme' has been dealt with as a special kind of FIGURE: an 'easy' one, a 'figure of sound', or, more simply, as a hazy synonym for 'trope'. To support such interpretations of Renaissance thought and practice requires the suppression of a considerable amount of evidence, not only because of the extreme scope of the viewpoint in the original texts, but also because 'figure', in Renaissance terms, is habitually referred to as a subordinate component of 'scheme'. Fortunately for those who prefer their history to be cyclical, the readers of 'scheme' as the more narrow critical term have thus far cleverly disagreed with each other in specifying it, allowing the conception much of the broad domain it originally entailed. Cf. FIGURE

TGW

scriptible
see PLEASURE

semiotics

deals with the study of signs: their production and communication, their systematic grouping in languages or codes, their social function. It is doubly relevant to the study of literature, for literature uses language, the primary sign system in human culture, and is further organized through various subsidiary codes, such as generic conventions. If, then, the sign-function is basic to both language and literature—and, beyond them, to culture in general—semiotics should repay attention.

Only recently, however, has this attention been directly sustained. Semiotics has an odd history. Various Western thinkers—the Stoics and Saint Augustine, Locke and Husserl—have treated signs and sign-functions, without quite constituting a separate study. Other disciplines can be seen, retrospectively, as crypto-semiotic; thus Tzvetan Todorov has discussed rhetoric from a semiotic point of view (*Theories of the Symbol*, 1977, trans. 1982). It is probable that any study as ambitiously inclusive as semiotics will always be plagued by problems of cohesion and demarcation. These problems are reflected in the double founding of modern semiotics from within different disciplines, by the American philosopher Charles Sanders Peirce (1839–1914) and by the Swiss linguist Ferdinand de Saussure (1857–1915).

Saussure's reorientation of linguistics from a diachronic to a synchronic approach, from the study of historical change to the systemization of a given state of language, conditions his treatment of the sign. 'Language is a system of signs that express ideas', and the interrelationship of signs thus determines meaning. The expressive function of the sign is achieved through its components of signifier (as image or form) and signified (as concept or idea); their linkage, with minor exceptions, is seen as arbitrary and unmotivated. Similarly, the system of signs that comprises a language expresses no given or predetermined meanings; these arise from the interrelations of the system: 'in language there are only differences *without positive terms*'. And since language is only one among sign systems (Saussure mentions writing, military signals, polite formulas) it is possible to envisage a future 'science that studies the life of signs within society', which Saussure calls 'semiology'—a term still common in French discussions, but elsewhere yielding to 'semiotics'.

While Saussure envisages an extension to the science of signs, Peirce begins with a generalized system, which he sees as a branch of logic. And while Saussure works with binaristic, dyadic relations, Peirce puts everything in threes, even coining the term 'triadomany' for his obsession. The triads make for a certain dynamism in Peirce's account; he is interested in semiosis, the act of signifying, and the triadic description of this act presents it as a mediation between two terms by a third. 'A *sign* is anything which is related to a Second thing, its Object . . . in such a way as to bring a Third thing, its *Interpretant*, into relation to the same Object'; the interpretant is itself a sign, so the process recurs. Peirce offers an exhaustive and exhausting taxonomy of all aspects of semiosis, but most of his terms are now neglected except those describing the relation between the sign and its object; Peirce differs from Saussure in allowing a greater role for motivated linkage. Besides the arbitrary 'symbol', he describes the 'icon' (linked through resemblance) and the 'index' (with an existential or causal linkage). These terms are now often applied to the signifier/signified pair.

Although Peirce may offer more scope as a critical tool, Saussure has exercised the greater influence until very recently. While Peirce's logic was neglected, Saussure's linguistics flourished, and drew his semiotics along with it. A crucial factor was the rise of STRUCTURALISM, in which the role of linguistics as a systematic model—either directly, or through its adaptation in anthropology—was paramount. Structuralism and semiotics, as they impinged on literary studies, were often indistinguishable, especially when semiotics concentrated on the production of meaning rather than its communication. And they raised similar problems for lettrists. Could the individual text be analysed as a sign-system? If not, of what system was it an instance? Was it justified to accord any essential privilege or particularity to literary language as an aesthetic code? These problems are still current, and it is always worth noting how they are handled by individual critics.

Semiotics should arguably be self-critical, and the fashionable structuralist semiotics of the 1960s did sometimes reflect on its procedures; thus Roland Barthes's *Elements of Semiology* (1964, trans. 1967) extends the Saussurean base, gives a greater role to motivation, and expresses doubts about binarism. But any expressed doubt in this period was counterbalanced by a surge of scientistic optimism about the development of what was seen as a rigorously objective and comprehensive study—especially when contrasted with impressionistic literary criticism. And there were undeniable advances; for example, in describing the signifying systems of NARRATIVE. But the last decade and a half has seen extensive 'post-structuralist' criticism of this semiotic enterprise. The positivist ideal of a closed and total structuration is itself subject to the metaphysical critique of DECONSTRUCTION. More particularly, the idealization of systems can lead to neglect of the dynamics of signification and a reductive account of the agents involved. To combat this reductionism, Julia Kristeva uses psychoanalysis to enlarge the notion of the speaking subject in semiotics; and the later work of Roland Barthes persistently strives to extend and to de-formalize the role of the reader. Umberto Eco's *Theory of Semiotics* (1976) actualizes the potential dynamism of Peirce and the social hints of Saussure. It emphasizes process through what Eco calls 'the mobility of semantic space'. Codes are subject to change in use: through undercoding, the simplification of alien systems, and through overcoding, the addition of extra signifying rules that are crucial in stylistic or ideological elaboration. And the 'unlimited semiosis' promised by Peirce's interpretant that is itself a sign means that for Eco any determinate meaning is replaced by something transitory, the provisional semantic stability of a given culture or subculture.

This is not to suggest that all semiotics has abjured determinate signification. A contrary example is Michael Riffaterre's *Semiotics of Poetry* (1978), which describes the reading of poems in terms of a 'semiotic transfer' between two systems. The first system is mimetic: for Riffaterre, prior readings are unpoetically referential. They suggest difficulties or 'ungrammaticalities' (predictably, as Riffaterre's examples are Symbolist and Surrealist), which are resolved by code-switching from mimesis to poetic semiosis proper. In the latter system all relationships are finally motivated. It is produced by transforming the 'matrix', a unifying node of significance which is variously encoded in text or intertext. The essentialist and organicist bias of Riffaterre's theory has been sharply questioned, but the brilliance of his readings is not in doubt.

The study of culture itself as a semiotic phenomenon was initiated by the work of Jan Mukařovský and the Prague school, which began in the 1930s. And the most ambitious approach to a semiotics of culture has also come from Eastern Europe, in the work of Jurij Lotman and the Moscow-Tartu school of semiotics. In 1971, Lotman produced one of the most thorough accounts of structuralist semiotics as applied to literature: *The Structure of the Artistic Text* (trans. 1977). This, predictably, uses a synchronic approach; but Lotman's cultural studies also encompass diachrony. In the first place, he makes typological distinctions between the semiotic practices of historical cultures: thus medievalism is marked by 'high semioticity', which 'proceeds from the assumption that everything is significant' (there is an overlap here with the work of Michel Foucault); whereas enlightenment culture sees the world of natural objects as real, so that 'signs become the symbols of falsehood'. Secondly, Lotman studies diachronic change by describing the interplay between culture as patterned information and an unpatterned 'non-culture', or by describing cultural 'translation' in which communicative needs encourage a creative recoding.

The semiotics of culture is still embryonic, but its promise is of special interest to lettrists in their attempts to advance interdisciplinary studies. Interdisciplinarity in practice often founders on the fact that two disciplines are merely *juxtaposed*; work at their interface, which should be most exciting, can become embarrassingly vague. The explanatory scope of cultural semiotics might help to provide a third term which, in proper Peircean fashion, could mediate between the other two.

See John Fiske, *Introduction to Communication Studies* (1982) ch. 3; R. W. Bailey, L. Matejka and P. Steiner (eds), *The Sign: Semiotics Around the World* (1978); M. E. Blanchard, *Description: Sign, Self, Desire; Critical Theory in the Wake of Semiotics* (1980). Current developments can be followed in the journal *Semiotica*. Robert E. Innis (ed.), *Semiotics: An Introductory Reader* (1986); a good selection, with particularly useful editorial comments.

EC

sensibility

The prestige of mathematical reasoning in seventeenth-century Europe was immense, and the end of the century might in England be called the Age of Reason. To some thinkers, it looked as if having accomplished so much in interpreting the natural world, reason could go on to solve problems hitherto left to less clear and distinct methods of investigation—matters of values and morals. But poets and critics in England never accepted the total primacy of reason, and they were very willing to take over a moral and aesthetic doctrine which was in reaction against a too great demand on reason. Such a doctrine existed: the elaboration of a notion of a personal, inner faculty, an emotional consciousness which came to be called *sensibility*. The doctrine assumed great importance in English thought in the eighteenth century, so much so that after mid-century, the Age of Sensibility would be a better label for the critical context of English literature. The book that crystallized this idea was the Earl of Shaftesbury's *Characteristics of Men, Manners, Opinions, Times* (1708–11). Shaftesbury develops a not very clear neo-Platonic argument and an ethic, based on this inner aesthetic sense, 'to learn what is *just* in Society and *beautiful* in Nature, and the Order of the World'. The natural moral sense is also the *individual* taste, though Shaftesbury did not abandon all traditional restrictions on its free workings.

It is too neat to see the development of the powerful idea of sensibility only as a reaction to prevalent philosophical doctrine, or as a component in the history of Western empiricism. Northrop Frye, in a valuable article 'Towards defining an age of feeling' (reprinted in J. L. Clifford (ed.), *Eighteenth-Century English Literature*, 1959) suggests that there are two polar views of literature. One is an aesthetic, Aristotelian view that considers works of literature as 'products', that seeks to distance the audience. The other view is psychological, seeing the creation of literature as a 'process', and seeking to involve the audience in this. Longinus's treatise *On the Sublime* is the classical Greek statement of the latter, and Longinus is an important source for eighteenth-century aesthetic theory. Sensibility is the important constituent in the eighteenth-century form of the second view. There had been a shift in critical interest from the late seventeenth century onwards, away from categorizing works of literature to investigating the psychological processes involved in creating and responding to art. 'Genius' is the fascinating concept in discussions of the artist, 'sensibility' both in discussing the artist and analysing the audience's response. Since 'process' is also to be seen in history and in nature, sensibility involves a sense of the past and is frequently the informing principle of reflective 'nature' poems like Thomson's *Seasons* (1726–30). Shaftesbury held that 'the *Beautiful*, the *Fair*, the *Comely* were never in the *Matter*, but in the *Art* and *Design*: never in Body it-self, but in the *Form* and *forming Power*'.

Wordsworth and Coleridge developed this idea of the 'aesthetic imagination', which leads to the Coleridgean 'primary imagination' where sensibility, man's perception, is 'a repetition in the finite mind of the eternal act of creation in the infinite I AM'. Shaftesbury's 'sensibility' was a little more modest than that, but it had an all-important moral side. This was later developed by Adam Smith in his *Theory of Moral Sentiment* (1759), which had great influence on critics in later discussions of sensibility. Smith added a related doctrine: the power of sympathy. Sympathy powered the benevolence that Shaftesbury advocated, and Shakespeare, it was agreed, had it to a sublime degree. A poet to be truly great also needed a concomitant of sensibility, the 'enthusiastic delight' of imagination. Sensibility was the particular faculty that responded to the greatest imaginative power, the *sublime*, another important part of the later eighteenth-century critical picture. This whole aesthetic was audience-based. Sensibility, though instinctive, could be cultivated, and the whole psychological theory gave greater and greater prominence to education, a 'sentimental education'. Obviously, sensibility and sentiment could become a cult. It did, giving rise to a good deal of bogus attitudinizing. It is the cult of 'sensibility' taken beyond the bounds of reason and common sense that Jane Austen portrays in *Sense and Sensibility* (1811), in the character of Marianne Dashwood, whose selfish concentration on her own feelings is contrasted with the self-control and consideration for other people's feelings shown by her 'sensible' sister, Elinor. See also IMAGINATION.

See W. J. Bate, 'The growth of individualism: the premise of feeling' in *From Classic to Romantic* (1961).

AMR

short fiction
Probably the most ancient of all literary forms; the term covers everything from the fable, folk-tale or fairy-story, to such sophisticated

and highly-developed structures as the German *Novelle*, via the stories of the *Decameron*, and Cervantes's *Exemplary Tales*. Like the EPIC, short fiction goes back in time far beyond the art of writing, and it was not until relatively recently in the history of literature that stories arose from anything but a common stock; praise went to the art of the teller rather than the originality of his material. It was only at the beginning of the nineteenth century that short fiction, because of the requirements of magazines of ever-widening circulation, came into its own and attracted great writers to practise it, like Pushkin, Edgar Allan Poe, Henry James, Anton Chekhov, James Joyce, Thomas Mann, Franz Kafka and D. H. Lawrence, as well as lesser men (like Maupassant) who excelled in this particular genre.

Perhaps because of its mercurial diversity—and despite its great popularity, which has however tended to decline in recent decades—short fiction has given rise to surprisingly little theoretical criticism. One of the earliest, and best attempts to define the genre was Poe's, in two reviews (1842 and 1847) of Nathaniel Hawthorne's tales: 'short prose narrative, requiring from a half-hour to one or two hours in its perusal', working towards a 'single effect' created by incidents chosen with economy and a rigorous sense of necessity in the design. Other critics (most of them in fact themselves practitioners of the art, such as H. E. Bates, Sean O'Faolain and V. S. Pritchett) have stressed the fact that short fiction must be exemplary and representative, a world in brief compass; that it establishes unity of impression and a feeling of totality, by concentrating on a single character, event or emotion, and by compression and the avoidance of digression or repetition; that it satisfies our craving for paradox and shape, our longing to perceive a dramatic pattern and significance in experience, even if this means sacrificing plausibility to effect (as sometimes in Pushkin and Maupassant, not to mention Poe). Truman Capote goes so far as to assert that 'a story can be wrecked by a faulty rhythm in a sentence—especially if it occurs towards the end—or a mistake in paragraphing, even punctuation'; James, he says, 'is the maestro of the semicolon', and Hemingway 'a first-rate paragrapher'. O'Faolain argues similarly that the language of short fiction should be 'spare', and that realistic detail is only a 'bore' if it simply seeks 'idle verisimilitude' rather than 'general revelation by suggestion'. All these theorists insist on meaningful openings (not of the anecdotal 'by the way' kind), and natural yet appropriate endings, either the 'whimper' sort as in Chekhov, or the 'whip-crack' variety practised by Maupassant. The sonorous last phrase of Joyce's closing story in *Dubliners*, for instance ('upon all the living and the dead'), is effective because it has been prepared for throughout by gradual and almost imperceptible shifts of tone from the breezy opening onwards ('Lily, the caretaker's daughter, was literally run off her feet'). In this story, as in other masterpieces of the genre like Pushkin's 'Queen of Spades' or Kafka's 'Metamorphosis', a central, controlling image maintains an essential unity which transcends as it complements the unity guaranteed by the more obvious devices catalogued by Poe and others. Nevertheless, we should not be tempted by enthusiasts of short fiction into the fallacious assumption that it requires the same degree of control and overall design as the SONNET, for example. It is obviously less diffuse than the NOVEL, just as the short story proper differs from the folk-tale of the *Thousand and One Nights* variety in that it does not easily tolerate loosely-connected episodes, digressions, and moral or bawdy commentary; but the closest analogy for short fiction probably lies outside literature proper. As Bates saw, the film and the short story are expressions of the same art, that of telling stories by a series of gestures, shots and suggestions, with little elaboration or explanation. It is certainly no coincidence that some of the most effective films are adaptations of short fiction.

See Caroline Gordon and Allen Tate, *The House of Fiction* (1960); Eugene Current-Garcia and Walton R. Patrick, *What is the Short Story?* (1961); Sean O'Faolain, *The Short Story* (1948, reprinted 1964); H. Bonheim, *The Narrative Modes: Techniques of the Short Story* (1982).

JWJF

sign
see SEMIOTICS

simile
While METAPHOR is a dramatic, absolute and intuited identification of two phenomena, simile is a comparison, discursive, tentative, in which the 'like' or 'as . . . as' suggests, from the viewpoint of reason, separateness of the compared items (Marston, *Antonio and Mellida*):

> and thou and I will live—
> Let's think like what—and thou and I will live
> Like unmatch'd mirrors of calamity.

Because simile is usually a pointedly rationalized perception, it has none of the revelatory suddenness of metaphor nor expresses and demands the same degree of mental commitment to the image. Instead it presents itself as a provisional, even optional, aid whose function is explanatory or illustrative. Simile appeals to what we already know about things, metaphor invites the imagination to break new ground; for this reason we can pass an evaluative judgment on simile, whereas we must either take or leave a metaphor. The temporariness of simile underlines, in the work of a Baudelaire or a Rilke, the fact that the universal analogy is only glimpsed, only fragments vouchsafed. And because simile is temporary, it and the totality of experience it promises are infinitely renewable. Simile is a figure with much stamina.

Because simile does not upset reality, but merely titillates our perception of it, keeping different phenomena discrete, it can be used with some irresponsibility. On the one hand this means it can play an important alleviatory role, letting air and whimsy into involved narrative or analysis (Proust) and on the other that poets not prepared to envisage the chaos of metaphor can use simile as the repository for their inventive boldnesses and keep their metaphors conventional (early Hugo, George).

The position of the 'like' phrase is significant. When it succeeds the justificatory adjective or verb ('thy beauty . . . stings like an adder'—Swinburne), we are given a metaphor defused; the figurative dimension of 'stings' is superseded by its literal dimension. When it precedes ('*Mon coeur, comme un oiseau, voltigeait . . .*'—Baudelaire), the relationship between phenomena is more complete; here the 'like' phrase not so much explains away the verb as supposes other verbs.

In calling simile provisional, we mean that the comparability is provisional, its appositeness dependent on a particular confluence of circumstances, and this has made simile a natural vehicle for a relativistic view of the world (Proust); the world of simile is a world of passing acquaintances, incessant sensory flirtation with objects never finally known. But within these limitations the simile, by using or implying the present tense, can lift an action or perception out of the fleeting and exceptional and install it in the constant and familiar. (As A *does* B, so X *did* Y.) This is a main function of the epic simile, where often a noble or complex sentiment is made accessible to the reader through being linked with a familiar external state of affairs. The same expository function is performed by those fantastic Renaissance conceits which take the form of similes. These two notorious stanzas from Donne's 'Valediction: Forbidding Mourning', for instance, externalize, in an exploratory fashion, a spiritual and emotional state which might be impenetrable without the similes:

> Our two soules therefore, which are one
>   Though I must goe, endure not yet
> A breach, but an expansion
>   Like gold to ayery thinnesse beate.
>
> If they be two, they are two so
>   As stiffe twin compasses are two,
> Thy soule the fixt foot, makes no show
>   To move, but doth, if th'other doe.

CS

sincerity

Prior to the eighteenth century, a term of little significance in criticism: the absence or otherwise of dissimulation on the part of a writer (though not necessarily of a fictional character such as Iago in *Othello*) was neither questioned nor thought worthy of comment. But in the late 1760s Jean-Jacques Rousseau's *Confessions*, an unprecedentedly frank if subtly edited autobiography, projected a persona of the author which the reader was beguiled or bludgeoned into taking at face value. Soon after this Goethe, in his early novel *The Sorrows of Young Werther* (1774), attacked calm rationalism and exalted instead sensibility and passionate feelings, all in the name of sincerity. Both these works were to prove of seminal importance in the Romantic movement, which arose in the late eighteenth century and lasted well into the nineteenth. During this period writers popularized the image of the poet suffering intense emotions of grief and joy which he then proceeded to enshrine directly and 'sincerely' in his works. But with E. T. A. Hoffmann's allegorical fairy-story *The Golden Pot* (1813), Byron's epic satire *Don Juan* (1819–24) and Baudelaire's figure of the poet as dandy (analysed in his essay *The Painter of Modern Life*, 1863) a new note is struck: the idea of pose, show, even outright duplicity begins to creep in. In the 1880s Nietzsche perceptively noted that 'every profound spirit needs a mask'. This tendency culminated in the life and art of such *fin-de-siècle* 'decadents' as J. K. Huysmans, the creator in *Against Nature* (1884) of the character Des Esseintes, whose neurasthenic extravagances fascinated Oscar Wilde and his contemporaries. It was Wilde who enunciated the pithiest of anti-sincerity paradoxes when he wrote that 'the first duty in life is to be as *artificial* as possible'. Around the same time the discrepancy between what a man may say or do in public and what he really thinks (betrayed through dreams or by involuntary slips of the tongue attracted Sigmund Freud's scientific curiosity, and led to the publication of such studies as *The Psychopathology of Everyday Life* in 1914 (see PSYCHOLOGY). After Freud it was no longer possible to take an innocent attitude towards the issue of sincerity, and this deepened awareness of complexity in matters hitherto thought relatively simple has been reflected in the work of modern novelists. The nocturnal persona of Molly Bloom, the speaker of the closing monologue in James Joyce's *Ulysses* (1922), is clearly more sincere, or at least more authentic, than her everyday self. Similarly, in bringing the titanic clashes of ancient tragedy into the demure and sedate drawing-rooms of her characters, Ivy Compton-Burnett (1892–1969) called into question the 'sincerity' of much that passes for polite conversation. Her French disciple Nathalie Sarraute (b. 1902) has concentrated on the phenomenon of 'sub-conversation', or the level of social intercourse which is never heard aloud but conveys unavowed animosities, conflicts and resentments, in fact all the unseemly deceptions hidden beneath urbane surfaces.

The evolution of attitudes towards insincerity in art and life is thus a complex one, and examination of it is not assisted by imprecision in the term 'sincerity' itself. All the intellectual historian can say with any assurance is that 'at a certain point in its history the moral life of Europe added to itself a new element, the state or quality of the self which we call sincerity' (Lionel Trilling); and that this point occurred somewhere around the middle of the eighteenth century. Trilling defines the current meaning of the term as 'congruence between avowal and actual feeling'. In this sense it tends, in discussions about literature, to become the amateur's panacea, used as a means of explaining or isolating literary excellence; in such naïve exercises in evaluation it serves as a loose form of approbation (cf. 'genuineness' or, more fashionably, 'authenticity'). But even where it is not positively inaccurate it is rarely a very helpful aid in what T. S. Eliot called 'the common pursuit of true judgment'. On examination the most apparently 'sincere' works usually turn out to have reached their final form long after the original emotions which gave rise to them, and should ultimately be seen to have more in common with a literary tradition than with the feelings of a particular individual. It is always much more instructive, in fact, to consider a work as an artefact more or less consciously fashioned and produced, rather than as pure lyrical effusion. Putting it negatively, Leo Tolstoy, himself an almost archetypally sincere man, also put it best when he saw 'poetry in the fact of not lying', by which he meant that the work of art has its own truthfulness, which has little or nothing to do with the honest transcription of feeling. Sincerity as usually understood is therefore not a very helpful word in the literary critic's vocabulary and should be sparingly employed. As Oscar Wilde discerned with his usual acuteness, 'Man is least himself when he talks in his own person. Give him a mask and he will tell you the truth.' That mask is, in fact, the most genuine of the faces the artist presents to us. See also PERSONA.

See I. A. Richards, *Principles of Literary Criticism* (1924), chs 23 and 34; Henri Peyre, *Literature and Sincerity* (1963); Lionel Trilling, *Sincerity and Authenticity* (1972).

JWJF

skaz

see FORMALISM

society

In critical usage, a term with two main senses: (1) the 'society' of a novel, play or poem, a social world created or imitated within the work,

(2) the 'society' of literature's creation and consumption, the world of customs, values, institutions and language-habits in which the work is created, published, and read, the culture in its broadest definition (cf. CULTURE). In autotelic theories of literature (those which assume that literary works are self-sustaining, coherent structures) the two usages are commonly held distinct. In realistic theories of literature (those which assume that literary works in some sense copy life) they blur. In historicist theories of literature (those which assume that the literary work is a personalized instance of some total complex of artistic expression) they become virtually indistinguishable.

Critics from Plato and Aristotle on have known that literature is essentially 'social'—has social causes, contents, and effects. The question is how valuable that insight is. With the personalization of romantic art, and the self-subsistence of symbolist art, the tendency to stress the distinctiveness of literary expression grew, reacting against deterministic social accounts of literature: those which saw it as a social mirror, a social product (e.g. Taine), a social criticism (e.g. naturalism), or an ideological instrument (e.g. some Marxist critics). Criticism tended to substitute median terms: 'culture' for the milieu, 'icon' for the work. But latterly there has been new interest in the complex transactions existing between 'literature' (meaning either the single text, or the entire corpus) and 'society' (meaning a particular community or the large-scale social metastructure). There are various reasons for this: the growth of sociology, linguistics, and structuralism; an increasing critical stress on fiction as opposed to poetry; a general tendency toward the politicalization of thought.

What is clear is that the term 'society' invites—or reveals—critical confusion, since it refers to something that can be thought of as primarily inside or outside the work. The society of, say, a Jane Austen novel can be thought of primarily as a fiction (a deliberately selective, conventionalized milieu which is an aspect of the composition) or a structure from outside 'reported' or analysed. Beyond this are larger issues. We can see literary works as social products and agents, and society as an envelope around literature, analysable in terms of reading publics, authors' *Weltanschauungen*, content-analysis, linguistics and ideologies. Or we can see them as creative centres lying outside such determinisms, though perhaps as potential powers *in* society. 'Society' raises all the problems of the territorial boundary separating 'art' from 'reality'; for that reason it will always constitute a critical crux, and remain a centre of attention for critics interested in the complex relationships between the fictional and formal and the world we observe round us. See also CULTURE.

See Malcolm Bradbury, *The Social Context of Modern English Literature* (1971); Richard Hoggart, 'Literature and society', *Speaking to Each Other* (1970); F. R. Leavis, 'Literature and society' and 'Sociology and literature', *The Common Pursuit* (1952); Jacques Leenhardt, 'The sociology of literature: some stages in its history' and Lucien Goldmann, 'The sociology of literature: status and problems of method', *International Social Science Journal*, 19, 4 (1967).

MSB

soliloquy

is a formal device by which a dramatic character, alone on the stage, reveals in speech his feelings, thoughts and motives to the audience. In its simplest form, as often in the Elizabethan drama before Shakespeare, it can be merely a means of directly communicating information that has not emerged in the course of the action or dialogue; for unskilful playwrights, therefore, it may be no more than a substitute for fully dramatic writing. But while it is obviously 'unrealistic' to present a character not otherwise out of his mind talking aloud while alone, audiences prepared to accept that they are in the theatre instead of the high street will no more question the dramatist's right to make audible the inner processes of reflection than readers question the novelist's frequent claim to know and articulate what goes on inside the heads and hearts of his characters.

The typical soliloquy is either a passionate speech giving vent to the immediate pressure of feeling at a point of crisis, or a deliberative speech in which a particular dilemma or choice of action is debated and resolved or, since one may lead naturally to the other, a combination of both. Thus the most effective soliloquies are introduced at moments of urgency for the character concerned, particularly when there is a reason for privacy and secrecy rather than public display of passion or reasoning. Sometimes however the soliloquy may be spoken directly to the audience by a character who wishes to take them into his confidence. Clowns and villains are inclined to this mode of address: the clowns because they often stand on the periphery of the plot and so invite the audience to join them in ridiculing situations in which they are not directly involved, and the villains (like Shakespeare's Richard III and Iago) because their awareness of the audience's presence adds to their stature as clever rogues in charge of events.

When the audience is eavesdropping on a meditative or impassioned soliloquy, the dramatist has the opportunity to internalize his presentation of character and to trace the dynamics of thought and feeling even beyond the level of the character's own awareness. In Shakespeare's subtlest soliloquies (those of Hamlet and Macbeth for instance) the audience is made to recognize ironies and ambiguities in what the character says, but of which he is unaware. Thus the actor is given the opportunity not only for a virtuoso performance of a set speech, but also for suggesting either the involuntary direction his thoughts and feelings move in, or the painful effort to articulate what lies almost out of reach of his words. In both cases the language and style of these great soliloquies do not describe the character's state of mind, they act it out.

See W. Clemen, *English Tragedy Before Shakespeare* (1961); L. Schücking, *Character Problems in Shakespeare's Plays* (1922).

DJP

sonnet

Technically the sonnet is easy to identify: fourteen lines divided (usually) by rhyme and argument into units of eight lines (octave) and six (sestet). The metre is normally the prevalent metre of the language—in English the iambic pentameter, in French the alexandrine, and in Italian (the original language of the *sonetto*, 'little song') the hendecasyllable. Petrarch (1304–74) was the first major sonneteer: his *Rime* to 'Laura' established the essential form and matter—a record of the intense and hazardous service of a lover, a service offering precarious local triumphs and the certainty of final defeat. Petrarch's rhyme-scheme (abba, abba, cde, cde, *or* cdc, dcd) was significantly different from Shakespeare's (abab, cdcd, efef, gg) which had more ironic possibilities. But the point of the proliferating formal rules which characterize the sonnet convention often gets lost in cataloguing variations: *every* sonnet is a 'variation' on the norm. What the convention means to the poet is a specialized 'vocabulary' of formal devices in addition to the normal rules of the language (cf. METRE), and his voluntary subjection to this discipline produces (hopefully) a high precision of utterance, a new and paradoxical freedom: 'rhyme is no impediment to his conceit, but rather gives him wings to mount and carries him, not out of his course, but as it were beyond his power to a far happier flight' (Samuel Daniel, *Defence of Rhyme*, 1603). The over-running of grammatical logic in the sonnet is analysed in Robert Graves and Laura Riding, *A Survey of Modernist Poetry* (1928) and William Empson, *Seven Types of Ambiguity* (1930), chapter II; the development of a sustained metaphoric argument, in Winifred Nowottny, *The Language Poets Use* (1962), and Murray Krieger, *A Window to Criticism* (1964).

It is clear that sonnets are often technical 'exercises', but it by no means follows that they are therefore insincere. In exploring his medium, the poet is exploring his own capacities to feel and think: Sidney's declaration (*Astrophel and Stella*, c. 1583), 'I am no pick-purse of another's wit' has an ironic edge, but is justified in the emotional thoroughness of his expropriations. Conventionality can be misunderstood and overstressed; it is perfectly possible to write insincere sonnets—to be facile, self-deceived, inexperienced or gross (Ben

Jonson, 'An Elegie'):

> Such songsters there are store of; witness he
> That chanced the lace, laid on a smock, to see, ·
> And straightway spent a sonnet . . .

The fragile idealism of the convention invited parody and self-parody (as in Shakespeare's *Love's Labour's Lost*), but proved inseparable from its ability to endure through time and change. Donne's famous lines form 'The Canonisation' catch both the permanence and the fragility:

> We'll build in sonnets pretty rooms;
> As well a well wrought urn becomes
> The greatest ashes, as half-acre tombs . . .

In the sonnet the individual poet may find a fullness and spaciousness of meaning he could not attain in isolation: 'The true father or shaping spirit of the poem is the form of the poem itself, and this form is a manifestation of the spirit of poetry, the "onlie begetter" of Shakespeare's sonnets who was not Shakespeare himself, much less that depressing ghost Mr W. H., but Shakespeare's subject, the master-mistress of his passion' (Northrop Frye, *Anatomy of Criticism*, 1957). The uncompromising technical discipline of the sonnet ensures that only the greatest poets—of the calibre of Shakespeare, Milton, Wordsworth—have excelled at it, but the logical and emotional intensity available in this form has preserved its fascination for many poets right down to the present day.

See J. W. Lever, *The Elizabethan Love Sonnet* (1956); Hallett Smith, *Elizabethan Poetry* (1952).

LS

sound

According to Mallarmé, versification (and therefore poetry) exists whenever a writer attempts style; when he gives equal prominence to sonority and to clarity of linguistic performance: *'Toutes les fois qu'il y a effort au style il y a versification'*. But sound is a primary aspect of poetry rather than of prose, and Mallarmé's dictum that the aesthetic impulse, the *'effort au style'*, renders prose and poetry indistinguishable visual vehicles of versification fails to convince: prose is a most unsatisfactory medium for writers concerned with sound (and for some poets, poetic writing is little better). The writer of prose can only control sound and attempt to indicate subtleties of sound, by means of punctuation.

A reviewer of essays by Robert Creeley, a poet obsessed with sound, was moved to comment 'One is puzzled by the exotic syntax'. The writer of poetry can not only produce exotic syntax, but can also counterpoint punctuation spatially with line endings; the pause at the end of the line offers an additional means of scoring sound to the comma, the semicolon, etc. Spatial 'punctuation', and typographical variation—innovated by Mallarmé in his '*Un Coup de Dés . . .*' (1897), and simplified yet more radically by Raoul Hausmann's *Optophonic Poems* of 1918—increased the poet's grammatical/spatial/typographical syntax, and partially solved the problems of scoring sound. Such problems are usually restricted to the work of poets for whom sound is of the same importance as meaning; work where variations of sound result from idiosyncrasies of the specific poet's voice and speech patterns, rather than being sonic variations within the confines of some pre-established communal verse structure such as the sonnet or the haiku, or variants within some similarly pre-established line/rhyme convention.

Whilst such conventions appeal to the collective 'mind's ear', their very visual nature—the fact that such stereotyped symmetrical structures can be charted diagrammatically—suggests that the poetry of such conventions subordinates sound to visual semantics; the extreme product of this tendency being 'CONCRETE' POETRY, a purely visual poetry of silent, spatially punctuated semantics.

It is thus essential that the visual experience of reading poetry motivated by both sonic and semantic considerations be complemented by the audial experience of the poet's voice. Clearly it is impossible to totally appreciate unrecorded poetry of the past, though phonetic reconstructions of such works as *Beowulf*, and reconstructed 'period' readings, such as Basil Bunting's approximations of Wordsworth's accent, may offer valuable insights into the sonic values of past works. Certainly it would be a mistake to neglect recording facilities today, when poets of the revived oral tradition, such as Creeley, have told audiences at readings that even to raise their voice would be to spoil the effect of the poem. Whilst it is incontestable that poetry exists whenever there is effort towards sonic or semantic style, the ear should not be neglected, for poetry aurally experienced may well transcend prose, verse, and book.

See Henri Chopin (ed.), *OU*, 33 (1968); Hans Richter, *Dada, Art and Anti-Art* (1965), 41–4, 118–21; Philip Steadman (ed.), *Form*, 3 (1966); Nicholas Zurbrugg (ed.), *Stereo Headphones*, 4 (1971), 'Futurism and after: Marinetti, Boccioni, and electroacoustic literature', *Comparative Criticism*, 4 (1982); Roland Barthes, 'The grain of the voice', *Image-Music-Text* (trans. 1977).

NCPZ

speech

see DECONSTRUCTION

speech act
see AUTHOR, DISCOURSE

stasis
see LITERATURE

story
see MYTH, NARRATIVE, NARRATIVE STRUCTURE, PICARESQUE, PLOT

stream of consciousness

A technique which seeks to record the random and apparently illogical flow of impressions passing through a character's mind. The best-known English exponents are Dorothy Richardson, Virginia Woolf and James Joyce. Later novelists have often employed the technique, though rarely with such thoroughness as its early proponents. For them it was a fresh weapon in the struggle against intrusive narration. By recording the actual flow of thought with its paradoxes and irrelevancies they sought to avoid the over-insistent authorial rhetoric of Edwardian novels. They felt that the traditional techniques could not meet the social pressures of the new age; believing that, in Virginia Woolf's words, 'human nature had changed . . . in or about December 1910', they rejected the socio-descriptive novel in favour of a novel centring on 'the character itself'. Inner thoughts and feelings now occupied the foreground of attention.

Theoretically, the aim is inclusiveness: 'No perception comes amiss' (Woolf). But, in practice, each novelist developed selective principles and personal structural procedures. Joyce and Woolf use the technique in quite different ways. Woolf's style is leisurely and repetitive, returning constantly to dominant images (e.g. the chimes of Big Ben in *Mrs Dalloway*, 1925). These images have no significance outside the novel: the novelist alone makes their meaning by the patterning she creates in the flow of recorded experience. Disconnected association is heightened and ordered by the passionate yet rational mind which conceives and controls it. Joyce's work, with its mastery of the abrupt shift from reflection to reflection, approaches the theory more nearly: 'Not there. In the trousers I left off. Must get it. Potato I have. Creaky wardrobe . . .' But he, too, inevitably imposes structures on the random. In *Ulysses* (1922), the ultimate order and meaning of events is related to those primary images which span human culture; each event is continuous with all other such events in human history, refracted through language into its radical meaning: Bloom/Stephen are Ulysses/Telemachus, as they are the eternal type of Father/Son.

Each writer seeks his own way of organizing, and so communicating, the arbitrary, and each finally gestures towards the inability of any single device to render fully the human condition.

See Leon Edel, *The Modern Psychological Novel* (revised ed., 1964); Melvin J. Friedman, *Stream of Consciousness: A Study of Literary Method* (1955); Robert Humphrey, *Stream of Consciousness in the Modern Novel* (1954); Dorrit Cohn, *Transparent Minds: Narrative Modes for Presenting Consciousness in Fiction* (1978).

GG

stress
see METRE

structuralism
as a concept is grand, controversial and elusive. For our purposes it is to be understood at two levels of generality: first, as a broad intellectual movement, one of the most significant ways of theorizing in the human sciences in the twentieth century; second, as a particular set of approaches to literature (and other arts and aspects of culture) flourishing especially in France in the 1960s but with older roots and continuing repercussions.

The basic premiss of structuralism is that human activity and its products, even perception and thought itself, are *constructed* and not *natural*. Structure is the principle of construction and the object of analysis, to be understood by its intimate reference to the concepts of *system* and *value* as defined in SEMIOTICS. A structure—for example the conventional sequencing of episodes in fairy stories, the geometry of perspective in post-medieval art, or something as apparently mundane as our arrangements for what, when and how we eat—is not merely an insignificantly mechanical ordering. Each element in the structure, whether 'unit' or 'transformation' or whatever, has meaning in the Saussurean sense of 'value' because it has been selected from a system of options and is therefore defined against the background of other possibilities. This is a radical view of meaning in its proposal that meanings do not come from nature or God, but are arbitrary, man-made. Clearly these assumptions encourage ANALYSIS and CRITIQUE and therefore disturb the complacency of traditional human inquiries. Hence the feeling of conservative scholars that structuralism is subversive, though their criticisms are usually misleadingly couched in other terms, e.g. structuralism is mechanistic and so against spontaneity and creativity.

Structuralist students of literature linked semiotic assumptions with ideas from other sources, principally Russian FORMALISM; Prague School structuralism (cf. FOREGROUNDING); the narrative analysis of Vladimir Propp; structuralist anthropology as blended from linguistics and Propp in the cooking-pot of Claude Lévi-Strauss; the new generative linguistics of Chomsky. Their activities and publications were too vast and diverse to summarize here, but I can mention the three most important, paradigmatic, models of analysis.

Theory of literature

The attempt to formulate general rules to distinguish literary from non-literary discourse: see POETICS. 'Poetics' is the theory of 'literariness' rather than the description of individual literary works. The late Roman Jakobson was the key figure in this ambitious enterprise: his seminal paper 'Linguistics and Poetics' (1960) proposed what would in Chomskyan terms constitute a set of 'substantive universals' to characterize the essence of literature, based on processes of repetition, parallelism and equivalence. Another version of poetic theory follows the lead of Chomsky and re-locates literariness: it is said to be not an objective property of texts but a faculty of (some) readers who are said to possess a 'literary competence' in addition to and analogous to the universal 'linguistic competence' postulated by Chomsky. See J. Culler, *Structuralist Poetics* (1975). Neither of these proposals seems very plausible; for a critique, see Fowler, 'Linguistics and, and versus, Poetics', reprinted in *Literature as Social Discourse* (1981). However, if the writing of generative rules for all and only those texts constituting Literature seems an impossible project, the more modest programme of generative grammars for specific *genres* seems a feasible enterprise, and this has been attempted by Tzvetan Todorov in a number of studies: see his *Grammaire du Décaméron* (1969) and *The Fantastic* (1973).

The analysis of verse

The reference-text here is the analysis by Jakobson and Lévi-Strauss of Baudelaire's 'Les chats' (translated in the DeGeorge and Lane anthologies). The analysts sift the poem for all kinds of linguistic symmetries, from rhyme to syntactic minutiae such as tense and number, and thus re-work it into an intensely patterned formal object, static and impersonal and remote from the communicative and interpersonal practices which language ordinarily serves. This analysis has been taken as a typical example of the abuse of linguistics in literary analysis, the application of a technique in an absolutely non-selective way, thus fabricating 'poetic' structures which the reader could not possibly perceive: see M. Riffaterre, 'Describing poetic structures' (1966), reprinted in Ehrmann; Fowler, 'Language and the reader' in *Style and Structure in Literature* (1975). But Jakobson is a very extreme example, and aspects of his theory, more discreetly applied, do provide illumination in verse analysis, as Riffaterre's own later work demonstrates: see his *Semiotics of Poetry* (1978).

More successful has been *the analysis of narrative structure*. The inspiration came from Vladimir Propp's *Morphology of the Folk-Tale* (1928), which appeared in French translation in 1957 and in English in 1958. Propp noted that, though the individual characters in Russian tales were very diverse, their *functions* (villain, helper, etc.) could be described in a limited number of terms (he suggested thirty-one, falling into seven superordinate categories). By reference to these elements, the narrative ordering of any tale could be analysed as a sequence of 'functions of the *dramatis personae*' and associated actions. This is in fact a generative grammar of narrative: a finite system (paradigm) of abstract units generates an infinite set of narrative sequences (syntagms). The linguistic analogy was seized on by Lévi-Strauss and made explicit by A. J. Greimas (*Sémantique structurale*, 1966), who provided a sophisticated reinterpretation of Propp's analysis in semantic terms. It became a standard assumption in narratology that the structure of a story was homologous with the structure of a sentence; this assumption allowed the apparatus of sentence-linguistics to be applied to the development of a metalanguage for describing narrative structure. The work of Roland Barthes, Tzvetan Todorov and Gérard Genette are particularly important in this development. See *Communications* 8 (1966): the contribution of Barthes is translated as 'Introduction to the structural analysis of narratives' in his *Image-Music-Text* (1977); this model has been applied to a story from Joyce's *Dubliners* by Seymour Chatman in 'New ways of analyzing narrative structure', *Language and Style*, 2 (1969). Genette's *Figures III* (1972), translated as *Narrative Discourse* (1980), achieves a masterly advance in the theory and description of POINT OF VIEW. Chatman's *Story and Discourse* (1978) applies many ideas from the French structural analysis of narrative in an English context. See also Fowler, *Linguistics and the Novel* (2nd ed., 1983). An informative general account of French structural narratology is Shlomith Rimmon-Kenan, *Narrative Fiction: Contemporary Poetics* (1983).

Anglo-Saxon reaction to structuralism has been almost universally hostile, deploring its mechanistic and reductive style and suspecting its exponents of a kind of left-wing philistinism. Fortunately, the response in France has been more subtle and more positively critical, confronting problems of what is neglected in the structuralist approach: reader, author, discourse as communicative practice and as ideology. See AUTHOR, DECONSTRUCTION, DISCOURSE, POSTSTRUCTURALISM, PSYCHOLOGY AND PSYCHOANALYSIS, READER, SEMIOTICS.

For an account of structuralism in the broader sense see Jean Piaget, *Structuralism* (1971). David Robey's *Structuralism: An Introduction* (1973) reprints a series of accessible lectures on structuralism in a variety of disciplines. Structuralism in literary studies is the subject of Jonathan Culler, *Structuralist Poetics* (1975); Terence Hawkes, *Struc-*

turalism and Semiotics (1977); Ann Jefferson, 'Structuralism and poststructuralism' in Jefferson and Robey (eds), *Modern Literary Theory* (1982). Anthologies of structuralist writings include R. T. and M. DeGeorge, *The Structuralists: From Marx to Lévi-Strauss* (1972); R. Macksey and E. Donato (eds), *The Structuralist Controversy* (1972); J. Ehrmann (ed.), *Structuralism* (1970); M. Lane (ed.), *Structuralism, A Reader* (1970).

RGF

structure

All critical theories have some notion of structure: the developing unity of a work. But, according to what characteristics are emphasized as providing that unity, the terms will vary: pattern, plot, story, form, argument, language, rhetoric, paradox, metaphor, myth. Starting from these dispositions, the term 'structure' then becomes an enabling reference; the reader is advised to consult potentially parallel entries (e.g. FORM, where structure is distinguished from texture, both being aspects of form) to see how this can be. The proposition is reversed here: such features are typologies of structure, organizational means for arriving at hypotheses about the principles of coherence in a given work. There are many such means, but they fall into two main categories: those derived from internal means and emphasizing features likely to be found especially in literature, and those derived from applying general principles of structure found in language, or the psychology of individuals or communities, or in broad areas of style in all the arts and in life, or in social structure, to works of literature for typological purposes.

I here assume what I think must be assumed for criticism effectively to exist: that every work is a distinct and verbally-created universe and must have a self-created logic or sequence for which the author is responsible. The work will have its own expectations and probabilities which constitute the unity of that universe. There is likely to be a coherence of social relationships and possibilities of relationship, constituting a society; a coherence of action, of probable behaviour in development, constituting a plot; coherence of attitude or value to these things, constituting a tone; coherence of rhetorical tactic, or point of perception and view, constituting a technique or (in a local sense) a language; there are likely to be other significant blocks of coherence— metrical and stanzaic features; acts and scenes; generic conventions— also inviting our sense of significant development. As we begin reading, we recognize that an author, starting writing, has made certain committing choices: where to commence his action, from which standpoints to see it, which language(s) and convention(s) to maintain. As we continue reading, we see that from these a logic flows—not a single logic of tone, technique, story or metaphor but a compound, total system of development or order which enables us to structure our own perceptions, acquire a sense of relevance, see what is persistent and significant in this universe. In some structures it will be apparent that one particular type of order—story, language, composition (in Nabokov's phrase) as hero—seems dominant. We are not engaged similarly from genre to genre or work to work; and as the significant dispositions, the sense of primary structure, vary so will our terminology.

Criticism's normal business will be to project the selective, one-for-all order of a fiction and discourse about it in the light of what is common to all fictions, so generalizing features like genre, rhetoric, motif and language into recurrent types in order to come to perceptions about what is distinctively literary. But developing order in fictions has analogues, deliberate or attributable, in order outside fiction. Thus while our typologies of order will concern what is distinctive about literary presentation, they are also likely to extend to structures in writings not fictional: to those in language in general; then to those in forms of expression or consciousness in the particular human society and then in the human mind at large. These things open literature to analogical explanation and to linguistic, psychological, sociological and ideological study; and they may creatively suggest the recurrence of structure analogously through all human experience (cf. STRUCTRUAL-ISM). The main danger here is that of applying methods of structural analysis assumed to be 'objective' because scientific, and derived in the first instance for other purposes, to literary works: an interesting case of the application of structural fictions to structural fictions.

See Kenneth Burke, *The Philosophy of Literary Form* (1957); R. S. Crane, *The Languages of Criticism and the Structure of Poetry* (1953); Northrop Frye, *Anatomy of Criticism* (1957); Frank Kermode, *The Sense of an Ending* (1967).

MSB

style

is one of the oldest and most tormented terms in literary criticism; its meaning is controversial, its relevance disputed. One usage can be discarded at once: criticism is not concerned with the belief that some authors or books have style (are 'stylish') whereas others do not. We must assume that all texts manifest style, for style is a standard feature of all language, not a *de luxe* extra peculiar to literature or just to some literature.

A style is a manner of expression, describable in linguistic terms, justifiable and valuable in respect of non-linguistic factors. The concept 'manner of expression' is controversial (see below), but the other two parts of the definition seem not to be: that it is a facet of language; and that it is given significance by personal or cultural, rather than verbal, qualities.

From 'style', 'stylistics' is derived as a branch of literary study. Some historians of criticism have called any approach to literature which pays close attention to aspects of language (imagery, sound-structure, syntax, etc.) 'stylistics'. This is misleading, since stylistics is a historically isolable division of criticism with its own principles and methods. Most modern criticism is verbally-oriented but, lacking the tenets, preoccupations and methodical spirit of figures like Auerbach, Croll, Spitzer, it should not be dubbed 'stylistics'. Stylistics is less diffuse, more single-minded, more mechanical, than criticism in general. Similarly, the word 'style' itself has relatively technical connotations; those not involved in (strict) stylistics tend to speak of 'tone' or, often, 'rhetoric'.

Linguistic form is not absolutely controlled by the concepts we want to express. There are alternative ways of putting messages into words, and the choice among alternatives is exercised along non-linguistic principles. Whether I say 'Shut the door!' or 'I wonder if you would mind closing the door, please?' is determined by a whole complex of personal and situational facts structuring the communicative event of which the sentence is a part. Stylistics posits that these extra-textual influences on the form of communication are organized systematically, and that the system brings about orderings of linguistic form which are themselves systematic and, more important, *characteristic*, i.e. symptomatic of one particular set of extra-verbal factors. This determination of style by context works outside literature as well as within it (see D. Crystal and D. Davy, *Investigating English Style*, 1969). Thus styles may be seen as characteristic of an author, of a period, of a particular kind of persuasion (rhetoric), or a genre. Literary stylisticians have generally been concerned to test such hypotheses as these: authors' styles—'linguistic fingerprints', allegedly—have been one focus; we also find such generalizations as 'Ciceronian', 'Senecan', 'Attic'; 'baroque', 'mannered'; 'grand', 'middle', 'low'; 'terse', 'expansive', 'florid', 'periodic', etc. These labels indicate that stylistics is a *classificatory* mode of literary study, generating categories of text arrived at on the basis of many different kinds of taxonomic criteria, generally a mixture of linguistic/formal and extra-linguistic/situational.

Style depends on a FOREGROUNDING of some selected feature, or set of features, of linguistic surface structure. A particular diction may be prominent, or a persistent rhythm, or a certain reiterated syntactic organization. This density in one part of the language may not catch our conscious attention, but it causes a certain stylistic impression in us: we feel that the text belongs to a familiar authorial or cultural milieu. 'Density' suggests counting, and indeed stylistics (unlike linguistics) is implicitly quantitative, and is sometimes explicitly so. Extreme instances of quantitative stylistics would be G. U. Yule's statistical work on literary vocabulary, and the more recent computer-assisted studies in authorship-detection. Here counting is directed to discovery; usually we count to confirm hypotheses—that there *is* a syntactic or lexical tendency which explains our perception of a peculiar period-style, for instance (see Josephine Miles's work).

The idea of style involves an idea of choice among equivalent ways of expressing the same thought. Such a proposal is anathema to the NEW CRITICS (cf. PARAPHRASE), for whom a change in wording is inevitably a change in meaning. The New Critical attitude relies on a false use of 'meaning'. Sentences may have the same propositional content (be synonymous) but express it in different ways so that the reader's *mode of apprehending* meaning is distinctively determined. Richard Ohmann has suggested that this distinction—between semantic *content* and stylistic or rhetorical *form*—is explained by the division between deep and surface structure found in generative linguistics. See Ohmann's 'Generative grammars and the concept of literary style' in D. C. Freeman (ed.), *Linguistics and Literary Style* (1970). The modern rapprochement between linguistics and criticism over the theory of style is very appropriate, for stylistics as an academic subject was born at the time of the birth of modern linguistics, and has continued to use some of the techniques of linguistics. Charles Bally, an eminent French stylistician, was a student of Saussure's; Leo Spitzer developed his methods in an attempt to bridge a gap between linguistics and literary history; and the late Stephen Ullmann, besides being an influential stylistician of French fiction, was also an expert on semantics.

The term 'stylistics' or 'linguistic stylistics' has come to designate any analytic study of literature which uses the concepts and techniques of modern linguistics, e.g. in the title of Anne Cluysenaar's excellent book *Introduction to Literary Stylistics* (1976) which is not a study of style as such but an introduction to practical textual criticism refined by linguistic ideas. It is preferable to restrict the term to the linguistic study of style in the sense indicated above, devising appropriate terms for other literary applications of linguistics. See LANGUAGE for discussion and references.

See R. W. Bailey and D. M. Burton, *English Stylistics: A Bibliography* (1968); M. W. Croll and J. Max Patrick (eds), *Style, Rhetoric and Rhythm* (1966); H. Hatzfeld, *A Critical Bibliography of the New Stylistics, Applied to the Romance Languages, 1900–1952* (1953); Graham Hough, *Style and Stylistics;* Josephine Miles, *Style and Proportion: The Language of Prose and Poetry* (1967); Louis T. Milic (ed.), *Stylists on Style: A Handbook with Selections for Analysis* (1969); Leo Spitzer, *Linguistics and Literary History* (1948); Stephen

Ullmann, *Style in the French Novel* (2nd ed., 1964), *Meaning and Style* (1973). Relevant journals include *Style* and *Language and Style*.

RGF

subject
see DISCOURSE

surfiction
see FICTION

Surrealism

grew directly out of DADA, its founder and chief spokesman, André Breton, having played an important role in Dada experiments. Yet where Dada reflected a sense of dissolution, providing public displays of artistic anarchy and images commensurate with the absurdity and uncertainty of the age, Surrealism propounded its own coherent anti-dote to the cant of nihilism and the facile mindlessness of public optimism. It did so with an evangelical enthusiasm which should have forewarned of its subsequent commitment to radical politics. Where the Dadaists had seen meaningless disorder, the Surrealists saw a synthesis which owed something to Hegel, the Romantics, the Symbolists. Breton was prepared to acknowledge that Surrealism could be seen as the 'prehensile tail' of Romanticism. Certainly it borrowed some of its methods—a concern with dreams, madness, hypnosis and hallucina-tion, deriving in part from Novalis, Coleridge, Nerval and Baudelaire. But the Surrealists were less dedicated to seeking visible evidence of a spiritual world than to creating the marvellous. Their aim was to change the world, partly through social revolution but more centrally through a revolution in consciousness. The techniques devised or borrowed—automatic texts and paintings (created in an attempt to evade conscious control and tap the intuitive, alogical, power of the subconscious), works inspired and shaped by chance, written accounts of dreams and paintings providing images of dream visions—were all designed to subvert aestheticism and precipitate a fundamental altera-tion in our understanding of 'reality'. To this end the Surrealists delighted in paradoxical images which mocked the process of rational thought and perception. They juxtaposed unrelated words and objects, thereby creating tantalizing images and iridescent verbal effects. Sur-realism is concerned with re-invigorating language, expanding our definition and perception of reality to incorporate the insights of the subconscious, and extending our appreciation of the central and liberat-ing role of chance, automatism and eroticism. It proposed the release of the imagination and stood as an implicit criticism of a restrictive rationalism in society and realism in literature. Though international in scope and influence, Surrealism is more firmly rooted in France than Dada had been. Its major writers and artists tend to be French (Breton, Soupault, Eluard, Aragon, Masson, Tanguy, Delvaux). Its impact in England came late (1936) and was largely ineffectual. But the United States benefited from the wartime presence of some of the leading European Surrealists, and its literature and art still bear the marks of this cultural transfusion.

The standard history of Surrealism is Maurice Nadeau, trans. R. Howard, *The History of Surrealism* (1968). For a book which counterbalances his tendency to see Surrealism as a movement contained within the years 1922–39, see Roger Cardinal and Robert Short, *Surrealism: Permanent Revelation* (1970). See also Savone Alexandrian, *Surrealist Art* (1970); Ferdinand Alguié, *The Philosophy of Surrealism* (1969); C. W. E. Bigsby, *Dada and Surrealism* (1972); J. H. Matthews, *An Introduction to Surrealism* (1965); Patrick Waldberg, *Surrealism* (1965).

CWEB

suspension of disbelief
see BELIEF

symbol
The literary symbol, defined straightforwardly by Kant (who, in his *Critique of Judgement*, 1790, calls it an 'aesthetic idea') in terms of the 'attributes' of an object 'which serve the rational idea as a substitute for logical presentation, but with the proper function of animating the mind by opening out for it a prospect into a field of kindred representations stretching beyond its ken' (his examples are the eagle that stands for Jove, and the peacock that represents Juno) takes on a special significance for Romantics early (Coleridge) and late (Yeats). Yeats indeed goes so far as to maintain that a 'continuous indefinable symbolism' is 'the substance of all style' (*The Symbolism of Poetry*, 1900), and for him the excellence of a symbol consists in the suggestiveness that derives from the suppression of a metaphor's directly apprehensible terms of reference: 'as a sword-blade may flicker with the light of burning towers', so the symbol evokes unseen worlds.

Between Jove's symbolic eagle (and the symbolism of medieval literature, not always distinguishable from allegory), and Yeats's mysticism, lies Blake's idiosyncratic appropriation of the symbolic language of the Bible ('Bring me my bow of burning gold/Bring me my arrows of desire') and the major literary movement known as *Symbolism*, where the almost autonomous symbol reveals the hidden order that lies behind our deceptive everyday reality.

The elaboration of a language of signs into what Arthur Symons (*The*

Symbolist Movement in Literature, 1899) calls 'a form of expression . . . for an unseen reality apprehended by the consciousness', a quasi-occult mode of knowledge deliberately opposed to the positivism of the age, stems from the work of Baudelaire (his Swedenborgian poem '*Correspondances*', for instance) and from the barely sane Gerard de Nerval's visions of a sentimental world lurking beneath natural forms, where ('*Vers Dorés*'):

> . . . *comme un œil naissant couvert par ses paupières,*
> *Un pur esprit s'accroît sous l'écorce des pierres!*

De Nerval's active world of occult correspondences mocks at free-thinking man's inability to penetrate reality; Baudelaire's poem is devoted to the proposition that nature is a temple wherein man hears '*de confuses paroles*' offering an imitation of an order he is not equipped to confront face to face. For later Symbolist writers, the artist becomes a high priest of this temple, communing with, and communicating (to the extent that the profane multitude can comprehend) the occult truths hidden by the veil called reality. Baudelaire's highly sensuous '*Correspondances*', which draws attention to the elaborate pattern of synaesthesia by which it isolates itself from linear discourse, fore-shadows an autonomous art which, in the work of Mallarmé, extends the ritualistic concern with the sacrosanct exactness of the incantation in the direction of an extreme preoccupation with technique: the connotative and associative functions of literary language and the evocative effects manipulated by the writer in the creation of a fictional world distinct from (often superior to) the world of everyday reality. The Art for art's sake of Gautier's *Émaux et Camées* (1858) had turned upon analogies between literature and the fine arts; the new AESTHETIC-ISM endorsed Pater's belief that 'all art aspires to the condition of music', praising Wagner's attempt to express the unconscious of his race in intricate structures of myth and symbol. The dedication of the Symbol-ists to the techniques of art, which, in Mallarmé's words, 'purify the language of the tribe', influenced many modern writers, including Eliot, Joyce, Valéry and Rilke, and engendered a literary criticism (that of the Russian Formalists and the English and American New Critics) which, stripping the Symbolist aesthetic of its late Romantic elements, evolved critical procedures delicate enough to describe the complex inner workings of modernist literature at the same time as it brought an unprecedented attention to bear on the linguistic devices of earlier writing. See also ALLEGORY.

See Maurice Bowra, *The Heritage of Symbolism* (1943); Guy Michaud (ed.), *La Doctrine Symboliste* (1947); Guy Michaud, *Message Poétique du Symbolisme* (1961); Arthur Symons, *The Symbolist*

Movement in Literature (1899, repr. 1958); Edmund Wilson, *Axel's Castle* (1935, repr. 1961).

GMH

synonym
see PARAPHRASE

syntax
The ordering of words, phrases and clauses in the structure of sentences: the 'left-to-right' principle of linguistic structure. Meaning—whatever thoughts we intend to communicate—is abstract; it is therefore not transferable from person to person directly: the mediation of a physical channel is needed. Meaning has to be made concrete, spread out in time and space ('left-to-right') for speaker, hearer, writer, reader. It is the arrangements of syntax which are responsible for this space-time ordering of abstract elements of meaning. And syntax is a major influence on STYLE: the way meanings are concretized, through syntax, affects the way an audience responds to those meanings.

One property of syntax is its capacity to provide different word-orders for the same meaning. Even though word-order is not strictly 'significant', it is nevertheless valuable and potent because it can determine the sequence in which a reader apprehends the elements of the complex structure of meanings embodied in a sentence. For example, the second and fifth words of the sentence *He put the book down* form one single meaning (cf. *deposit*) but are, because of the word-order, experienced discontinuously. The meaning of *put* must be incomplete, provisional, until the sentence is completed by *down*. This interrupted or delayed perception of meaning does not occur when we listen to the synonymous sentence *He put down the book*. Meaning is the same, but the mode of experiencing meaning is importantly different, because of the difference in syntax. Here, the meaning of *put* is immediately completed by *down*, there is no suspense, and no subsequent part of the sentence disturbs the firmly apprehended meaning' ('deposit'). A different kind of syntactic influence on the reader's reception of meaning is illustrated by the sentence *He put down the rebellion*. It is obvious, once one has read the whole sentence, that *put down* does not mean 'deposit' but 'subdue'. But this fact is obvious *only* after one has taken in the whole of the sentence (unless one guesses from context). In the temporal experience of reading, or listening, this figurative meaning for *put down* is supplied retrospectively, the basic, physical meaning being assumed first. Here the temporal sequence of mental operations demanded by the syntactic order is the reverse of that required for the processing of meaning. The ways in which syntax determines, assists, or even impedes the reader's apprehension of meaning are manifold.

To proceed to a literary example, the indirect and interrupted first sentence of Henry James's novel *The Ambassadors*—'Strether's first question, when he reached the hotel, was about his friend'— appropriately gives one time to wonder what this question is to be, sets up the tone of tentative enquiry which characterizes the whole narrative. (See Ian Watt's important paper in *Essays in Criticism*, 10, 1960.) Syntax can be mimetic; as the following lines from *Paradise Lost* demonstrate, the contrast between action and guile is imitated in first direct, then contorted, syntax:

> My sentence is for open war. Of wiles,
> More unexpert, I boast not: them let those
> Contrive who need, or when they need; not now.

Because syntax is inevitable and, in a sense, imperceptible, critics may fail to attend to its power. But as Winifred Nowottny observes, we should not regard syntax as merely ' "a harmless, necessary drudge" holding open the door while the pageantry of words sweeps through' (*The Language Poets Use*, 1962, 10). We must recognize that syntax exercises a continuous and inexorable control over our apprehension of literary meaning and structure—and that its influence is not limited to the spectacular grammatical games of Pope or Browning or Cummings.

The importance of syntax is acknowledged by the French pedagogic tradition of *explication de texte*, but has only recently received proper notice in Anglo-American criticism. Donald Davie's *Articulate Energy* (1955) is a brilliant exposition of different kinds of poetic syntax. Syntax has been more extensively and technically analysed in modern linguistic stylistics, using techniques drawn from transformational-generative grammar. See, for example, S. Chatman, *The Later Style of Henry James* (1972), and many of the papers in D. C. Freeman (ed.), *Essays in Modern Stylistics* (1981), in which it is often claimed or implied that artistic design is embodied in FOREGROUNDED syntactic patterns. Advocates of functional linguistics have made another bold claim that syntactic patterns encode a 'vision of things' (Halliday) or 'mind-style' (Fowler). See M. A. K. Halliday, 'Linguistic function and literary style: An inquiry into the language of William Golding's *The Inheritors*', in S. Chatman (ed.), *Literary Style: A Symposium* (1971); R. Fowler, *Linguistics and the Novel* (2nd ed., 1983), *Linguistic Criticism* (1986). There has also begun some interesting work on psycholinguistic implications of syntax for readers: e.g. G. L. Dillon,

Language Processing and the Reading of Literature (1978). See also LANGUAGE, STYLE.

RGF

syuzhet

see FORMALISM, NARRATIVE STRUCTURE

T

taste
see CLASSIC, CULTURE, EVALUATION

technique
Style as a deliberate procedure; literary and artistic craftsmanship, connoting formal rather than affective or expressive values. Every writer has, of course, employed a (more or *less* conventional) technique, but the insistence on technique rather than on inspiration, or the reverse, has been related to changing modes of sensibility. Thus, René Wellek follows other critics in maintaining that the distrust of inspiration and an accompanying faith in technique are the major points which set off Symbolism from Romanticism. In this, there exists an unbroken continuity from Poe, Baudelaire and Flaubert to Pound, Eliot and Valéry. Pound has declared that he believes in technique 'as the test of a man's sincerity' and Eliot has praised Valéry's *On Literary Technique* for projecting the image of the poet as a 'cool scientist' rather than as a 'dishevelled madman'.

NZ

tenor
see METAPHOR

tension
Conflict or friction between complementaries, converses, opposites. In literary criticism, a much-used term relying on its context for whatever particular meaning it may have. Endemic in dialectic thought, it has been variously employed in the analysis of the Romantic sensibility, and in criticism involving such polarizing conceptions as the Classicism-Romanticism antithesis, the Freudian opposites or Lévi-Strauss's dynamic dualisms. It is particularly common in discussions of twentieth-century poetics, reflecting the contemporary writer's increased awareness of tension, whether psychological, social, or that within the frame of his own linguistic medium. Thus, Gottfried Benn describes the Expressionist's medium as that of 'tension-laden words'. Generally, tension has been located wherever opposing forces, impulses

or meanings could be distinguished and related to one another.

The Russian Formalists and their followers describe verse rhythm in terms of the tension between the force of the rhythmical impulse and that of the syntactical pattern (cf. METRE). Other critics have pointed to the tensions inherent in metaphor. Empson's types of ambiguity are studies in different manifestations of tension between simultaneous meanings, while Cleanth Brooks's theory of paradox posits the power of the tensions involved in poetry as an evaluative criterion, in accord with the notion of a poem as drama. John Crowe Ransom defines a tension between the logical argument of a poem and its local texture, W. K. Wimsatt implies a tension between the concrete and the universal or the particular and the general, and Allen Tate attempts a theory in which tension means the simultaneity of literal and metaphoric or figurative meaning (*ex*Tension and *in*Tension). Such preoccupations with tension are responsible for the critical bias in favour of such lyrical or dramatic poetry in which it prevails as against poetry of tensionless sentiment or narrative and descriptive poetry.

See Brian Lee, 'The New Criticism and the language of poetry' in Roger Fowler (ed.), *Essays on Style and Language* (1966), 29–52, and references.

NZ

text

We should beware of regarding the printed text of a literary work as 'the work itself'. Many interesting questions arise when we consider the process of recovering 'the work' from 'the text'. In *Principles of Literary Criticism* (1924) I. A. Richards attempted to describe the process of reading and reacting to a text, and his analysis is suggestive. Modern descriptive linguistics has, more recently, clarified certain aspects of the decoding process, as applied to written or spoken 'text'. Two important points arise for literary criticism. First, an adequate understanding of the language-system involves a recognition of the important role played by stress, speed, loudness, pitch and voice-quality in the communication of meanings. All these features are more or less effaced by transposition into the written code, and much of the writer's work is to find means of replacing or reorganizing them. Gerard Manley Hopkins resorted to modifications of the written system which are far from precious or irrelevant. In fact, the full implications of this point for written poetic and prose form have still to be explored. Second, our new knowledge of how the members of a community learn the meanings of words (through their use in contexts of language and situation) leads to a distinction between subjective and intersubjective responses to the text. Subjective responses rely on meanings derived from the use of a word in special circumstances unique to the individual, while intersubjective responses rely on uses which are widespread throughout the community. Clearly there is nothing so simple as a dichotomy: some contexts are peculiar to a section of a community or to a family. The possibility of communication, however, in the community at large depends on the widest type of intersubjective response. And literary criticism, if it is not to be local or (at worst) autobiographical, must appeal to that wider system of meanings. It must also be remembered that since the socio-linguistic background against which we decode a text constantly changes through time, marks on paper and recorded sound give only an illusion of total stability. But then, as Gombrich shows in *Art and Illusion* (1960), the same applies to the apparent permanence of stone and pigment. Attempts to restore the past can be partially successful only and cannot govern our overall response to the text.

AAAC

texture

Strictly, the word *texture* when applied to language, describes the tactile images employed to represent various physical surfaces, but by extension has come to mean the representation in words of all sensible phenomena. The widespread use of the term is based upon the assumption that words have an expressive or simulative aspect which helps to illustrate their meanings more immediately. This belief in the onomatopoeic properties of language has not always gone unchallenged, but the existence of techniques for producing particular sensory effects in the reader is undisputed, and it is thus possible to describe the texture of language in terms either of the means used or the effects obtained. Assonance (identity of vowel sounds), consonance (identity of consonant sounds), and alliteration (repetition of initial consonants) may each be used to produce such effects as cacophony (a sense of strain in pronunciation) or euphony (a sense of ease in pronunciation). All are exemplified in Pope's famous exercise 'An Essay on Criticism':

> When Ajax strives some rock's vast weight to throw,
> The line too labours, and the words move slow;
> Not so, when swift Camilla scours the plain,
> Flies o'er th'unbending corn, and skims along the main.

Samuel Johnson, however, attempting to prove that the mind governs the ear and not the reverse, quotes more lines with similar textural qualities and demonstrates quite convincingly that not even 'the greatest master of numbers can fix the principles of representative harmony' (*Life of Pope*).

Many other critics and theorists from Aristotle to I. A. Richards have disputed the possibility of any natural connection between the sound of any language and the things signified. Richards in *The Philosophy of Rhetoric* (1936), 62 asks:

> What resemblance or natural connection can there be between the semantic and phonetic elements in the morpheme? One is a sound, the other a reference. Is (fl-) [in *flicker, flash, flare*] really like 'moving light' in any way in which (sl-) or (gl-) is not? Is that not like asking whether the taste of turkey is like growing in some way that the taste of mint is not?

One need not go quite so far as this to agree with his conclusion that most expressive words get their feeling of peculiar aptness from other words sharing the morpheme and supporting them in the background of the reader's mind.

The relation of texture to structure is dealt with elsewhere (see FORM) but it should be stated here that Richards's views on the inter-inanimation of words avoid the implicit fallacies in the traditional notion of texture as verbal decor, and preserve verse analysis as an intelligent, and not merely a mechanical exercise.

BCL

theme

traditionally means a recurrent element of subject-matter, but the modern insistence on simultaneous reference to form and content emphasizes the formal dimension of the term. A theme is always a subject, but a subject is not always a theme: a theme is not usually thought of as the *occasion* of a work of art, but rather a branch of the subject which is indirectly expressed through the recurrence of certain events, images, or symbols. We apprehend the theme by inference—it is the rationale of the images and symbols, not their quantity. There is a case for restricting the loosely formal use of the term; if we use 'theme' to mean a certain *quantity* of features in a work (iterative imagery or stylistic mannerism), we are confusing a symptom with a cause. For example, if we talk about the 'theme of drowning' in Dickens's *Our Mutual Friend*, we are only saying that it is a novel in which people are repeatedly drowned or drowning is frequently mentioned, whereas the 'theme of Christian redemption' offers an explanation of the *significance* of drowning. Recurrent local features are better designated by the term *motif*.

The degree of abstraction of the term depends on the nature of the work under consideration. It makes more sense, for example, to talk of the 'theme of waiting' in Beckett's *Waiting for Godot* (1956) than the 'theme of drowning' in Dickens, because the play offers the action itself as an important part of its subject-matter, not simply one kind of event which becomes 'thematic' by repetition. The epithet *thematic* should thus mean 'symptomatic of the presence of a theme' rather than merely 'iterative' or 'recurrent'.

However, the term is sensitive and useful precisely because it admits of degrees of abstract reference; it is neither possible nor desirable to restrict all quantitative usages, because theme implies the linearity or extension of a work in a way that other subject-matter terms do not. Compared, for example, with *thesis*, a qualitative term meaning the core of argument or attitudes a work promotes or reveals, theme is a more concrete and formalistic term with structural implications. We think of a theme as a line or thread running through a work, linking features which are un- or otherwise related (cf. PLOT). The thesis of a work is paraphrasable, but a theme might not be so. Thesis is also an intentionalist term, whereas theme may or may not be. Proust's themes, for example, modelled on the analogy of music, are a conscious part of his creative method; but in other, less self-conscious cases, to use the term is to talk about structure, not intended content. Thus a critic may use 'theme' to refer to those repeated parts of a subject which control aspects of a work which he perceives as formal as well as conceptual.

'Theme' is also used to refer beyond the individual work. We speak of 'perennial themes' such as the theme of the Fall. Here, theme pre-exists the individual work and borders on *archetype* or even MYTH. On the other hand works of literature may express themes which condition other works (e.g. the *carpe diem* theme) in which case the term is starting to overlap with CONVENTION.

VRLS

threnody
see ELEGY

topos
see COMPARATIVE LITERATURE

tradition
is a historical scheme made up of formal, stylistic and ideological attributes common to large numbers of works over a long time. It generally implies a causal nexus linking individual works. The literary historian may use the idea of tradition either in a strictly historical way or as an aid to criticism. In the first case, he will use individual works to demonstate a process of literary change; in the second, the procedure will be reversed to illumine the individual work.

Tradition tends to be defined either in formal and stylistic terms, or in terms of ideas and attitudes: the 'oral tradition' and the 'radical tradition', for example. Placing a work raises many questions. Can styles determine ways of thinking? In what lies the originality of a work?

How does the individual work contribute to the evolution of the tradition? How far do social changes, how far individual genius contribute to changing literary forms? Paradoxically, placing a work in an intellectual tradition may draw one's attention to specifically literary problems to explain why one work is more effective than another when both express similar ideas. And vice versa: the extra subtlety of thought of one work may become obvious through comparison with lesser works in the same convention. Most basic of all, an awareness of tradition may be indispensable to establish the original meaning of a text, especially if works are closely linked by literary influence or imitation, as in (say) an oral tradition, or in the 'Classical tradition'.

Two methodological problems arise. We derive our definition of the tradition from individual works, but we decide which works are relevant according to our definition. The way out is the dialectical process of measuring the works against the tradition, modifying the tradition in the light of the works.

The second problem concerns how the tradition works (if it works at all). Is the tradition all in the eye of the beholder? If not, in what way are works linked together? The principal agency is surely the author's mind. To this we have no access, but can deduce from the work many of the influences which he has transmitted into and transmuted in his work. The causal link between works may be the influence of a common environment, including a common literary environment of aesthetic conventions and the language itself. It may be ideological or religious. It may be the direct link of literary borrowing. The attempt to determine the varying proportions of such influences by placing a work in a tradition can help immensely to reveal the total structure of a literary work.

Traditional is sometimes opposed to *original* (see ORIGINALITY), or to 'new-fangled', with corresponding pejorative or laudatory undertones. Such oppositions rest on misconception and misapplication. Few works, if any, exist in such a vacuum that they cannot be related to any sort of tradition. And 'traditional' should not be equated with the negative sense of 'conservative': there are radical traditions. 'Traditional' is more properly a neutral descriptive term, with approving or disapproving undertones depending on one's attitude to the tradition in question. See also CONVENTION, CREATION, DISCOURSE, EXPERIMENTAL.

See T. S. Eliot, 'Tradition and the individual talent', *The Sacred Wood* (1920).

EJB

tragedy

As a species of drama *tragedy* can be defined only in the most general terms, such as Aristotle's 'the imitation of an action that is serious . . .

with incidents arousing pity and fear'. His *Poetics* attempts a classification of the elements proper to tragedy but, despite his inductive methodology, few Greek tragedies conform to his model. However, his concept of *hamartia*, the act of the hero which initiates the fatal process, suggests a basis for any more developed theory of tragedy. This hamartia may be anything from a mistake over identity to deliberate crime or sin, but is always horrifyingly out of proportion to the consequences of pain and destruction. The act of the hero, a man 'better than ourselves', a 'great-souled' man, opens a gap in the fragile fabric of morality and civilization through which the primeval forces of anarchy and destruction pour. Tragedy is a dramatization of man's sense of his humanity and society as constantly under threat from the arbitrary chances of fate and his own innate savagery. In tragedy's heroic phase (e.g. Sophocles's *Oedipus*) man accepts a measure of responsibility for the destructive action and asserts against it a quality of heroic suffering and knowledge. But in its ironic phase tragedy emphasizes the arbitrariness of evil, rather than simply its disproportion to human action, and moves towards a kind of savage farce (e.g. Euripides's *Electra*) in which the heroic stance degenerates into futile posturing.

The tragic gap and the shift from the heroic to the ironic phase are evident in Elizabethan and Jacobean tragedy. The fates of Marlowe's Tamburlaine and Faustus are consequent on their hubristic error—denial of man's mortality—but the tragic structure of these morality situations insists on the hostility, even the malevolence, of the 'gods' or 'God' that exact their rights. In Shakespeare's heroic tragedies—*Othello, Coriolanus, Antony and Cleopatra*—the heroes' psychologies are involved in a destruction that is limited in scope—domestic or political, not metaphysical—and the hero, in his final speech, asserts his enduring *virtù* against the facts of defeat and death. But the psychological factors—pride, lust, jealousy—are the *données* of the action, not its significant *causes*; they provide a context in which the forces of destruction can work. Similarly the tragedies of Racine are not really explorations of the psychology of 'passion'; in their world a monstrous primeval power infiltrates man's social and moral order through the intoxicating irrationality of sexual desire.

The gap between human and ultimate causes widens in Elizabethan developments of the Senecan tragedy of blood; in Kyd's *Spanish Tragedy* and Marston's *Antonio's Revenge* the revenge structure becomes a metaphor for an irruption of evil. Whatever the superficial moral realities of the situation, and the calls of the revenger on nature, honour, and blood, the acting out of revenge is a descent into a chaos of horror and savagery urged on by a malignant and insatiable ghost. The revenger can only carry out his 'duty' by distancing himself from the reality of the act by elaborate mimes, masks, and plays. It is the unbearable knowledge of the nature of revenge that makes Hamlet a prisoner in his own play. T. S. Eliot's complaint that Hamlet's emotion was 'in excess of the facts as they appear' is unwitting testimony to the gap between human motive and action and the pressure of evil behind them that defines the tragic experience. In *Macbeth*, a revenge structure in reverse, the commitment to crime is specific and deliberate, albeit fearful, but the tragedy again lies in the enormity and universality of the evil that enters through the gap in nature that Macbeth has opened. The darkness and chaos of Scotland are not *caused* by the murder of Duncan; the forces that the weird sisters testify to are given licence by it. The symbolism of evil is not merely explanatory or emblematic; similarly, in *King Lear* the tempest is not a symbolic extension of Lear's disintegration so much as an expression of the primeval chaos that now engulfs him and his action. But at least in *Macbeth* the act and the consequence are still clearly related; in *Lear* the gap is appallingly wide. An act of senile folly precipitates the disintegration of human society—the basic ties of nature fall apart to reveal a chaos where humanity 'must prey on itself like monsters of the deep'. The causal element, the hamartia, has become almost incidental; evil is immanent and overflows from the smallest breach in nature. In this phase of tragedy the protagonist is forbidden even the luxury of stoicism; Lear's pathetic submission to fate is merely the prelude to the final cruelty. Beyond this there is only the surrealist horror of Webster: in *The White Devil* and *The Duchess of Malfi* tragedy is a horrible and inconsequential farce relieved only by magnificent rhetorical gestures; insanity, disease, and corruption inform a world in which man is an arbitrary actor.

If tragedy has not been an available mode since the eighteenth century this may have to do with the growth of rationalism and the bourgeoisie. The tradition of REALISM in the new form of the NOVEL was antipathetic to the extraordinary or inexplicable; the great English novels in this tradition lack a metaphysical dimension, a sense of active evil pressing on the edges of civilization. Evil is redefined as moral or social *error* and the scrutiny of psychology and motive becomes the animating structural concern. The tragic gap closes and man is wholly responsible for the disorder he creates. In this situation the drama of external evil finds expression only in the melodramatic modes of the GOTHIC fantasy and, later, the ghost story; in these the evil is external to the hero and the 'normal' society he represents, whereas in tragedy it is inherent. Some of the dramas of Ibsen attempt to express a sense of tragic destiny with insistent symbolism, but even at its most impressive and dramatic, as in *Ghosts*, the requirement of realism, of explicability, inhibits the symbolism of transcendence. Hereditary syphilis is undoubtedly horrific, but as a symbol of evil it lacks universality, it is too specifically a disease.

In fact a finer sense of tragic structure informs the symbolic fictions of Henry James and Conrad. A comparison of the similar moral situation in James's *Portrait of a Lady* and George Eliot's *Middlemarch* and *Daniel Deronda* shows James's symbolic rhetoric creating a sense of active, immanent, evil where Eliot was content with terms of moral responsibility and guilt. And Conrad's work is full of pressures from the heart of darkness. Tragedy is a possible form for these novelists because they collapse the realistic opposition of the 'real' and the 'poetic'; their symbolisms of evil are not illustrative or exemplary, but functions of their language. As Jorge Luis Borges said, 'Conrad and Henry James wrote novels of reality because they judged reality to be poetic'. The tragic structure depends on such a judgment. See also CATHARSIS, DRAMA.

See A. C. Bradley, *Shakespearèan Tragedy* (1904); J. Jones, *On Aristotle and Greek Tragedy* (1962); Dorothea Krook, *Elements of Tragedy* (1969); F. L. Lucas, *Tragedy: Serious Drama in Relation to Aristotle's Poetics* (1927, repr. 1961); F. W. Nietzsche, trans. W. Kaufmann, *The Birth of Tragedy* (1967); G. Steiner, *The Death of Tragedy* (1961); N. Frye, *Fools of Time* (1967); R. P. Draper (ed.), *Tragedy: Developments in Criticism* (1980); R. B. Sewall, *The Vision of Tragedy* (1980).

PM

translations

are commonly abused and translators undervalued: yet the literary translator has at all times been extremely influential, and the branch of literary criticism concerned with translation brings close analysis of language to bear on cross-cultural literary questions in a way central to COMPARATIVE LITERATURE, since a unique creative energy is generated where languages converge. H. A. Mason's *Humanism and Poetry in the Early Tudor Period* (1959) admirably demonstrates the value of such studies.

In our own time NEW CRITICAL insistence on the inseparability of form and content has questioned the possibility of translation: and one could cite a number of poets, from Shelley's likening of translation to subjecting a violet to chemical analysis to Robert Frost's working definition of poetry as 'what gets left out in translation' to demonstrate that writers have had grave doubts about it. Yet Shelley (for example) was himself an admirable translator: and it seems that he was primarily stressing the impossibility of exact correspondence between source and target texts, rather than rejecting translation; he believed that 'the plant must spring again from the seed, or it will bear no flower'. Some elements in the source text elude the net of the target language: others stretch it and call attention to the device by which they are admitted: the process is controlled by the translator, who must be a scrupulous critic and a creative writer; he locates the 'seed' and makes it grow.

Dryden, regrounding the classics in a contemporary idiom, was much concerned with translation. Unaware of modern conceptions of the relation between form and content, he could happily advocate reasonable freedom, demanding that the translator should first 'know what is peculiar to the author's style', and then

> 'tis time to look into ourselves, to conform our genius to his, to give his thoughts either the same turn, if our tongue will bear it, or, if not, to vary but the dress, not alter or destroy the substance.

This kind of translation, called by Dryden paraphrase, is, however, sharply distinguished from impermissibly free imitations. Modern translators, not sharing Dryden's conviction that human nature is everywhere the same, and concerned, like modern critics, with the phenomenology of a given work, have paid more attention to imitation as a mode of translating at least lyric poetry, and have often worked in the territory between two languages, rather than offering to reconstruct one on the foundations of another. Lowell's 'Imitations' are representative or, fifty years earlier, Pound's 'Homage to Sextus Propertius'. Louis Zukovsky's recent translations of Catullus have created an even more striking synthetic language that mimes or mouths the Latin of the original in a way that is deliberately indecent. See also PARAPHRASE.

See W. Arrowsmith and R. Shattuck (eds), *The Craft and Context of Translation* (1961); W. Benjamin, 'The Task of the Translator', in *Illuminations* (1970); R. A. Brower (ed.), *On Translation* (1966); G. Mourin, *Les Belles Infidèles* (1955); E. Nida, *Toward a Science of Translating* (1964); G. Steiner, Introduction to his anthology of verse translation first published as *The Penguin Book of Modern Verse Translation* (1966), reissued as *Poem into Poem* (1971); S. Bassnett-Maguire, *Translation Studies* (1980); R. W. Brislin (ed.), *Translation: Approaches and Research* (1976); G. Toury, *In Search of a Theory of Translation* (1980).

GMH

travesty
see PARODY

typicality
Although types and typologies have long been traditional ideas in literary criticism, modern MARXIST CRITICISM has deployed this notion in new ways. The Hungarian Marxist critic Georg Lukács, heavily influenced by the aesthetics of the German philosopher Hegel, has used

the idea of 'typicality' to indicate the process whereby, in classical REALIST literature, events and individuals are at once uniquely particularized, and representative of broader, deeper trends in history itself. A George Eliot character, for example, is neither an isolated 'personality' nor a mere emblem of some underlying reality; the peculiar complexity of such a character lies in its dialectical unity of the individual and the representative. For Lukács, such a fusion avoids at once an 'alienated' presentation of character which divorces it from its social context, and a pure reduction of individuals or situations to abstract 'symptoms' of impersonal forces. Lukács finds MODERNIST literature characterized by both forms of representation, and dogmatically regards them as absolute errors. Characters in such fictions are either damagingly 'privatized', reduced to mere abstract consciousness, or allegorically presented. But the latter defect is also, for Lukács, typical of the 'socialist realist' literature to which he was privately hostile: socialist realism in this sense perpetuates the weaknesses of 'naturalism', which represents a declension from the major realist tradition. Scott and Balzac, writing at a period when the bourgeoisie was still a progressive force, were able to create 'typical' events and characters, intuitively sensing the shaping forces of history within particular phenomena. By the time of Flaubert, Zola and Conrad, the bourgeoisie had endured a crisis of political confidence, could no longer make living connections between individuals and their world, and found itself confronted by an opaque, impenetrable reality. It took refuge either in dispassionate description of this supposedly immutable society (Flaubert, naturalism), or in the private recesses of consciousness (SYMBOLISM). In the work of such exceptional writers as Thomas Mann, Lukács found the great tradition of typicality perpetuated into the twentieth century.

See J. Bernstein, *The Philosophy of the Novel* (1984); G. Lukács, *The Historical Novel* (1962), *Studies in European Realism* (1950); R. Williams, *Drama from Ibsen to Brecht* (1968).

TE

V

value

see EVALUATION, REFUNCTIONING

variation,
the calculated avoidance of uniformity of expression, seems to be a
feature of all art-forms (music, literature, etc.) having a time dimension. A pervasive characteristic of literary language, it occurs on lexical,
syntactic and phonological levels.

Lexical variation has its most commonplace manifestation in the
'elegant variation' of fictional and journalistic prose: avoidance of
repeated use of the same expression by choosing an alternative expression having the same reference; e.g. by successively referring to a
character as *Parson Smith, the man of God, Mr Smith, our clerical
friend*, etc. Lexical variation is also a stylistic convention of much
heroic poetry, e.g. Old English verse, where the use of variant core-
ferential phrases is an inseparable part of the technique of alliterative
composition. *Syntactic* variation can take the form of repeating the
same structure but with different ordering (often with a chiasmic, or
mirror-image pattern), as in Whitman's *Jehovah am I/Old Brahm I,
and I Saturnius am* (from 'Chanting the Square Deific'). *Phonological*
variation can take the form of 'ringing the changes' on stressed vowel
sounds (particularly long vowels and diphthongs) for euphonious
effect (*Paradise Lost*, 3):

> Then feed on thoughts that voluntary move
> Harmonious numbers; as the wakeful bird . . .

A further kind of variation is the breaking up of excessive regularity in
parallelistic patterns, whether these are patterns on a metrical or a
lexico-syntactic level. *Metrical* variation is an accepted licence of
English verse whereby (under certain conditions) the positions of
stressed and unstressed syllables may be reversed. A similar phenomenon is the final twist in the verbal pattern of (*Merchant of Venice*,
3, 1):

If you prick us, do we not bleed? if you tickle us, do we not laugh?
if you poison us, do we not die? and if you wrong us, shall we not
revenge?

Whatever the differences between the above cases, they all illustrate
enhancement of the element of unpredictability in language, often
where in ordinary language the orderliness of repetition might have
been expected. It is notable that whereas verbal parallelism characteristically follows a strictly predictable pattern in 'sub-literary' compositions such as folk-songs and language games, it rarely does so in
literature. Similarly, metrical variation is found in serious poetry, but
not in doggerel verse or nursery rhymes. Such observations suggest that
variation has a more significant role in literature than the mere negative
one of avoiding the tedium of mechanical repetition. One possible
explanation is prompted by the Russian formalist thesis that art 'makes
strange' the experience it describes, and hence that the language of art
has to be a 'twisted', oblique mode of discourse. Variation, unexpected-
ness, establishes a medium or 'scenario' of poetic heightening, in which
daring departures from linguistic norms become acceptable. See also
FORMALISM.

GNL

vehicle
see METAPHOR

verbal irony
see IRONY

verisimilitude
see BELIEF, REALISM

vers libre
see FREE VERSE

verse
is the minimal condition of poetry if poetry is to mean anything even as a
metaphor—'Poetry is only in verse and nowhere else' (Vigny). The
degree of expressivity of language depends upon the frame of mind in
which we approach it and that frame of mind is in turn determined by
conventions of presentation, lay-out, etc. Free verse might perhaps be
printed as prose, but, printed as verse, 'the words are more *poised* than
in prose' and 'are to be attended to, in passing, for their own sake'
(MacNeice, *Modern Poetry*, 1938; 2nd ed., 1968).

Verse is the line of poetry; a line of verse differs from the line of prose
in that it has an active relationship with the page on which it may be

written; it asks the page to proclaim its self-sufficiency, to make it portentous and to make room for its mental and emotional extension, the infra-line (Claudel calls the primordial line 'an idea isolated by blank space'); the prose line merely undergoes the physical limitations of the page which thwarts its urge for continuous linearity (the paragraph is a concession to the page, the stanza collusion with it). And the poem differs from the shopping list in that the poem turns sequence into the formally consequential.

A line of verse will be a line of verse as long as it can point to an authority of a higher order than grammar. By this standard, many lines need the corroboration of others, derive their 'lineness' from accompanying evidence. This authority of course need not be metric or rhythmic; it may be as arbitrary as it pleases; enjambment is enough to suggest an unseen entity imposing itself, to look like compliance with a formal structure. Indeed there is a sense in which in free verse enjambment is a psychological need for both writer and reader, and more a purely formal than an expressive device.

Perhaps the first line of a lyric poem is more line than any of the subsequent ones. Its formulation is an act of perfect faith, it is invocation, libation, abstracted utterance. It can be neither good nor bad, because however the poet came by it, it is the absolutely given, the only assumption the poem can allow itself. Many poems are a making sense of and a giving quality to the first line. And if the first line can so often stand for a title, it is because, while being part of the poem, it partakes also of a paradigmatic existence.

If we call prose 'poetic' we must recognize that it is poetic not for any intrinsic reasons but because it alludes to itself in a verse context. Prose is a manner, verse a form; there is no language called poetry, there is only a poetic language in the verse instance. Verse is verse before it is anything else, meaning, vision, etc. If highly imaged language is called poetic, it is because verse alone has enough formal presence to give direction to the caprice of invention and equilibrium to semantic violence, just as it has enough formal presence to re-animate the semantically sedate. See also METRE, POETRY, PROSE.

See V. Forrest-Thompson, *Poetic Artifice* (1978); P. Fussell, *Poetic Meter and Poetic Form* (revised ed., 1979).

CS

verse epistle

is one of the neo-classical forms of familiar and complimentary poetry which flourished in England during the seventeenth century. Imitating the epistles of the Roman poet Horace, such verse was addressed to friends, patrons and fellow-poets in a style that approximated to the informal candour and civility of conversation, allowing the poet to expatiate freely in a personal manner on moral and literary themes. Among the principal themes of the Horatian epistle, for instance, are the pleasures and virtues of friendship, the values of self-knowledge and integrity of mind, the praise of the temperate life in country retirement, and general or specific reflections on the art and status of poetry (Horace's *Ars Poetica* is in the form of an epistle). Many of the complimentary poems with which Jonson and the Tribe of Ben commended and appraised each other's work are related to the epistolary form in their tone of personal familiarity. The extravagance of Donne's epistles to noble ladies has not drawn much critical approval, but the epistles of Daniel, Drayton, Carew and Herrick are justly admired. The full capacities of the form, however, are best exemplified by Jonson and Pope; like Horace himself they are also great satirists, and the kinship between verse epistle and satire rests in a common emphasis upon moral and critical realism. The Horatian familiar epistle should not be confused with the Ovidian elegiac epistle (e.g. Drayton's *Englands Heroicall Epistles* and Pope's *Eloisa to Abelard*) in which historical characters are fictitiously supposed to lament their misfortunes.

See R. A. Brower, 'The Image of Horace', in *Alexander Pope: The Poetry of Allusion* (1959); D. J. Palmer, 'The Verse Epistle' in Bradbury and Palmer (eds), *Metaphysical Poetry, Stratford-upon-Avon Studies*, 11 (1970).

DJP

voice

see DIALOGIC STRUCTURE, FORMALISM

W

wit

The term first comes into critical importance applied to literature in the
seventeenth century, though it was used in the previous century in a
general way to denote liveliness and brilliance of conversation. 'Witty
Jack Donne' is an Elizabethan man-about-town, but when he turns up
in Carew's 'Elegie upon the Death of the Deane of Pauls' (1623) as

> . . . a King, that rul'd as hee thought fit
> The universall Monarchy of *wit* . . .

we are moving into a time when *wit* was a powerful if disputed critical
concept or basis for value-judgment, though such a time was more
surely after the Restoration. The clue to the reason for this may lie in a
meaning of *wit* which is assigned to the Restoration years: 'the seat of
consciousness or thought, the mind'. Dryden, living in this critical
climate, defined wit as 'sharpness of conceit'. His emphasis is on
self-consciousness on the part of both the poet and the audience. It is no
accident, then, that at this time 'the wits' emerged—a group of gentle-
men, conscious of their nimble minds and cultural awareness. Apart
from self-consciousness itself, there are several other characteristics of
Restoration and eighteenth-century wit that come from such an in-
group attitude. Comparison is stressed. The wit demands to be used in
a context of accepted ideas and reading, though the opposite side of this
is also valued, namely unexpected justness. Cleverness and quickness
are parts of it, too, and the idea of the marshalled disposition of
material. Lastly, ideas are important: the most famous characterization
of wit, echoed by later critics and poets, is that of the most influential
philosopher of the age, John Locke, who defines it as 'the Assemblage
of Ideas, and putting those together with quickness and variety'.

Locke is here, however, acting as the spokesman for the new highly
developed and articulate consciousness of the self in moral thinking,
scientific observation and poetry, which begins to assume special
importance in England in the seventeenth century. The consciousness
of the self as initiator, user and arbiter of ideas produced the problem of
establishing a communal, standard judgment, a point of rest which
became increasingly the goal of the succeeding Augustan age. The

arrogance of wit was resisted. There was a backlash of sensibility, from men who followed their hearts; and there was a conservative backlash from men who distrusted unsupported human daring. Addison devoted several *Spectator* papers to discussing wit (see nos 35, 61–3, 140 and 249). In No. 62, he elaborates his famous distinctions between 'true wit' and 'false wit' allowing an escape hole of 'mix'd wit' to avoid condemning writers whom he half admired. There is a see-saw between admiration for quick cleverness and admiration for the harmony of the assemblage. 'False wit' appears to Addison to be '*Gothick*', that is without proportion, fussy, entertaining but lacking overall control. 'True wit' he sees as majestic and 'natural'.

It would be possible to give a historical account of the use of 'wit' as a critical term. Pope, for example, makes it one of the primary topics of his 'Essay on Criticism'. Dr Johnson was himself a witty writer. His *Rasselas* depends for much of its powerful and moving moral judgment on the witty juxtaposition of ideas and judgments. At the same time, he is firmly committed to total control in literature. In his *Life of Cowley*, a 'witty' writer of the seventeenth century, he gave two of the most widely quoted critical definitions of wit: 'that which though not obvious, is, upon its first production, acknowledged to be just; a kind of *discordia concors* . . .'. It is perhaps more important, however, to see the prizing of wit in poetry and writing in general as one of the ends of an arc through which taste can swing, from admiring the unconscious, the area of FEELING. In the 1890s, the writers in the *Yellow Book*, very conscious rebels against a suffocating Victorian tide of feeling, cultivated wit. T. S. Eliot, later, developed a poetic which made use of wit and selected for admiration certain seventeenth-century writers such as Donne and especially Marvell, in whose work he saw the successful realization of wit, which he defines in his essay on 'Andrew Marvell' (1921) as 'tough reasonableness beneath the slight lyric grace': knowledgeable technical skill united with a total self-consciousness. Here wit is not arrogant as in the seventeenth century, but a defensive personal attitude. Cleanth Brooks was a member of a group of American writers and critics who seized on wit as a personal style of writing and of living, in defence against the blanketing megalopolis of American capitalism. In *The Well Wrought Urn* (1947), he refers to wit as 'an awareness of the multiplicity of possible attitudes to be taken towards a given situation'. This is also a defensive position against the mass 'feeling' of communism, or fascism. The value of wit as a personal protection and a weapon had been recognized by earlier writers, though they also saw its divisive disadvantages. As Pope wrote:

> Thus wit, like faith, by each man is apply'd
> To one small sect, and all are damned beside . . .

See A. Alvarez, *The School of Donne* (1961), ch. 6; W. Empson, *The Structure of Complex Words* (1951), ch. 3; C. S. Lewis, *Studies in Words* (1961), ch. 4; D. J. Millburn, *The Age of Wit: 1650–1750* (1966), useful bibliography, 315–16.

AMR

writing

see DECONSTRUCTION